The
Black
Woman

Also by Toni Cade Bambara

The Black Woman

An Anthology

Toni Cade Bambara

WITH AN INTRODUCTION BY

Eleanor W. Traylor

WASHINGTON SQUARE PRESS
PUBLISHED BY POCKET BOOKS

New York   London   Toronto   Sydney

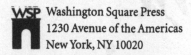 Washington Square Press
1230 Avenue of the Americas
New York, NY 10020

Copyright © 1970 by Toni Cade
Introduction copyright © 2005 by Toni Cade Bambara

All rights reserved, including the right to reproduce
this book or portions thereof in any form whatsoever.
For information address Washington Square Press,
1230 Avenue of the Americas, New York, NY 10020

ISBN: 978-0-7434-7697-3

First Washington Square Press trade paperback edition March 2005

10   9   8   7   6   5   4   3   2   1

WASHINGTON SQUARE PRESS and colophon are registered trademarks of
Simon & Schuster, Inc.

Designed by Christine Weathersbee

Manufactured in the United States of America

For information regarding special discounts for bulk purchases,
please contact Simon & Schuster Special Sales at 1-800-456-6798
or business@simonandschuster.com

"And What About the Children," from *Chosen Poems: Old and New* by
Audre Lorde. Copyright © 1982, 1976, 1974, 1973, 1970, 1968 by Audre Lorde.
Used by permission of W. W. Norton & Company, Inc.

"Naturally," Copyright © 1968 by Audre Lorde, from *Collected Poems* by
Audre Lorde. Used by permission of W. W. Norton & Company, Inc.

Contents

Contents

Contents

CONTENTS

Re Calling the Black Woman

Eleanor W. Traylor
for Karma Bene

This time, as I listened to her talk over the stretch of one long night, she made vivid without knowing it what is perhaps the most critical fact of my existence—that definition of me, of her and millions like us, formulated by others to serve out their fantasies, a definition we have to combat at an unconscionable cost to the self and even use, at times, in order to survive; the cause of so much shame and rage as well as, oddly enough, a source of pride: simply, what it has meant, what it means, to be a Black woman in America.

Paule Marshall, "Reena" in *The Black Woman: An Anthology*

Talking to Toni Cade Bambara is not only antidote for "snake bite," as she would say, it is perfect assurance that "bad hair day" and "bad self-esteem day" are demons existing to be exorcised by Karma, alias "Scout," "Squeaky," "Ms. Muffin," "Hazel," "Thunderbun," or "Hazel Elizabeth Deborah Parker" (alias "TCB")—agents of revolutionary thought in the facto-fictive world of Toni Cade Bambara.

The rigorous healing of that thought persists as palpably today as it did in 1970 when it appeared in print as *The Black Woman: An Anthology* edited by Toni Cade. When a book as well as a life pluck the "weasel" of thought and fire the pistol of action in their time, liberating a future of ever new audiences "to think better than they've been trained" (9), then that book and that life receive, through the years, an everlasting *yes.* At millennium 147 studies of that life and work have been produced by readers who love conversations with Toni Cade Bambara (consummate teacher, activist, editor, essayist, storyteller, filmmaker, and novelist). Of these, 28 have targeted *The Black Woman: An Anthology* as founding text of a "womanist" evolutionary enunciation.

The book has been a cause of self-discovery, as evidenced by the testimony of Jasmine Farah Griffin who, "at seven or eight years old . . . spotted *The Black Woman*" at Robins Bookstore in Philadelphia.

> Staring from the cover directly at me was a beautiful brown woman with a large Afro that merged with the black background of the book's cover. . . . In the still color-conscious black world of McDaniel Elementary School in South Philadelphia, I was constantly reminded that I was "black" (which always seemed to be qualified by phrases such as "and ugly," "and shiny," "and crispy"), not at all like Angela or Kathleen who were light-skinned. . . . So you see I was in desperate need of a browner, Afroed revolutionary image. And this anonymous sister on the Cade anthology was going to be the one. . . . By possessing the book, I could possess the woman, could become the woman—or so I reasoned. (Glaude 113–14)

This is the voice of the Jasmine of 2002 remembering the Jasmine of 1970 in the insistence that many young "Scouts" will find *The*

Black Woman peeping from the windows of bookstores across the world. Indeed, not only did *The Black Woman* launch a face, it unveiled and named a landscape as resplendent as the world of literature offers. For in 1970, the year of its publication, *The Bluest Eye* introduced Toni Morrison and *The Third Life of Grange Copeland* introduced Alice Walker as commanders in the field of fiction. Both these stunning novels, on the level of sublimity, unmask what happens when a "Scout" or "Squeaky" cannot find her inspiring portrait anywhere. *I Know Why the Caged Bird Sings* introduced Maya Angelou as progenitor of the contemporary life narrative. And, in that year of wonders, the already published voices of stellar poets received more resonance in the publications of *Family Pictures* and *Riot* by Gwendolyn Brooks, *Prophets for a New Day* by Margaret Walker, *Cables to Rage* by Audre Lorde, *We a Baddddd People* by Sonia Sanchez, and *I Am a Black Woman* by Mari Evans. Wondrously, Toni Cade's *The Black Woman: An Anthology* (hereafter referred to as *Anthology*) heralded what its editor later named an *Afrafemme* view of the world.

In the collection of poetry, stories, and essays that is the *Anthology,* a definition of this worldview emerges as a sensibility, not as an *ism.* Its awareness explores first the interiority of an in-the-head, in-the-heart, in-the-gut region of a discovery called the *self.* It tests the desires, the longings, the aspirations of this discovered self with and against its possibilities for respect, growth, fulfillment, and accomplishment (see the poetry and essays of Lindsey, Lincoln, Clark, Brown, and Beale in *Anthology*). It finds sisterly empathy with complementary selves (see Beale, Cade, Cook, Robinson, Williams, Lindsay, Giovanni, and Grant in *Anthology*). It discovers a voice by which to end its own entrapping silence and to end its silencing in the media of traditional and prevailing expressive modes (see all contributions to *Anthology*). It refuses the assumptions and terminology of colonial, capitalist, racist, and gendered versions of reality; linguistically, its aspirations include the subversion of terms that reduce the ever-wide dimensions of the self (see all contributions to *Anthology*). In fact, such self-referential terms as *Afrafemme* and *womanist* (coined by contributor Alice Walker) liberate the agents of self and world revolutionary thought and change from imposed hegemonic interpretation or labeling.

The speakers whose voices sound through *The Black Woman: An Anthology* were (and remain) active participants in an ever-evolving movement whose impact at mid-twentieth century was perhaps the most revolutionary cultural and intellectual re-imagining to have occurred in the United States since the birth of America in The Declaration of Independence. Undoubtedly, the evolving civil rights, Black Power, black nationalism, and black arts movements tilled the soil of thought in which the seeds of mid-century and later liberation struggles over the world sprouted and grew strong. Yet, though black liberational movements, seminal as they were at mid-century, "caused a disruption of the totalizing production of public consciousness" (Lubiano 163), succeeding brilliantly, though not fully, toward "a radical reordering" (Neal 62–78)[1] of the word and toward "dismantling the dominant categories of interpretation [establishing] fresh perspectives from which to displace the limiting horizons of [received] understanding" (Sharabi 105)[2], they did not escape the versions of gendered reality, as Frances Beale argues in *Anthology:*

> Since the advent of Black Power, the Black male has exerted a
> more prominent leadership role in our struggle for justice in
> this country. He sees the system for what it is for the most

---

[1] Neal, Larry. "The Black Arts Movement" (1964) in *Visions of a Liberated Future.* New York: Thunder's Mouth Press, 1989.

[2] Sharabi, Hisham. *NeoPatriachy: A Theory of Distorted Change in Arab Society.* New York: Oxford University Press, 1988.

part, but where he rejects its values and mores on many issues, when it comes to women, he seems to take his guidelines from the pages of the *Ladies Home Journal.* Certain Black men are maintaining that they have been castrated by society but that Black women somehow escaped this persecution and even contributed to the emasculation. (93)

And as Wahneema Lubiano notes at millennium, those movements (ongoing as they are) have not yet produced a "critique . . . that would lead to the overthrow of global capitalism and/or homophobic patriarchy" (Lubiano 163).

Moreover, as Kimberly Springer observes, "[T]he recuperation of the self in a racist and sexist society is a political enterprise and a Black feminist one that deprioritizes generational difference in the interest of historical, activist continuity" (*Signs* 1059). Writing in 2002, this thoroughgoing historian of Black feminism is supported by corroborating recent historians of the Women's Liberation Movement of the mid-twentieth century in the assertion that "African American women have historically had a stronger tradition of honoring women's independence than have White women," for even though " 'women of color have shaped the feminist movement from its inception in this country, yet the public face of feminism is often seen as White' " (Baxandall/Toledo 230). Remembering nineteenth-century "Black women involved in antislavery, antilynching, and suffrage work" like Maria Stewart, Mary Ann Shadd Carey, and Anna Julia Cooper, Kimberly Springer reminds us of the argument of Cooper in *A Voice from the South by a Black Woman of the South* (1892), namely that "Black Women [need] to work separately from White feminists because of racism experienced personally, political betrayal, and the strategic need for separatism" (1061). This argument resounds in Paula Giddings's crucial text *When and Where I Enter: The Impact of Black Women on*

Race and Sex in America (1984). And V.P. Franklin, writing in 2002, finds Giddings's observation that "historically 'white women had been the bane of Black women's existence' " to be in accordance with her own thesis in *Hidden in Plain View: African American Women, Radical Feminism, and the Origins of Women's Studies Programs,* (1967–1974). Similarly she remembers an earlier ancestor:

> Frances Beale also declared in "Double Jeopardy" that "another major differentiation is that the white women's liberation movement is basically middle class. Very few of these women suffer the extreme economic exploitation that most Black women are subjected to day by day. This is a crucial factor for us." Beale argued that "if the white groups do not realize that they are in fact fighting capitalism and racism, we do not have common bonds."
>
> (Franklin 456)

Again, the assertions of millennial scholars locate the contemporary grounding of "gender talk," as Beverly Guy-Sheftall and Johnnetta Cole entitle their 2004 publication, in *The Black Woman: An Anthology.*

To earn honor as a groundbreaking work, a book could achieve a single distinction: it could launch a face or propel self-discovery, name a landscape or herald an emerging sensibility, or inspire new historic scholarship. But in 1970, the *Anthology* did this and more. It inscribed conversations that emerge from the kitchen as in Verta Mae Smart-Grosvenor's "The Kitchen Crisis" and land in the large world as in Francee Covington's "Are the Revolutionary Techniques Employed in *The Battle of Algiers* Applicable to Harlem?" It raised questions as provocative as Jean Carey Bond's and Pat Peery's "Is the Black Male Castrated?" and as in Pat Robinson and Group's "Poor Black Women's Study Papers" and "A Historical and

Critical Essay for Black Women in the Cities." It peeks through the yet undiscovered places of a self who cannot yet esteem itself as in Shirley Williams's poignant story "Tell Martha Not to Moan." It illuminates the deep conflict of a divided self as in Alice Walker's beautiful "The Diary of an African Nun." It shines the light of courage on the brilliant discovered self seeking to be whole in Paule Marshall's "Reena." It embraces Nikki Giovanni's "Woman Poem" and "Nikki-Rosa," Kay Lindsey's "Poem," and Audre Lorde's "Naturally" and "And What About the Children." In short, it negotiates "the political/economic/social/cultural/aesthetic/military/psychosocial/psychosexual mix" (Bambara, *The Salt Eaters* 259). And what is more, *The Black Woman: An Anthology* erases muleminded boundaries as between orality and the written word, beautiful writing and investigative prose, professional writers and newly awakened rising voices, man and woman at the level of awakening self-discovery. In the process, it detonates "texts" that neutralize the achievement of wonderful possibilities and enunciations of what has yet to be deemed.

Toni Cade Bambara leaves a legacy of gathering congregations of the unlikely as in the hilarious meeting among the "quick and the dead" in the chapel scene of her jam session must-read novel *The Salt Eaters* (1980) and in the paradigm-informing design of *Those Bones Are Not My Child* (2000, published posthumously). Just as in *The Black Woman: An Anthology* and in *Tales and Stories for Black Folks* (1971) published one year later, she again gathers the work of acclaimed writers like Langston Hughes, Birago Diop, James Aggrey, Pearle Crayton, Albert Murray, and Ernest J. Gaines in company with never-before-published writers: her students from the Fort Greene Young Writer's Project in Brooklyn and "the Newark Mamas—mothers back in school, working for their college degrees at Livingston College, Rutgers University" (1) where she taught. In this collection, we gain the pedagogy of those who think better than they've been trained. We learn—à la student Linda Holmes—that it was not a piece of sky but that "out of the clear blue sky and for no apparent reason, a policeman hit Chicken Licken on her head" (146). And that the protests of a flock of testifiers, "Cocky Locky, Duckey Luckey, Drake Lake, Hen Len, Goosey Loosey, Gander Lander, Turkey Lurkey," like the researchers Zala gathers in *Those Bones*, "could not convince authorities that it is not a piece of the sky but a billie-club that makes chicken-licken so anti-police" (*Tales* 146–9). We also learn (à la Bambara) that for at least two centuries a small villain called Goldilocks—burglar, vandal, usurper, colonialist—had fouled the reputation of children. And that is why "the exacting ceremonies" (*SE* 145) of the most adorable and sassy youngsters, like little Hazel Elizabeth Deborah Parker (alias "Squeaky"), who enliven the story world of T.C.B. and who currently live in *The Boondocks* created by the genius of young cartoonist Aaron McGruder,[3] award prizes to the most embarrassing but celebrated adults and Goldilocks/Puffy's at millennium.

Story-talking-back-to-story or story-in-response-to-story or story-creating-reception-theory is the practice of the *Tales and Stories* anthology and of the two collections gathering the short stories of Toni Cade Bambara written between 1960 and 1972, the publication date of *Gorilla, My Love* and the 1974 publication of *The Sea Birds Are Still Alive.* Appearing before "the formalist paradigm for literary studies slowly collapsed [and] theory broke out" in the American Academy (Richter 20),[4] these stories and her novels *The Salt Eaters* (1980) and *Those Bones Are Not My Child* (2000) exemplify the new paradigm informing contemporary Black women's narratological practice to date. "Gathering"—a storyword used often by the "agents for change" (*SE* 12) to guide their reluctant

---

[3] McGruder, Aaron. *The Boondocks.* Kansas City: Andrews McMeet, 2000.

[4] Richter, David H. *Falling into Theory: Conflicting Views on Reading Literature.* Boston: Bedford/St. Martin's Press, 2000.

students in the fiction of Toni Cade Bambara—means also "research" and means as well the rigorous method by which this indefatiguable author worked to recommend to ever-new reading audiences the absolute necessity and the joy of *gathering* together to think deeply and act decisively in behalf of "salvation"—another of her most frequently used words.

The fecund gift she offers to ever-new audiences that this republication makes possible is what we may call *womanword:* an eye-to-eye, word-to-word encounter in which language explores itself as talking-text-in-writing. Womanword is music talking to Velma—the voice in the music saying, "Don't cheat the body, don't cheat the spirit" (*SE* 166); saying, "We have not been scuffling in this waste-howling wilderness for the right to be stupid" (*SE* 46); saying, "she would not have cut Medusa's head off . . . she would simply have told the sister to go and comb her hair" (*SE* 257). Womanword is, as well, a re-creative disturbance of conventional expectations as in the textual encounter between Gail (creed) and Sugar (heretic) in "The Johnson Girls" story of *Gorilla, My Love.* Womanword is also prescient. It is awesome in the "Going Critical" story where a mother foresees her own death and prepares her daughter in the most wonderful of irreductive ways in Bambara's *Deep Sightings & Rescue Missions* (1996, published posthumously). Womanword—which sometimes growls—is sometimes "breathless with laughter," sometimes profane, sometimes "don't ever let up, always teaching," and as ready for cookin' as a black-eyed pea that's been soaking all night—womanword is also Toniword is blackwomanword everywhere alive in the universe of word that talks and writes better than it has been trained.

Who is the Black Woman

She is a college graduate. *A drop-out.* A student. *A wife.* A divorcee. *A mother.* A lover. *A child of the ghetto.* A product of the bourgeoisie. *A professional writer.* A person who never dreamed of publication. *A solitary individual.* A member of the Movement. *A gentle humanist.* A violent revolutionary. *She is angry and tender, loving and hating. She is all these things—and more. And she is represented in a collection that for the first time truly lets her bare her soul and speak her mind.*

(Cade, First Edition)

She is also a must-read text to be delivered into the hands of all of us who work to achieve the wonderful light of knowledge, love, and beauty. She is an everlasting *yes.*

Bibliography

Primary Sources: Works by Toni Cade Bambara

Anthologies

The Black Woman: An Anthology. New York: New American Library, 1970.

Tales and Stories for Black Folks. Garden City, N.Y.: Zenith, 1971.

Collections of Short Stories

Gorilla, My Love. New York: Random House, 1972.

Raymond's Run. Mankato, Minn.: Creative Education, 1990.

The Sea Birds Are Still Alive: Collected Stories. New York: Random House, 1977.

Novels

Those Bones Are Not My Child. New York: Vintage, 2000.

The Salt Eaters. New York: Random House, 1980.

Collections of Essays and Conversations

Deep Sightings & Rescue Missions: Fiction, Essays, and Conversations. New York: Pantheon, 1996.

Secondary Sources: Recent Scholarship on Toni Cade Bambara's The Black Woman: An Anthology

Breines, Wini. "What's Love Got to Do with It? White Women, Black Women, and Feminism in the Movement Years." *Signs: Journal of Women in Culture and Society* 27 (2002): 1095.

Brown, Anita C., Gene H Brody, and Zolinda Stoneman. "Rural Black Women and Depression: A Contextual Analysis." *Journal of Marriage and the Family* 62.1 (February 2000): 187–198.

Browne, Irene, and Joya Misra. "The Intersection of Gender and Race in the Labor Market." *Annual Review of Sociology* 29 (Annual 2003): 487.

Caron, Simone M. "Birth Control and the Black Community in the 1960s: Genocide or Power Politics?" *Journal of Social History.* 10 August 2004 http://www.findarticles.com/p/articles/mi_m2005/is_n3_v31/ai_20574139

Denmark, Florence, Vita Rabinowitz, and Jeri Sechzer. *Engendering Psychology: Bringing Women into Focus.* Vol. Xvi. MA: Allyn and Bacon, 2000. 527.

Franklin, V.P. "Hidden in Plain View: African American Women, Radical Feminism, and the Origins of Women's Studies Programs, 1967–1974." *The Journal of African American History* 87.4 (Fall 2002): 433–445.

Gordon, Ann D., and Bettye Collier-Thomas. *African American Women and the Vote, 1837–1965.* Amherst: U of Massachusetts P, 1997.

Griffin, Farah Jasmine. "Conflict and Chorus: Reconsidering Toni Cade's *The Black Woman: An Anthology.*" *Is It Nation Time?: Contemporary Essays on Black Power and Black Nationalism.* Ed. Eddie S. Glaude Jr. Chicago: U of Chicago Press, 2002.

Hernton, Calvin. "The Sexual Mountain and Black Women Writers." *Black American Literature Forum* 18.4 (Winter 1984): 139–145.

Hodgson, Dennis, and Susan Cotts Watkins. "Feminists and Neo-Malthusians: Past and Present Alliances." *Population and Development Review* 23.3 (Fall 1997): 469.

John, Catherine A. "Complicity, Revolution and Black Female Writing." *Race and Class* 10 August 2004 http://static.highbeam.com/r/raceandclass/april011999/complicityrevolutionand blackfemalewriting/index.html

Joseph, Peniel E. "Black Liberation Without Apology: Reconceptualizing the Black Power Movement. *Black Scholar* 31.3 (Fall 2001): 2–19.

Liddell, Janice Lee, and Yakini Belinda Kemp. *Arms Akimbo: Africana Women in Contemporary Literature.* Tallahassee: UP of Florida, 1999.

Lubiano, Wahneema. "Standing in for the State: Black Nationalism and 'Writing' the Black Subject." *Is It Nation Time?: Contemporary Essays on Black Power and Black Nationalism.* Ed. Eddie S. Glaude, Jr. Chicago: University of Chicago Press, 2002.

May, Vivian M. "Thinking from the Margins, Acting at the Intersection: Anna Julia Cooper's *A Voice from the South.*" *Hypatia* 19.2 (Spring 2004): 74–91.

Musser, Judith. "African American Women's Short Stories in the Harlem Renaissance: Bridging a Tradition." *Melus* 23.2 (Summer 1998): 27.

Muther, Elizabeth. "Bambara's Feisty Girls: Resistance Narratives in *Gorilla, My Love.*" *African American Review* 36.3 (Fall 2002): 447.

Nubukpo, Komia Messan. "Through Their Sisters' Eyes: the Representation of Black Men in the Novels of Toni Morrison, Alice Walker, and Toni Cade Bambara." Diss. Boston U, 1987. *DAI* 48: 2009A.

Roberts, Dorothy. "Black Women and the Pill." *Family Planning Perspective* 32. 2. March-April 2000. 10 August 2004 http://www.agiusa.org/pubs/journals/3209200.html.

Rooney, Ellen. "What's the Story? Feminist Theory, Narrative, Address." *Differences: a Journal of Feminist Cultural Studies* 8.1 (Spring 1996): 1.

Roth Benita. "Race, Class and the Emergence of Black Feminism in the 1960s and 1970s." 10 August 2004. http://www.uga.edu/~womanist/roth3.1htm.

Rubin, Lillian B. "Worlds of Pain: Life in the Working-Class Family." 1992.

Ryan, Katy. "Revolutionary Suicide in Toni Morrison's Fiction." *African American Review.* 22 September 2000. 10 August 2004

Sanchez, Marta E. "La Malinche at the Intersection: Race and Gender in *Down These Mean Streets.*" *PMLA* 113.1 (January 1998): 117–128.

Smith, Barbara. "Feisty Characters and 'Other People's Causes': Memories of White Racism in U.S. Feminism." *The Feminist Memoir Project: Voices from Women's Liberation.* Eds. Rachel Blau DuPlessis and Ann Snitow. New York: Three Rivers Press, 1998. 478–79.

———. "Building Black Women's Studies." *The Politics of Women's Studies: Testimony from Thirty Founding Mothers.* Ed. Flowrence Howe. New York: Feminist Press, 2000. 194–203.

Smith, Dianne. "Critical Pedagogy and Disturbing the Pleasures of Silence." Online Posting 28 February 2003. University Council for Educational Administration Annual Convention. 2 November 2002. 10 August 2004

Springer, Kimberly. "Third Wave Black Feminism?" *Signs* 27.4 (Summer 2002): 1059–1082.

Thomas, Greg. "Bourgeois Cancer vs. Revolutionary Love: A Taste of Power Revisited." *Proud Flesh: A New Afrikan Journal of Culture, Politics, and Consciousness.* 2003. 10 August 2004

Wilcox, Janelle. "Constructed Silences: Voice and Subjectivity in Resistance Texts of Gayl Jones, Alice Walker, and Toni Cade Bambara." Diss. Washington State U, 1995. *DAI.* 57:224A.

Wilkinson, Doris. "The Clinical Irrelevance and Scientific Invalidity of the 'Minority' Notion: Deleting it from the Social Science Vocabulary." *Journal of Sociology and Social Welfare.* 1 June 2002.10 August 2004 http://www.findarticles.com/p/articles/mi mOCYZ/is_2_29/ai_89076680

"Women's Liberation Movement." 10 August 2004 http://www .glbtq.com/social-sciences/womens_liberation_movement .html.

Preface

We are involved in a struggle for liberation: liberation from the exploitive and dehumanizing system of racism, from the manipulative control of a corporate society; liberation from the constrictive norms of "mainstream" culture, from the synthetic myths that encourage us to fashion ourselves rashly from without (reaction) rather than from within (creation). What characterizes the current movement of the 60's is a turning away from the larger society and a turning toward each other. Our art, protest, dialogue no longer spring from the impulse to entertain, or to indulge or enlighten the conscience of the enemy; white people, whiteness, or racism; men, maleness, or chauvinism: America or imperialism . . . depending on your viewpoint and your terror. Our energies now seem to be invested in and are in turn derived from a determination to touch and to unify. What typifies the current spirit is an embrace, an embrace of the community and a hardheaded attempt to get basic with each other.

If we women are to get basic, then surely the first job is to find out what liberation for ourselves means, what work it entails, what benefits it will yield. To do that, we might turn to various fields of studies to extract material, data necessary to define that term in respect to ourselves. We note, however, all too quickly the lack of relevant material.

Psychiatrists and the like, while compiling data on personality traits and behavioral patterns, tend to reinforce rather than challenge social expectations on the subject of woman; they tell us in paper after paper that first and foremost the woman wishes to be the attractive, cared-for companion of a man, that she desires above all else motherhood, that her sense of self is nourished by her ability to create a comfortable home. Hollywood and other dream factories delight in this notion and reinforce it, and it becomes the social expectation. The woman who would demand more is "immature," "anti-social," or "masculine."

And on the subject of her liberation, when it is considered at all, the experts (white, male) tell us that ohh yes she must be free to enjoy orgasm. And that is that.

When the experts (white or Black, male) turn their attention to the Black woman, the reports get murky, for they usually clump the men and women together and focus so heavily on what white people have done to the psyches of Blacks, that what Blacks have done to and for themselves is overlooked, and what distinguishes the men from the women forgotten.

Commercial psychologists, market researchers, applied psychologists (who by any other name are still white, male) further say, on the subject of women and their liberation, that she must feel free to buy new products, to explore the new commodities, to change brands. So thousands of dollars are spent each year to offer her a wide range of clothes, cosmetics, home furnishings, baby products so that she can realize herself and nourish her sense of identity.

The biologists are no help either. Either they are busily assisting the psychologist in his paper on the Sex Life of the Swan or they are busily observing some primate group or other and concluding, on the basis of two or three weeks, acting as voyeurs to captive monkeys, that the female of the species is "basically" submissive, dependent, frivolous; all she wants to do is be cared for and be played with. It seems not to occur to these scientists (white, male) that the behavioral traits they label "basic" and upon which the psychologists breezily build their theories of masculine/feminine are not so "basic" at all; they do not exist, after all, in a context-free ether. They may very well be not inherent traits but merely at-the-moment traits. What would happen to the neat rows of notes if alterations were made in the cage, if the situation were modified, if the laboratory were rearranged. Add another monkey or two; introduce a water wheel or a water buffalo. Would other traits then be in evidence? Would the "basic" traits change or disappear? People, after all, are not only not rhesus monkeys, they also do not live in a static environment.

The biochemists have been having their day on the podium too. They, too, have much to say on the subject of woman. Chemical agents, sex hormones or enzymes, are the base of it all. They do make an excellent case for sex hormones' influencing physiological differences. But when it comes to explaining the role of either the hormones or the physiological differences in the building of personality, the fashioning of the personality that will or will not adapt to social expectations—all the objective, step-by-step training is out the window. As for woman and the whole question of her role, they seem to agree with Freud: anatomy is destiny.

History, of course, offers us much more data . . . and much more difficulty. For the very movements that could provide us with insights are those movements not traditionally taught in the schools or made available without glamorized distortions by show business: the movement against the slave trade, the abolitionist movement, the feminist movement, the labor movement. But even our skimpy knowledge of these phenomena show us something: the need for unified effort and the value of a vision of a society substantially better than the existing one.

I don't know that literature enlightens us too much. The "ex-

perts" are still men, Black or white. And the images of the woman
are still derived from their needs, their fantasies, their second-hand
knowledge, their agreement with the other "experts." But of course
there have been women who have been able to think better than
they've been trained and have produced the canon of literature
fondly referred to as "feminist literature": Anais Nin, Simone de
Beauvoir, Doris Lessing, Betty Friedan, etc. And the question for us
arises: how relevant are the truths, the experiences, the findings of
white women to Black women? Are women after all simply women?
I don't know that our priorities are the same, that our concerns and
methods are the same, or even similar enough so that we can afford
to depend on this new field of experts (white, female).

It is rather obvious that we do not. It is obvious that we are
turning to each other.

Throughout the country in recent years, Black women have
been forming work-study groups, discussion clubs, cooperative
nurseries, cooperative businesses, consumer education groups,
women's workshops on the campuses, women's caucuses within existing organizations, Afro-American women's magazines. From
time to time they have organized seminars on the Role of the Black
Woman, conferences on the Crisis Facing the Black Woman, have
provided tapes on the Attitude of European Men Toward Black
Women, working papers on the Position of the Black Women in
America; they have begun correspondence with sisters in Vietnam,
Guatemala, Algeria, Ghana on the Liberation Struggle and the
Woman, formed alliances on a Third World Women plank. They are
women who have not, it would seem, been duped by the prevailing
notions of "woman," but who have maintained a critical stance.

Unlike the traditional sororities and business clubs, they seem
to use the Black Liberation struggle rather than the American
Dream as their yardstick, their gauge, their vantage point. And
while few have produced, or are interested in producing at this

time, papers for publication, many do use working papers as part of their discipline, part of their effort to be clear, analytical, personal, basic; part of their efforts to piece together an "overview," an overview of ourselves too long lost among the bills of sale and letters of transit; part of their effort to deal with the reality of being Black and living in twentieth-century America—a country that has more respect for the value of property than the quality of life, a country that has never valued Black life as dear, a country that regards its women as its monsters, celebrating wherever possible the predatory coquette and the carnivorous mother.

Some of the papers representing groups and individuals are presented here along with poems, stories, and essays by writers of various viewpoints. What is immediately noticeable are the distinct placements of stress, for some women are not so much concerned with demanding rights as they are in clarifying issues; some demand rights as Blacks first, women second. Oddly enough, it is necessary to point out what should be obvious—Black women are individuals too.

For the most part, the work grew out of impatience: an impatience with the all too few and too soon defunct Afro-American women's magazines that were rarely seen outside of the immediate circle of the staff's and contributors' friends. It grew out of an impatience with the half-hearted go-along attempts of Black women caught up in the white women's liberation groups around the country. Especially out of an impatience with all the "experts" zealously hustling us folks for their doctoral theses or government appointments. And out of an impatience with the fact that in the whole bibliography of feminist literature, literature immediately and directly relevant to us, wouldn't fill a page. And perhaps that impatience has not allowed me to do all that needs to be done in this volume.

I had thought, in the overly ambitious beginnings, that what we had to do straightaway was (1) set up a comparative study of the woman's role as she saw it in all the Third World Nations; (2) examine the public school system and blueprint some viable alternatives; (3) explore ourselves and set the record straight on the matriarch and the evil Black bitch; (4) delve into history and pay tribute to all our warriors from the ancient times to the slave trade to Harriet Tubman to Fannie Lou Hamer to the woman of this morning; (5) present the working papers of the various groups around the country; (6) interview the migrant workers, the quilting-bee mothers, the grandmothers of the UNIA; (7) analyze the Freedom Budget and design ways to implement it; (8) outline the work that has been done and remains to be done in the area of consumer education and cooperative economics; (9) thoroughly discuss the whole push for Black studies programs and a Black university; (10) provide a forum of opinion from the YWCA to the Black Women Enraged; (11) get into the whole area of sensuality, sex; (12) chart the steps necessary for forming a working alliance with all non-white women of the world for the formation of, among other things, a clearing house for the exchange of information . . .

And the list grew and grew. A lifetime's work, to be sure. But I am comforted by the fact that several of the contributors here have begun books; several women contacted have begun books; several magazines are in the making; several groups are talking about doing documentary films. So in the next few months, there will be appearing books dealing exclusively with the relationships between Black men and women, with the revolutionary Black women of the current period, with the Black abolitionists, with the whole question of Black schools.

This then is a beginning—a collection of poems, stories, essays, formal, informal, reminiscent, that seem best to reflect the preoccupations of the contemporary Black woman in this country. Some items were written especially for the collection. Some were discovered tucked away in notebooks. Many of the contributors are professional writers. Some have never before put pen to paper with publication in mind. Some are mothers. Others are students. Some are both. All are alive, are Black, are women. And that, I should think, is credentials enough to address themselves to issues that seem to be relevant to the sisterhood.

I should like to thank Marvin Gettleman; my agent, Cyrilly Abels; my editor, Nina Finkelstein; my typists, Jean Powell of City College and Nat White of the Lower East Side. And especial thanks to my man Gene.

The book is dedicated to the uptown mammas who nudged me to "just set it down in print so it gets to be a habit to write letters to each other, so maybe that way we don't keep treadmilling the same ole ground."

—Toni Cade

Two Poems

Nikki Giovanni

Woman Poem*

you see, my whole life
is tied up
to unhappiness
it's father cooking breakfast
and me getting fat as a hog
or having no food
at all and father proving
his incompetence
again
i wish i knew how it would feel
to be free

it's having a job
they won't let you work
or no work at all
castrating me
(yes it happens to women too)

* Copyright © 1969 by Nikki Giovanni.

it's a sex object if you're pretty
and no love
or love and no sex if you're fat
get back fat black woman be a mother
grandmother strong thing but not woman
gameswoman romantic woman love needer
man seeker dick eater sweat getter
fuck needing love seeking woman

it's a hole in your shoe
and buying lil sis a dress
and her saying you shouldn't
when you know
all too well that you shouldn't

but smiles are only something we give
to properly dressed social workers
not each other
only smiles of i know
your game sister
which isn't really
a smile

joy is finding a pregnant roach
and squashing it
not finding someone to hold
let go get off get back don't turn
me on you black dog
how dare you care
about me
you ain't got no good sense
cause i ain't shit you must be lower
than that to care

it's a filthy house
with yesterday's watermelon
and monday's tears
cause true ladies don't
know how to clean

it's intellectual devastation
of everybody
to avoid emotional commitment
"yeah honey i would've married
him but he didn't have no degree"

it's knock-kneed mini skirted
wig wearing died blond mamma's scar
born dead my scorn your whore
rough heeled broken nailed powdered
face me
whose whole life is tied
up to unhappiness
cause it's the only
for real thing
i
know

September, 1968

Nikki-Rosa*

childhood remembrances are always a drag
if you're Black

* Copyright © 1969 by Nikki Giovanni.

[11]

you always remember things like living in Woodlawn
with no inside toilet
and if you become famous or something
they never talk about how happy you were to have your mother
all to yourself and
how good the water felt when you got your bath from one
    of those
big tubs that folk in chicago barbecue in
and somehow when you talk about home
it never gets across how much you
understood their feelings
as the whole family attended meetings about Hollydale
and even though you remember
your biographers never understand
your father's pain as he sells his stock
and another dream goes
and though you're poor it isn't poverty that
concerns you
and though they fought a lot
it isn't your father's drinking that makes any difference
but only that everybody is together and you
and your sister have happy birthdays and very good
    christmases
and I really hope no white person ever has cause to write
    about me
because they never understand Black love is Black wealth
    and they'll
probably talk about my hard childhood and never
    understand that
all the while I was quite happy

April, 1968

Poem

Kay Lindsey

I'm not one of those who believes
That an act of valor, for a woman
Need take place inside her.

My womb is packed in mothballs
And I hear that winter will be mild.

Anyway I gave birth twice
And my body deserves a medal for that
But I never got one.

Mainly because they thought
I was just answering the call of nature.

But now that the revolution needs numbers
Motherhood got a new position
Five steps behind manhood.

And I thought sittin' in the back of the bus
Went out with Martin Luther King.

Two Poems

Audre Lorde

Naturally

Since Naturally Black is Naturally Beautiful
I must be proud
And, naturally,
Black and
Beautiful
Who always was a trifle
Yellow
And plain though proud
Before.

I've given up pomades
Having spent the summer sunning
And feeling naturally free
    (If I die of skin cancer
    oh well—one less
    black and beautiful me)
Yet no Agency spends millions
To prevent my summer tanning

And who trembles nightly
With the fear of their lily cities being swallowed
By a summer ocean of naturally woolly hair?

But I've bought my can of
Natural Hair Spray
Made and marketed in Watts
Still thinking more
Proud beautiful black women
Could better make and use
Black bread.

And What About the Children

Now we've made a child.
And the dire predictions
Have changed into wild
Grim
Speculations.
Yet the negatives
Are still waiting
Watching
While the relatives
Keep Right On
Touching . . .
        (and how much curl
        is right for a girl?)

But if he's said—
At some future date—

To have a head
That's put on straight
My son won't care
About his
Hair

Nor give a damn
Whose wife I am.

Reena*

Paule Marshall

Like most people with unpleasant childhoods, I am on constant guard against the past—the past being for me the people and places associated with the years I served out my girlhood in Brooklyn. The places no longer matter that much since most of them have vanished. The old grammar school, for instance, P.S. 35 ("Dirty 5's" we called it and with justification) has been replaced by a low, coldly functional arrangement of glass and Permastone which bears its name but has none of the feel of a school about it. The small, grudgingly lighted stores along Fulton Street, the soda parlor that was like a church with its stained-glass panels in the door and marble floor have given way to those impersonal emporiums, the supermarkets. Our house even, a brownstone relic whose halls smelled comfortingly of dust and lemon oil, the somnolent street upon which it stood, the tall, muscular trees which shaded it were leveled years ago to make way for a city housing project—a stark, graceless warren for the poor. So that now whenever I revisit that

* Copyright © 1962 by Paule Marshall.

[19]

old section of Brooklyn and see these new and ugly forms, I feel nothing. I might as well be in a strange city.

But it is another matter with the people of my past, the faces that in their darkness were myriad reflections of mine. Whenever I encounter them at the funeral or wake, the wedding or christening—these ceremonies by which the past reaffirms its hold—my guard drops and memories banished to the rear of the mind rush forward to rout the present. I almost become the child again—anxious and angry, disgracefully diffident.

Reena was one of the people from that time, and a main contributor to my sense of ineffectualness then. She had not done this deliberately. It was just that whenever she talked about herself (and this was not as often as most people) she seemed to be talking about me also. She ruthlessly analyzed herself, sparing herself nothing. Her honesty was so absolute it was a kind of cruelty.

She had not changed, I was to discover on meeting her again after a separation of twenty years. Nor had I really. For although the years had altered our positions (she was no longer the lord and I the lackey) and I could even afford to forgive her now, she still had the ability to disturb me profoundly by dredging to the surface those aspects of myself that I kept buried. This time, as I listened to her talk over the stretch of one long night, she made vivid without knowing it what is perhaps the most critical fact of my existence—that definition of me, of her and millions like us, formulated by others to serve out their fantasies, a definition we have to combat at an unconscionable cost to the self and even use, at times, in order to survive; the cause of so much shame and rage as well as, oddly enough, a source of pride: simply, what it has meant, what it means, to be a Black woman in America.

We met—Reena and myself—at the funeral of her aunt who had been my godmother and whom I had also called aunt, Aunt Vi, and loved, for she and her house had been, respectively, a source of understanding and a place of calm for me as a child. Reena entered the church where the funeral service was being held as though she, not the minister, were coming to officiate, sat down among the immediate family up front, and turned to inspect those behind her. I saw her face then.

It was a good copy of the original. The familiar mold was there, that is, and the configuration of bone beneath the skin was the same despite the slight fleshiness I had never seen there before; her features had even retained their distinctive touches: the positive set to her mouth, the assertive lift to her nose, the same insistent, unsettling eyes which when she was angry became as black as her skin—and this was total, unnerving, and very beautiful. Yet something had happened to her face. It was different despite its sameness. Aging even while it remained enviably young. Time had sketched in, very lightly, the evidence of the twenty years.

As soon as the funeral service was over, I left, hurrying out of the church into the early November night. The wind, already at its winter strength, brought with it the smell of dead leaves and the images of Aunt Vi there in the church, as dead as the leaves—as well as the thought of Reena, whom I would see later at the wake.

Her real name had been Doreen, a standard for girls among West Indians (her mother, like my parents, was from Barbados), but she had changed it to Reena on her twelfth birthday—"As a present to myself"—and had enforced the change on her family by refusing to answer to the old name. "Reena. With two e's!" she would say and imprint those e's on your mind with the indelible black of her eyes and a thin threatening finger that was like a quill.

She and I had not been friends through our own choice. Rather, our mothers, who had known each other since childhood, had forced the relationship. And from the beginning, I had been at a disadvantage. For Reena, as early as the age of twelve, had had a quality that was unique, superior, and therefore dangerous. She seemed defined, even then, all of a piece, the raw edges of her adolescence smoothed over; indeed, she seemed to have escaped adolescence altogether and made one dazzling leap from childhood into the very arena of adult life. At thirteen, for instance, she was reading Zola, Hauptmann, Steinbeck, while I was still in the thrall of the Little Minister and Lorna Doone. When I could only barely conceive of the world beyond Brooklyn, she was talking of the Civil War in Spain, lynchings in the South, Hitler in Poland—and talking with the outrage and passion of a revolutionary. I would try, I remember, to console myself with the thought that she was really an adult masquerading as a child, which meant that I could not possibly be her match.

For her part, Reena put up with me and was, by turns, patronizing and impatient. I merely served as the audience before whom she rehearsed her ideas and the yardstick by which she measured her worldliness and knowledge.

"Do you realize that this stupid country supplied Japan with the scrap iron to make the weapons she's now using against it?" she had shouted at me once.

I had not known that.

Just as she overwhelmed me, she overwhelmed her family, with the result that despite a half-dozen brothers and sisters who consumed quantities of bread and jam whenever they visited us, she behaved like an only child and got away with it. Her father, a gentle man with skin the color of dried tobacco and with the nose Reena had inherited jutting out like a crag from his nondescript face, had come from Georgia and was always making jokes about having married a foreigner—Reena's mother being from the West Indies. When not joking, he seemed slightly bewildered by his large family and so in awe of Reena that he avoided her. Reena's mother, a small, dry, formidably Black woman, was less a person to me than the abstract principle of force, power, energy. She was alternately strict and indulgent with Reena and, despite the inconsistency, surprisingly effective.

They lived when I knew them in a cold-water railroad flat above a kosher butcher on Belmont Avenue in Brownsville, some distance from us—and this in itself added to Reena's exotic quality. For it was a place where Sunday became Saturday, with all the stores open and pushcarts piled with vegetables and yard goods lined up along the curb, a crowded place where people hawked and spat freely in the streaming gutters and the men looked as if they had just stepped from the pages of the Old Testament with their profuse beards and long, black, satin coats.

When Reena was fifteen her family moved to Jamaica in Queens and since, in those days, Jamaica was considered too far away for visiting, our families lost contact and I did not see Reena again until we were both in college and then only once and not to speak to. . . .

I had walked some distance and by the time I got to the wake, which was being held at Aunt Vi's house, it was well under way. It was a good wake. Aunt Vi would have been pleased. There was plenty to drink, and more than enough to eat, including some Barbadian favorites: coconut bread, pone made with the cassava root, and the little crisp codfish cakes that are so hot with peppers they bring tears to the eyes as you bite into them.

I had missed the beginning, when everyone had probably sat around talking about Aunt Vi and recalling the few events that had distinguished her otherwise undistinguished life. (Someone, I'm sure, had told of the time she had missed the excursion boat to Atlantic City and had held her own private picnic—complete with pigeon peas and rice and fricassee chicken—on the pier at 42nd Street.) By the time I arrived, though, it would have been indiscreet to mention her name, for by then the wake had become—and this would also have pleased her—a celebration of life.

I had had two drinks, one right after the other, and was well into my third when Reena, who must have been upstairs, entered the basement kitchen where I was. She saw me before I had quite seen her, and with a cry that alerted the entire room to her presence and charged the air with her special force, she rushed toward me.

"Hey, I'm the one who was supposed to be the writer, not you! Do you know, I still can't believe it," she said, stepping back, her blackness heightened by a white mocking smile. "I read both your books over and over again and I can't really believe it. My Little Paulie!"

I did not mind. For there was respect and even wonder behind the patronizing words and in her eyes. The old imbalance between us had ended and I was suddenly glad to see her.

I told her so and we both began talking at once, but Reena's voice overpowered mine, so that all I could do after a time was listen while she discussed my books, and dutifully answer her questions about my personal life.

"And what about you?" I said, almost brutally, at the first chance I got. "What've you been up to all this time?"

She got up abruptly. "Good Lord, in here's noisy as hell. Come on, let's go upstairs."

We got fresh drinks and went up to Aunt Vi's bedroom, where in the soft light from the lamps, the huge Victorian bed and the pink satin bedspread with roses of the same material strewn over its surface looked as if they had never been used. And, in a way, this was true. Aunt Vi had seldom slept in her bed or, for that matter, lived in her house, because in order to pay for it, she had had to work at a sleeping-in job which gave her only Thursdays and every other Sunday off.

Reena sat on the bed, crushing the roses, and I sat on one of the numerous trunks which crowded the room. They contained every dress, coat, hat, and shoe that Aunt Vi had worn since coming to the

United States. I again asked Reena what she had been doing over the years.

"Do you want a blow-by-blow account?" she said. But despite the flippancy, she was suddenly serious. And when she began it was clear that she had written out the narrative in her mind many times. The words came too easily, the events, the incidents had been ordered in time, and the meaning of her behavior and of the people with whom she had been involved had been painstakingly analyzed. She talked willingly, with desperation almost. And the words by themselves weren't enough. She used her hands to give them form and urgency. I became totally involved with her and all that she said. So much so that as the night wore on I was not certain at times whether it was she or I speaking.

From the time her family moved to Jamaica until she was nineteen or so, Reena's life sounded, from what she told me in the beginning, as ordinary as mine and most of the girls we knew. After high school she had gone on to one of the free city colleges, where she had majored in journalism, worked part-time in the school library, and, surprisingly enough, joined a houseplan. (Even I hadn't gone that far.) It was an all-Negro club, since there was a tacit understanding that Negro and white girls did not join each other's houseplans. "Integration, Northern style," she said, shrugging.

It seems that Reena had had a purpose and a plan in joining the group. "I thought," she said with a wry smile, "I could get those girls up off their complacent rumps and out doing something about social issues. . . . I couldn't get them to budge. I remember after the war when a Negro ex-soldier had his eyes gouged out by a bus driver down South I tried getting them to demonstrate on campus. I talked until I was hoarse, but to no avail. They were too busy planning the annual autumn frolic."

Her laugh was bitter but forgiving and it ended in a long reflective silence. After which she said quietly, "It wasn't that they didn't give a damn. It was just, I suppose, that like most people they didn't want to get involved to the extent that they might have to stand up and be counted. If it ever came to that. Then another thing. They thought they were safe, special. After all, they had grown up in the North, most of them, and so had escaped the Southern-style prejudice; their parents, like mine, were struggling to put them through college, they could look forward to being tidy little schoolteachers, social workers, and lab technicians. Oh, they were safe!" The sarcasm scored her voice and then abruptly gave way to pity. "Poor things, they weren't safe, you see, and would never be as long as millions like themselves in Harlem, on Chicago's South Side, down South, all over the place, were unsafe. I tried to tell them this—and they accused me of being oversensitive. They tried not to listen. But I would have held out and, I'm sure, even brought some of them around eventually if this other business with a silly boy hadn't happened at the same time. . . ."

Reena told me then about her first, brief, and apparently innocent affair with a boy she had met at one of the houseplan parties. It had ended, she said, when the boy's parents had met her. "That was it," she said, and the flat of her hand cut into the air. "He was forbidden to see me. The reason? He couldn't bring himself to tell me, but I knew. I was too black.

"Naturally, it wasn't the first time something like that had happened. In fact, you might say that was the theme of my childhood. Because I was dark I was always being plastered with Vaseline so I wouldn't look ashy. Whenever I had my picture taken they would pile a whitish powder on my face and make the lights so bright I always came out looking ghostly. My mother stopped speaking to any number of people because they said I would have been pretty if I hadn't been so dark. Like nearly every little black girl, I had my share of dreams of waking up to find myself with long blond curls, blue eyes, and skin like milk. So I should have been prepared. Besides, that boy's parents were really rejecting themselves in rejecting me.

"Take us"—and her hands, opening in front of my face as she suddenly leaned forward, seemed to offer me the whole of black humanity. "We live surrounded by white images, and white in this world is synonymous with the good, light, beauty, success, so that, despite ourselves sometimes, we run after that whiteness and deny our darkness, which has been made into the symbol of all that is evil and inferior. I wasn't a person to that boy's parents, but a symbol of the darkness they were in flight from, so that just as they— that boy, his parents, those silly girls in the houseplan—were running from me, I started running from them. . . ."

It must have been shortly after this happened when I saw Reena at a debate which was being held at my college. She did not see me, since she was one of the speakers and I was merely part of her audience in the crowded auditorium. The topic had something to do with intellectual freedom in the colleges (McCarthyism was coming into vogue then), and aside from a Jewish boy from City College, Reena was the most effective—sharp, provocative, her position the most radical. The others on the panel seemed intimidated not only by the strength and cogency of her argument but by the sheer impact of her blackness in their white midst.

Her color might have been a weapon she used to dazzle and disarm her opponents. And she had highlighted it with the clothes she was wearing: a white dress patterned with large blocks of primary colors I remember (it looked Mexican) and a pair of intricately wrought silver earrings—long and with many little parts which clashed like muted cymbals over the microphone each time she moved her head. She wore her hair cropped short like a boy's and it was not straightened like mine and the other Negro girls' in the audience, but left in its coarse natural state: a small forest under which her face emerged in its intense and startling handsomeness. I remember she left the auditorium in triumph that day, surrounded by a noisy entourage from her college—all of them white.

"We were very serious," she said now, describing the left-wing group she had belonged to then—and there was a defensiveness in her voice which sought to protect them from all censure. "We believed—because we were young, I suppose, and had nothing as yet to risk—that we could do something about the injustices which everyone around us seemed to take for granted. So we picketed and demonstrated and bombarded Washington with our protests, only to have our names added to the Attorney General's list for all our trouble. We were always standing on street corners handing out leaflets or getting people to sign petitions. We always seemed to pick the coldest days to do that." Her smile held long after the words had died.

"I, we all, had such a sense of purpose then," she said softly, and a sadness lay aslant the smile now, darkening it. "We were forever holding meetings, having endless discussions, arguing, shouting, theorizing. And we had fun. Those parties! There was always somebody with a guitar. We were always singing. . . ." Suddenly, she began singing—and her voice was sure, militant, and faintly self-mocking.

"But the banks are made of marble
 With a guard at every door
 And the vaults are stuffed with silver
 That the workers sweated for . . ."

When she spoke again the words were a sad coda to the song. "Well, as you probably know, things came to an ugly head with McCarthy reigning in Washington, and I was one of the people temporarily suspended from school."

She broke off and we both waited, the ice in our glasses melted and the drinks gone flat.

"At first, I didn't mind," she said finally. "After all, we were right. The fact that they suspended us proved it. Besides, I was in the middle of an affair, a real one this time, and too busy with that to care about anything else." She paused again, frowning.

"He was white," she said quickly and glanced at me as though to surprise either shock or disapproval in my face. "We were very involved. At one point—I think just after we had been suspended and he started working—we even thought of getting married. Living in New York, moving in the crowd we did, we might have been able to manage it. But I couldn't. There were too many complex things going on beneath the surface," she said, her voice strained by the hopelessness she must have felt then, her hands shaping it in the air between us. "Neither one of us could really escape what our color had come to mean in this country. Let me explain. Bob was always, for some odd reason, talking about how much the Negro suffered, and although I would agree with him I would also try to get across that, you know, like all people we also had fun once in a while, loved our children, liked making love—that we were human beings, for God's sake. But he only wanted to hear about the suffering. It was as if this comforted him and eased his own suffering—and he did suffer because of any number of things: his own uncertainty, for one, his difficulties with his family, for another . . .

"Once, I remember when his father came into New York, Bob insisted that I meet him. I don't know why I agreed to go with him . . ." She took a deep breath and raised her head very high. "I'll never forget or forgive the look on that old man's face when he opened his hotel room door and saw me. The horror. I might have been the personification of every evil in the world. His inability to believe that it was his son standing there holding my hand. His shock. I'm sure he never fully recovered. I know I never did. Nor can I forget Bob's laugh in the elevator afterwards, the way he kept repeating: 'Did you see his face when he saw you? Did you . . . ?' He had used me, you see. I had been the means, the instrument of his revenge.

"And I wasn't any better. I used him. I took every opportunity to treat him shabbily, trying, you see, through him, to get at that white world which had not only denied me, but had turned my own against me." Her eyes closed. "I went numb all over when I understood what we were doing to, and with, each other. I stayed numb for a long time."

As Reena described the events which followed—the break with Bob, her gradual withdrawal from the left-wing group ("I had had it with them too. I got tired of being 'their Negro,' their pet. Besides, they were just all talk, really. All theories and abstractions. I doubt that, with all their elaborate plans for the Negro and for the workers of the world, any of them had ever been near a factory or up to Harlem")—as she spoke about her reinstatement in school, her voice suggested the numbness she had felt then. It only stirred into life again when she talked of her graduation.

"You should have seen my parents. It was really their day. My mother was so proud she complained about everything: her seat, the heat, the speaker; and my father just sat there long after everybody had left, too awed to move. God, it meant so much to them. It was as if I had made up for the generations his people had picked cotton in Georgia and my mother's family had cut cane in the West Indies. It frightened me."

I asked her after a long wait what she had done after graduating.

"How do you mean, what I did. Looked for a job. Tell me, have you ever looked for work in this man's city?"

"I know," I said, holding up my hand. "Don't tell me."

We both looked at my raised hand which sought to waive the

discussion, then at each other and suddenly we laughed, a laugh so loud and violent with pain and outrage it brought tears.

"Girl," Reena said, the tears silver against her blackness. "You could put me blindfolded right now at the Times Building on 42nd Street and I would be able to find my way to every newspaper office in town. But tell me, how come white folks is so hard?"

"Just bo'n hard."

We were laughing again and this time I nearly slid off the trunk and Reena fell back among the satin roses.

"I didn't know there were so many ways of saying 'no' without ever once using the word," she said, the laughter lodged in her throat, but her eyes had gone hard. "Sometimes I'd find myself in the elevator, on my way out, and smiling all over myself because I thought I had gotten the job, before it would hit me that they had really said no, not yes. Some of those people in personnel had so perfected their smiles they looked almost genuine. The ones who used to get me, though, were those who tried to make the interview into an intimate chat between friends. They'd put you in a comfortable chair, offer you a cigarette, and order coffee. How I hated that coffee. They didn't know it—or maybe they did—but it was like offering me hemlock. . . .

"You think Christ had it tough?" Her laughter rushed against the air which resisted it. "I was crucified five days a week and half-day on Saturday. I became almost paranoid. I began to think there might be something other than color wrong with me which everybody but me could see, some rare disease that had turned me into a monster.

"My parents suffered. And that bothered me most, because I felt I had failed them. My father didn't say anything but I knew because he avoided me more than usual. He was ashamed, I think, that he hadn't been able, as a man and as my father, to prevent this. My mother—well, you know her. In one breath she would try to comfort me by cursing them: 'But Gor blind them' "—and Reena's voice captured her mother's aggressive accent—" 'if you had come looking for a job mopping down their floors they would o' hire you, the brutes. But mark my words, their time goin' come, 'cause God don't love ugly and he ain't stuck on pretty . . .' And in the next breath she would curse me, 'Journalism! Journalism! Whoever heard of colored people taking up journalism. You must feel you's white or something so. The people is right to chuck you out their office . . .' Poor thing, to make up for saying all that she would wash my white gloves every night and cook cereal for me in the morning as if I were a little girl again. Once she went out and bought me a suit she couldn't afford from Lord and Taylor's. I looked like a Smith girl in blackface in it. . . . So guess where I ended up?"

"As a social investigator for the Welfare Department. Where else?"

We were helpless with laughter again.

"You too?"

"No," I said, "I taught, but that was just as bad."

"No," she said, sobering abruptly. "Nothing's as bad as working for Welfare. Do you know what they really mean by a social investigator? A spy. Someone whose dirty job it is to snoop into the corners of the lives of the poor and make their poverty more vivid by taking from them the last shred of privacy. 'Mrs. Jones, is that a new dress you're wearing?' 'Mrs. Brown, this kerosene heater is not listed in the household items. Did you get an authorization for it?' 'Mrs. Smith, is that a telephone I hear ringing under the sofa?' I was utterly demoralized within a month.

"And another thing. I thought I knew about poverty. I mean, I remember, as a child, having to eat soup made with those white beans the government used to give out free for days running, sometimes, because there was nothing else. I had lived in Brownsville, among all the poor Jews and Poles and Irish there. But what I saw in Harlem where I had my case load was different somehow. Perhaps because it seemed so final. There didn't seem to be any way to escape from those dark hallways and dingy furnished rooms . . . all that defeat." Closing her eyes, she finished the stale whiskey and soda in her glass.

"I remember a client of mine, a girl my age with three children already and no father for them and living in the expensive squalor of a rooming house. Her bewilderment. Her resignation. Her anger. She could have pulled herself out of the mess she was in? People say that, you know, including some Negroes. But this girl didn't have a chance. She had been trapped from the day she was born in some small town down South.

"She became my reference. From then on and even now, whenever I hear people and groups coming up with all kinds of solutions to the quote Negro problem, I ask one question. What are they really doing for that girl, to save her or to save the children? . . . The answer isn't very encouraging."

It was some time before she continued and then she told me that after Welfare she had gone to work for a private social-work agency, in their publicity department, and had started on her master's in journalism at Columbia. She also left home around this time.

"I had to. My mother started putting the pressure on me to get married. The hints, the remarks—and you know my mother was never the subtle type—her anxiety, which made me anxious about getting married after a while. Besides, it was time for me to be on my own."

In contrast to the unmistakably radical character of her late adolescence (her membership in the left-wing group, the affair with Bob, her suspension from college), Reena's life of this period sounded ordinary, standard—and she admitted it with a slightly self-deprecating, apologetic smile. It was similar to that of any number of unmarried professional Negro women in New York or Los Angeles or Washington: the job teaching or doing social work which brought in a fairly decent salary, the small apartment with kitchenette which they sometimes shared with a roommate; a car, some of them; membership in various political and social action organizations for the militant few like Reena; the vacations in Mexico, Europe, the West Indies, and now Africa; the occasional date. "The interesting men were invariably married," Reena said and then mentioned having had one affair during that time. She had found out he was married and had thought of her only as the perfect mistress. "The bastard," she said, but her smile forgave him.

"Women alone!" she cried, laughing sadly, and her raised opened arms, the empty glass she held in one hand made eloquent their aloneness. "Alone and lonely, and indulging themselves while they wait. The girls of the houseplan have reached their majority only to find that all those years they spent accumulating their degrees and finding the well-paying jobs in the hope that this would raise their stock have, instead, put them at a disadvantage. For the few eligible men around—those who are their intellectual and professional peers, whom they can respect (and there are very few of them)—don't necessarily marry them, but younger women without the degrees and the fat jobs, who are no threat, or they don't marry at all because they are either queer or mother-ridden. Or they marry white women. Now, intellectually I accept this. In fact, some of my best friends are white women . . ." And again our laughter—that loud, searing burst which we used to cauterize our hurt mounted into the unaccepting silence of the room. "After all, our goal is a fully integrated society. And perhaps, as some people believe, the only solution to the race problem is miscegenation. Besides, a man should be able to marry whomever he wishes. Emotionally, though, I am less kind and understanding, and I resent like hell the reasons some Black men give for rejecting us for them."

"We're too middle-class-oriented," I said. "Conservative."

"Right. Even though, thank God, that doesn't apply to me."

"Too threatening . . . castrating . . ."

"Too independent and impatient with them for not being more ambitious . . . contemptuous . . ."

"Sexually inhibited and unimaginative . . ."

"And the old myth of the excessive sexuality of the black woman goes out the window," Reena cried.

"Not supportive, unwilling to submerge our interests for theirs . . ."

"Lacking in the subtle art of getting and keeping a man . . ."

We had recited the accusations in the form and tone of a litany, and in the silence which followed we shared a thin, hopeless smile.

"They condemn us," Reena said softly but with anger, "without taking history into account. We are still, most of us, the Black woman who had to be almost frighteningly strong in order for us all to survive. For, after all, she was the one whom they left (and I don't hold this against them; I understand) with the children to raise, who had to make it somehow or other. And we are still, so many of us, living that history.

"You would think that they would understand this, but few do. So it's up to us. We have got to understand them and save them for ourselves. How? By being, on one hand, persons in our own right and, on the other, fully the woman and the wife. . . . Christ, listen to who's talking! I had my chance. And I tried. Very hard. But it wasn't enough."

The festive sounds of the wake had died to a sober murmur beyond the bedroom. The crowd had gone, leaving only Reena and myself upstairs and the last of Aunt Vi's closest friends in the basement below. They were drinking coffee. I smelled it, felt its warmth and intimacy in the empty house, heard the distant tapping of the cups against the saucers and voices muted by grief. The wake had come full circle: they were again mourning Aunt Vi.

And Reena might have been mourning with them, sitting there amid the satin roses, framed by the massive headboard. Her hands lay as if they had been broken in her lap. Her eyes were like those of someone blind or dead. I got up to go and get some coffee for her.

"You met my husband," she said quickly, stopping me.

"Have I?" I said, sitting down again.

"Yes, before we were married even. At an autograph party for you. He was free-lancing—he's a photographer—and one of the Negro magazines had sent him to cover the party."

As she went on to describe him I remembered him vaguely, not his face, but his rather large body stretching and bending with a dancer's fluidity and grace as he took the pictures. I had heard him talking to a group of people about some issue on race relations very much in the news then and had been struck by his vehemence. For the moment I had found this almost odd, since he was so fair-skinned he could have passed for white.

They had met, Reena told me now, at a benefit show for a Harlem day nursery given by one of the progressive groups she belonged to, and had married a month afterwards. From all that she said they had had a full and exciting life for a long time. Her words were so vivid that I could almost see them, she with her startling blackness and extraordinary force and he with his near-white skin and a militancy which matched hers; both of them moving among the Black bourgeoisie of St. Albans or Teaneck, cal and social issues equally uncompromising, the line of their allegiance reaching directly to all those trapped in Harlem. And they had lived the meaning of this allegiance, so that even when they could have afforded a life among the black bourgeoisie of St. Albans or Teaneck, they had chosen to live it not in Harlem so close that there was no difference.

"I—we—were so happy I was frightened at times. Not that anything would change between us, but that someone or something in the world outside us would invade our private place and destroy us out of envy. Perhaps this is what did happen. . . ." She shrugged and even tried to smile but she could not manage it. "Something slipped in while we weren't looking and began its deadly work.

"Maybe it started when Dave took a job with a Negro magazine. I'm not sure. Anyway, in no time, he hated it, the routine, unimaginative pictures he had to take and the magazine itself, which dealt only in unrealities: the high-society world of the Black bourgeoisie and the spectacular strides Negroes were making in all fields—you know the type. Yet Dave wouldn't leave. It wasn't the money, but a kind of safety which he had never experienced before which kept him there. He would talk about free-lancing again, about storming the gates of the white magazines downtown, of opening his own studio—but he never acted on any one of these things. You see, despite his talents—and he was very talented—he had a diffidence that was fatal.

"When I understood this I literally forced him to open the studio—and perhaps I should have been more subtle and indirect, but that's not my nature. Besides, I was frightened and desperate to help. Nothing happened for a time. Dave's work was too experimental to be commercial. Gradually, though, his photographs started appearing in the prestige camera magazines and money from various awards and exhibits and an occasional assignment started coming in.

"This wasn't enough somehow. Dave also wanted the big, gaudy commercial success that would dazzle and confound that white world downtown and force it to see him. And yet, as I said before, he couldn't bring himself to try—and this contradiction began to get to him after a while.

"It was then, I think, that I began to fail him. I didn't know how to help, you see, I had never felt so inadequate before. And this was very strange and disturbing for someone like me. I was being submerged in his problems—and I began fighting against this.

"I started working again (I had stopped after the second baby). And I was lucky because I got back my old job. And unlucky because Dave saw it as my way of pointing up his deficiencies. I couldn't convince him otherwise: that I had to do it for my own sanity. He would accuse me of wanting to see him fail, of trapping him in all kinds of responsibilities. . . . After a time we both got caught up in this thing, an ugliness came between us, and I began to answer his anger with anger and to trade him insult for insult.

"Things fell apart very quickly after that. I couldn't bear the pain of living with him—the insults, our mutual despair, his mocking, the silence. I couldn't subject the children to it any longer. The divorce didn't take long. And thank God, because of the children, we are pleasant when we have to see each other. He's making out very well, I hear."

She said nothing more, but simply bowed her head as though waiting for me to pass judgment on her. I don't know how long we remained like this, but when Reena finally raised her head, the darkness at the window had vanished and dawn was a still, gray smoke against the pane.

"Do you know," she said, and her eyes were clear and a smile had won out over pain, "I enjoy being alone. I don't tell people this because they'll accuse me of either lying or deluding myself. But I do. Perhaps, as my mother tells me, it's only temporary. I don't think so, though I feel I don't ever want to be involved again. It's not that I've lost interest in men. I go out occasionally, but it's never anything serious. You see, I have all that I want for now."

Her children first of all, she told me, and from her description they sounded intelligent and capable. She was a friend as well as a mother to them, it seemed. They were planning, the four of them, to spend the summer touring Canada. "I will feel that I have done well by them if I give them, if nothing more, a sense of themselves and their worth and importance as Black people. Everything I do with them, for them, is to this end. I don't want them ever to be confused about this. They must have their identifications straight from the beginning. No white dolls for them!"

Then her job. She was working now as a researcher for a small progressive news magazine with the promise that once she completed her master's in journalism (she was working on the thesis now) she might get a chance to do some minor reporting. And like most people she hoped to write someday. "If I can ever stop talking away my substance," she said laughing.

And she was still active in any number of social action groups. In another week or so she would be heading a delegation of mothers down to City Hall "to give the mayor a little hell about conditions in the schools in Harlem." She had started an organization that was carrying on an almost door-to-door campaign in her neighborhood to expose, as she put it, "the bloodsuckers: all those slumlords and storekeepers with their fixed scales, the finance companies that never tell you the real price of a thing, the petty salesmen that leech off the poor . . ." In May she was taking her two older girls on a nationwide pilgrimage to Washington to urge for a more rapid implementation of the school-desegregation law.

"It's uncanny," she said and the laugh which accompanied the words was warm, soft with wonder at herself, girlish even, and the air in the room which had refused her laughter before rushed to absorb this now. "Really uncanny. Here I am, practically middle-aged, with three children to raise by myself and with little or no money to do it and yet I feel, strangely enough, as though life is just beginning—that it's new and fresh with all kinds of possibilities. Maybe it's because I've been through my purgatory and I can't ever be overwhelmed again. I don't know. Anyway, you should see me on evenings after I put the children to bed. I sit alone in the living room (I've repainted it and changed all the furniture since Dave's gone, so that it would at least look different)—I sit there making plans and all of them seem possible. The most important plan right now is Africa. I've already started saving the fare."

I asked her whether she was planning to live there permanently and she said simply, "I want to live and work there. For how long, for a lifetime, I can't say. All I know is that I have to. For myself and for my children. It is important that they see Black people who have truly a place and history of their own and who are building for a new and, hopefully, more sensible world. And I must see it, get close to it, because I can never lose the sense of being a displaced person here in America because of my color. Oh, I know I should remain and fight not only for integration (even though, frankly, I question whether I want to be integrated into America as it stands now, with its complacency and materialism, its soullessness) but to help change the country into something better, sounder—if that is still possible. But I have to go to Africa. . . .

"Poor Aunt Vi," she said after a long silence and straightened one of the roses she had crushed. "She never really got to enjoy her bed of roses what with only Thursdays and every other Sunday off. All that hard work. All her life. . . . Our lives have got to make more sense, if only for her."

We got up to leave shortly afterwards. Reena was staying on to attend the burial later in the morning, but I was taking the subway to Manhattan. We parted with the usual promise to get together and exchanged telephone numbers. And Reena did phone a week or so later. I don't remember what we talked about, though.

Some months later I invited her to a party I was giving before leaving the country. But she did not come.

The Diary of an African Nun*

Alice Walker

Our Mission School is at the foot of lovely Uganda mountains and is a resting place for travelers. Classrooms in daylight, a hotel when the sun sets.

The question is in the eyes of all who come here; why are you, so young, so beautiful perhaps, a nun? The Americans cannot understand my humility. I bring them clean sheets and towels and return their too much money and candid smiles. They cannot understand this, but they think it a good thing. The German guests are very different. They do not offer money but praise. The sight of a Black nun strikes their sentimentality; and, as I am unalterably rooted in native ground they consider me a work of primitive art, housed in a magical color; the incarnation of civilization, anti-heathenism, and the fruit of a triumphing idea. They are coolly passionate and smile at me lecherously with speculative crystal eyes of bright historical blue. The French find me charmante and would like to paint

* Reprinted from *Freedomways*, Summer 1968.

a picture. The Italians, used as they are to the habit, concern themselves with the giant cockroaches in the latrines and give me hardly a glance, except in reproach for them.

I am, perhaps, as I should be. *Gloria Deum. Gloria in excelsis Deo.*

I am a wife of Christ, a wife of the Catholic church. The wife of a celibate martyr and saint. I was born in this township, a village "civilized" by American missionaries. All my life I have lived here within walking distance of the Ruwenzori mountains—mountains which show themselves only once a year under the blazing heat of spring.

II

When I was younger, in a bright blue school uniform and bare feet, I came every day to the mission school. "Good morning," I chanted to the people I met. But especially to the nuns and priests who taught at my school. I did not then know that they could not have children. They seemed so productive and full of intense, regal life. I wanted to be like them, and now I am. Shrouded in whiteness like the mountains I see from my window.

At twenty I earned the right to wear this dress, never to be without it, always to bathe myself in cold water even in winter, and to wear my mission-cropped hair well covered, my nails clean and neatly clipped. The boys I knew as a child are kind to me now and gentle, and I see them married and kiss their children, each one of them so much what our Lord wanted—did he not say, "Suffer little children to come unto me"?—but we have not yet been so lucky, and we never shall.

III

At night I sit in my room until seven, then I go, obediently, to bed. Through the window I can hear the drums, smell the roasting goat's meat, feel the rhythm of the festive chants. And I sing my own chants in response to theirs, *"Pater noster, qui est in caelis, sanctificetur nomen tuum, adveniat regnum tuum, fiat voluntas tua, sicut in caelo et in terra . . ."* My chant is less old than theirs. They do not know this—they do not even care.

Do I care? Must I still ask myself whether it was my husband, who came down bodiless from the sky, son of a proud father and flesh once upon the earth, who first took me and claimed the innocence of my body; or was it the drum beats, messengers of the sacred dance of life and deathlessness on earth? Must I still long to be within the black circle around the red, glowing fire, to feel the breath of love hot against my cheeks, the smell of love strong about my waiting thighs—! Must I still tremble at the thought of the passions stifled beneath this voluminous rustling snow!

How long must I sit by my window before I lure you down from the sky? Pale lover who never knew the dance and could not do it! I bear your colors, I am in your livery, I belong to you. Will you not come down and take me? Or are you even less passionate than your father who look but could not show his face?

IV

Silence, as the dance continues—now they will be breaking the wine, cutting the goat's meat in sinewy strips. Teeth will clutch it, wring it. Cruel, greedy, greasy lips will curl over it in an ecstasy which has never ceased wherever there were goats and men.

The wine will be hot from the fire; it will cut through the obscene clutter on those lips and turn them from their goat's meat to that other.

At midnight a young girl will come to the circle, hidden in black. She will not speak to anyone. She has said "good morning" to them all, many mornings, and has decided to be like them. She will begin the dance—every eye following the flashes of her oiled, slippery body, every heart pounding to the flat clacks of her dusty feet. She will dance to her lover with arms stretched upward to the sky, but her eyes are leveled at her lover, one of the crowd. He will dance with her. The tempo will increase. All the crowd can see the weakening of her knees, can feel in their own loins the loosening of her rolling thighs. Her lover makes her wait until she is in a frenzy, tearing off her clothes and scratching at the narrow cloth he wears. The eyes of the crowd are forgotten. The final taking is unbearable as they rock through the oldest dance. The flames roar and the purple bodies crumple and are still. And the dancing begins again and the whole night is a repetition of the dance of life and the urgent fire of creation. Dawn breaks finally to the acclaiming cries of babies.

V

"Our Father, which art in heaven, hallowed be Thy name, Thy kingdom come, Thy will be done on earth—" And in heaven, would the ecstasy be quite as fierce and sweet?

"Sweet, Sister," they will say. "Have we not yet made a convert of you? Will you yet be a cannibal and eat up the life that is Christ because it eases your palate?"

What must I tell my husband? To say the truth would mean

oblivion, to be forgotten for another thousand years. Still, perhaps I shall answer this to him who took me:

"Dearly Beloved, let me tell you about the mountains and the Spring. The mountains that we see around us are black, it is the snow that gives them their icy whiteness. In the Spring, the hot black soil melts the crust of snow on the mountains, and the water as it runs down the sheets of fiery rock burns and cleanses the naked bodies that come to wash in it. It is when the snows melt that the people here plant their crops; the soil of the mountains is rich, and its produce plentiful and good.

"What have I or my mountains to do with a childless marriage, or with eyes that can see only the snow; or with you or friends of yours who do not believe that you are really dead—pious faithful who do not yet realize that barrenness is death?"

Or perhaps I might say: "Leave me alone; I will do your work." Or, what is more likely, I will say nothing of my melancholia at your lack of faith in the Spring . . . for what is my faith in the Spring and the Eternal Melting of Snows (you will ask) but your belief in the Resurrection? Could I convince one so wise that my belief bears more fruit?

How teach a barren world to dance? It is a contradiction that divides the world.

My mouth must be silent, then, though my heart jumps to the booming of the drums, as to the last strong pulse of life in a dying world.

For the drums will soon, one day, be silent. I will help muffle them forever. To assure life for my people in this world I must be among the lying ones and teach them how to die. I will turn their dances into prayers to an empty sky, and their lovers into dead men, and their babies into unsung chants that choke their throats each spring.

VI

In this way will the wife of a loveless, barren, hopeless Western marriage broadcast the joys of an enlightened religion to an imitative people.

Tell Martha Not to Moan*

Shirley Williams

My mamma is a big woman, tall and stout, and men like her cause she soft and fluffy-looking. When she round them it all smiles and dimples and her mouth be looking like it couldn't never be fixed to say nothing but darling and honey.

They see her now, they sho see something different. I should not even come today. Since I had Larry things ain't been too good between us. But—that's my mamma and I know she gon be there when I need her. And sometime when I come, it okay. But this ain't gon be one a them times. Her eyes looking all ove me and I know it coming. She snort cause she want to say god damn but she don't cuss. "When it due, Martha?"

First I start to say, what. But I know it ain't no use. You can't fool old folks bout something like that, so I tell her.

"Last part of November."

* Reprinted from the *Massachusetts Review*. Copyright © 1968 by *Massachusetts Review, Inc.*

"Who the daddy?"

"Time."

"That man what play piano at the Legion?"

"Yeah."

"What he gon do bout it?"

"Mamma, it ain't too much he can do, now is it? The baby on its way."

She don't say nothing for a long time. She sit looking at her hands. They all wet from where she been washing dishes and they all wrinkled like yo hand be when they been in water too long. She get up and get a dish cloth and dry em, then sit down at the table. "Where he at now?"

"Gone."

"Gone? Gone where?" I don't say nothing and she start cussing then. I get kinda scared cause mamma got to be real mad foe she cuss and I don't know who she cussing—me or Time. Then she start talking to me. "Martha, you just a fool. I told you that man wan't no good first time I seed him. A musician the worst kind of men you can get mixed up with. Look at you. You ain't even eighteen years old yet, Larry just barely two, and here you is pregnant again." She go on like that for a while and I don't say nothing. Couldn't no way. By the time I get my mouth fixed to say something, she done raced on so far ahead that what I got to say don't have nothing to do with what she saying right then. Finally she stop and ask, "What you gon do now? You want to come back here?" She ain't never liked me living with Orine and when I say no, she ask, "Why not? It be easier for you."

I shake my head, again. "If I here, Time won't know where to find me, and Time coming; he be back. He gon to make a place for us, you a see."

"Hump, you just played the fool again, Martha."

"No Mamma, that not it at all; Time want me."

"Is that what he say when he left?"

"No, but . . ."

Well, like the first night we met, he come over to me like he knowed me for a long time and like I been his for awmost that long. Yeah, I think that how it was. Cause I didn't even see him when we come in the Legion that first night.

Me and Orine, we just got our checks that day. We went downtown and Orine bought her some new dresses. But the dress she want to wear that night don't look right so we go racing back to town and change it. Then we had to hurry home and get dressed. It Friday night and the Legion crowded. You got to get there early on the weekend if you want a seat. And Orine don't want just any seat; she want one right up front. "Who gon see you way back there? Nobody. You don't dance, how you gon meet people? You don't meet people, what you doing out?" So we sit up front. Whole lots a people there that night. You can't even see the bandstand cross the dance floor. We sharing the table with some more people and Orine keep jabbing me, telling me to sit cool. And I try cause Orine say it a good thing to be cool.

The set end and people start leaving the dance floor. That when I see Time. He just getting up from the piano. I like him right off cause I like men what look like him. He kind of tall and slim. First time I ever seed a man wear his hair so long and nappy—he tell me once it an African Bush—but he look good anyway and he know it. He look round all cool. He step down from the bandstand and start walking toward me. He come over to the table and just look. "You," he say, "you my Black queen." And he bow down most to the floor.

Ah shit! I mad cause I think he just trying to run a game. "What you trying to prove, fool?" I ask him.

"Ah man," he say and it like I cut him. That the way he say it. "Ah man. I call this woman my Black queen—tell her she can rule my life and she call me a fool."

"And sides what, nigga," I tell him then, "I ain't black." And I ain't, I don't care what Time say. I just a dark woman.

"What's the matter, you shamed of being Black? Ain't nobody told you Black is pretty?" He talk all loud and people start gathering round. Somebody say, "Yeah, you tell her bout it, soul." I embarrassed and I look over at Orine. But she just grinning, not saying nothing. I guess she waiting to see what I gon do so I stand up.

"Well if I is black, I is a fine black." And I walk over to the bar. I walk just like I don't know they watching my ass, and I hold my head up. Time follow me right on over to the bar and put his arm round my shoulder.

"You want a drink?" I start to say no cause I scared. Man not supposed to make you feel like he make me feel. Not just like doing it—but, oh, like it right for him to be there with me, touching me. So I say yes. "What's your name?" he ask then.

I smile and say, "They call me the player." Orine told a man that once in Berkeley and he didn't know what to say. Orine a smart woman.

"Well they call me Time and I know yo mamma done told you Time ain't nothing to play with." His smile cooler than mine. We don't say nothing for a long while. He just stand there with his arm round my shoulder looking at us in the mirror behind the bar. Finally he say, "Yeah, you gon be my Black queen." And he look down at me and laugh. I don't know what to do, don't know what to say neither, so I just smile.

"You gon tell me your name or not?"

"Martha."

He laugh. "That a good name for you."

"My mamma name me that so I be good. She name all us kids from the Bible," I tell him laughing.

"And is you good?"

I nod yes and no all at the same time and kind of mumble cause

I don't know what to say. Mamma really did name all us kids from the Bible. She always saying, "My mamma name me Veronica after the woman in the Bible and I a better woman for it. That why I name all my kids from the Bible. They got something to look up to." But mamma don't think I'm good, specially since I got Larry. Maybe Time ain't gon think I good neither. So I don't answer, just smile and move on back to the table. I hear him singing soft-like, "Oh Mary don't you weep, tell yo sister Martha not to moan." And I kind of glad cause most people don't even think bout that when I tell em my name. That make me know he really smart.

We went out for breakfast after the Legion close. Him and me and Orine and German, the drummer. Only places open is on the other side of town and at first Time don't want to go. But we finally swade him.

Time got funny eyes, you can't hardly see into em. You look and you look and you can't tell nothing from em. It make me feel funny when he look at me. I finally get used to it, but that night he just sit there looking and don't say nothing for a long time after we order.

"So you don't like Black?" he finally say.

"Do you?" I ask. I think I just ask him questions, then I don't have to talk so much. But I don't want him to talk bout that right then, so I smile and say, "Let's talk bout you."

"I am not what I am." He smiling and I smile back, but I feel funny cause I think I supposed to know what he mean.

"What kind of game you trying to run?" Orine ask. Then she laugh. "Just cause we from the country don't mean we ain't hip to niggas trying to be big-time. Ain't that right, Martha?"

I don't know what to say, but I know Time don't like that. I think he was going to cuss Orine out, but German put his arm round Orine and he laugh. "He just mean he ain't what he want to be. Don't pay no mind to that cat. He always trying to blow some shit." And he start talking that talk, rapping to Orine.

I look at Time. "That what you mean?"

He all lounged back in the seat, his legs stretched way out under the table. He pour salt in a napkin and mix it up with his finger. "Yeah, that's what I mean. That's all about me. Black is pretty, Martha." He touch my face with one finger. "You let white people make you believe you ugly. I bet you don't even dream."

"I do too."

"What do you dream?"

"Huh?" I don't know what he talking bout. I kind of smile and look at him out the corner of my eye. "I dreams bout a man like you. Why, just last night, I dream—"

He start laughing. "That's all right. That's all right."

The food come then and we all start eating. Time act like he forgot all bout dreams. I never figure out how he think I can just sit there and tell him the dreams I have at night, just like that. It don't seem like what I dream bout at night mean as much as what I think bout during the day.

We leaving when Time trip over this white man's feet. That man's feet all out in the aisle but Time don't never be watching where he going no way. "Excuse me," he say kind of mean.

"Say, watch it buddy." That white man talk most as nasty as Time. He kind of old and maybe he drunk or an Okie.

"Man, I said excuse me. You the one got your feet in the aisle."

"You," that man say, starting to get up, "you better watch yourself boy."

And what he want to say that for? Time step back and say real quiet, "No, motherfucker. You the one. You better watch yourself and your daughter too. See how many babies she gon have by boys like me." That man get all red in the face, but the woman in the booth with him finally start pulling at him, telling him to sit down, shut up. Cause Time set to kill that man.

I touch Time's arm first, then put my arm round his waist. "Ain't no use getting messed behind somebody like that."

Time and that man just looking at each other, not wanting to back down. People was gon start wondering what going on in a few minutes. I tell him, "Got something for you, baby," and he look down at me and grin. Orine pick it up. We go out that place singing, "Good loving, good, good loving, make you feel so clean."

"You like to hear me play?" he ask when we in the car.

"This the first time they ever have anybody here that sound that good."

"Yeah," Orine say. "How come you all staying round a little jive-ass town like Ashley?"

"We going to New York pretty soon," Time say kind of snappy.

"Well, shit, baby, you—"

"When you going to New York?" I ask real quick. When Orine in a bad mood, can't nobody say nothing right.

"Couple of months." He lean back and put his arm round me. "They doing so many things with music back there. Up in the City, they doing one maybe two things. In L.A. they doing another one, two things. But, man, in New York, they doing everything. Person couldn't never get stuck in one groove there. So many things going on, you got to be hip, real hip to keep up. You always growing there. Shit, if you 'live and playing, you can't help but grow. Say, man," he reach and tap German on the shoulder, "let's leave right now."

We all crack up. Then I say, "I sorry but I can't go, got to take care of my baby."

He laugh, "Sugar, you got yo baby right here."

"Well, I must got two babies then."

We pull in front of the partment house then but don't no one move. Finally Time reach over and touch my hair. "You gon be my Black queen?"

I look straight ahead at the night. "Yeah," I say. "Yeah."

We go in and I check first on Larry cause sometimes that girl don't watch him good. When I come in some nights, he be all out the cover and shivering but too sleepy to get back under em. Time come in when I'm pulling the cover up on Orine two kids.

"Which one yours," he ask.

I go over to Larry bed. "This my baby," I tell him.

"What's his name?"

"Larry."

"Oh, I suppose you name him after his daddy?"

I don't like the way he say that, like I was wrong to name him after his daddy. "Who else I gon name him after?" He don't say nothing and I leave him standing there. I mad now and I go in the bedroom and start pulling off my clothes. I think, That nigga can stand up in the living room all night, for all I care; let Orine talk to German and him, too. But Time come in the bedroom and put his arms round me. He touch my hair and my face and my tittie, and it scare me. I try to pull away but he hold me too close. "Martha," he say, "Black Martha." Then he just stand there holding me, not saying nothing, with his hand covering one side on my face. I stand there trembling but he don't notice. I know a woman not supposed to feel the way I feel bout Time, not right away. But I do.

He tell me things nobody ever say to me before. And I want to tell him that I ain't never liked no man much as I like him. But sometime you tell a man that and he go cause he think you liking him a whole lot gon hang him up.

"You and me," he say after we in bed, "we can make it together real good." He laugh. "I used to think all I needed was that music, but it take a woman to make that music sing, I think. So now stead of the music and me, it be the music and me and you."

"You left out Larry," I tell him. I don't think he want to hear that. But Larry my baby.

"How come you couldn't be free," he say real low. Then, "How you going when I go if you got a baby?"

"When you going?"

He turn his back to me. "Oh, I don't know. You know what the song say, 'When a woman take the blues, She tuck her head and cry. But when a man catch the blues, he grab his shoes and slide.' Next time I get the blues," he laugh a little, "next time the man get too much for me, I leave here and go someplace else. He always chasing me. The god damn white man." He turn over and reach for me. "You feel good. He chasing me and I chasing dreams. You think I'm crazy, huh? But I'm not. I just got so many, many things going on inside me I don't know which one to let out first. They all want out so bad. When I play—I got to be better, Martha. You gon help me?"

"Yes, Time, I help you."

"You see," and he reach over and turn on the light and look down at me, "I'm not what I am. I uptight on the inside but I can't get it to show on the outside. I don't know how to make it come out. You ever hear Coltrane blow? That man is together. He showing on the outside what he got on the inside. When I can do that, then I be somewhere. But I can't go by myself. I need a woman. A Black woman. Them other women steal your soul and don't leave nothing. But a Black woman—" He laugh and pull me close. He want me and that all I care bout.

Mamma come over that next morning and come right on in the bedroom, just like she always do. I kind of shamed for her to see me like that, with a man and all, but she don't say nothing cept scuse me, then turn away. "I come to get Larry."

"He in the other bedroom," I say, starting to get up.

"That's okay; I get him." And she go out and close the door.

I start to get out the bed anyway. Time reach for his cigarettes and light one. "Your mamma don't believe in knocking, do she?"

I start to tell him not to talk so loud cause Mamma a hear him, but that might make him mad. "Well, it ain't usually nobody in here with me for her to walk in on." I standing by the bed buttoning my house coat and Time reach out and pull my arm, smiling.

"I know you ain't no tramp, Martha. Come on, get back in bed."

I pull my arm way and start out the door. "I got to get Larry's clothes together," I tell him. I do got to get them clothes together cause when Mamma come for Larry like that on Sadday morning, she want to keep him for the rest of the weekend. But—I don't know. It just don't seem right for me to be in the bed with a man and my mamma in the next room.

I think Orine and German still in the other bedroom. But I don't know; Orine don't too much like for her mens to stay all night. She say it make a bad impression on her kids. I glad the door close anyway. If Mamma gon start talking that "why don't you come home" talk the way she usually do, it best for Orine not to hear it.

Orine's two kids still sleep but Mamma got Larry on his bed tickling him and playing with him. He like that. "Boy, you sho happy for it to be so early in the morning," I tell him.

Mamma stop tickling him and he lay there breathing hard for a minute. "Big Mamma," he say laughing and pointing at her. I just laugh at him and go get his clothes.

"You gon marry this one?" Every man I been with since I had Larry, she ask that about.

"You think marrying gon save my soul, Mamma?" I sorry right away cause Mamma don't like me to make fun of God. But I swear I gets tired of all that. What I want to marry for anyway? Get somebody like Daddy always coming and going and every time he go leave a baby behind. Or get a man what stay round and beat me all the time and have my kids thinking they big shit just cause they got a daddy what stay with them, like them saddity kids at school. Shit, married or single they still doing the same thing when they goes to bed.

Mamma don't say nothing else bout it. She ask where he work. I tell her and then take Larry in the bathroom and wash him up.

"The older you get, the more foolish you get, Martha. Them musicians ain't got nothing for a woman. Lots sweet talk and babies, that's all. Welfare don't even want to give you nothing for the one you got now, how you gon—" I sorry but I just stop listening. Mamma run her mouth like a clatterbone on a goose ass sometime. I just go on and give her the baby and get the rest of his things ready.

"So your mamma don't like musicians, huh?" Time say when I get back in the bedroom. "Square-ass people. Everything they don't know about, they hate. Lord deliver me from a square-ass town with square-ass people." He turn over.

"You wasn't calling me square last night."

"I'm not calling you square now, Martha."

I get back in the bed then and he put his arm round me. "But they say what they want to say. Long as they don't mess with me things be okay. But that's impossible. Somebody always got to have their little say about your life. They want to tell you where to go, how to play, what to play, where to play it—shit, even who to fuck and how to fuck em. But when I get to New York—"

"Time, let's don't talk now."

He laugh then. "Martha, you so Black." I don't know what I should say so I don't say nothing, just get closer and we don't talk.

That how it is lots a time with me and him. It seem like all I got is lots little pitchers in my mind and can't tell nobody what they look like. Once I try to tell him bout that, bout the pitchers, and he just laugh. "Least your head ain't empty. Maybe now you got some pictures, you get some thoughts." That make me mad and I start cussing, but he laugh and kiss me and hold me. And that time, when we doing it, it all—all angry and like he want to hurt me. And I think bout that song he sing that first night bout having the blues. But that the only time he mean like that.

Time and German brung the piano a couple days after that. The piano small and all shiny black wood. Time cussed German when German knocked it against the front door getting it in the house. Time went to put it in the bedroom but I want him to be thinking bout me, not some damn piano when he in there. I tell him he put it in the living room or it don't come in the house. Orine don't want it in the house period, say it too damn noisy—that's what she tell me. She don't say nothing to Time. I think she halfway scared of him. He pretty good bout playing it though. He don't never play it when the babies is sleep or at least he don't play loud as he can. But all he thinking bout when he playing is that piano. You talk to him, he don't answer; you touch him, he don't look up. One time I say to him, "Pay me some tention," but he don't even hear. I hit his hand, not hard, just playing. He look at me but he don't stop playing. "Get out of here, Martha." First I start to tell him he can't tell me what to do in my own self's house, but he just looking at me. Looking at me and playing and not saying nothing. I leave.

His friends come over most evenings when he home, not playing. It like Time is the leader. Whatever he say go. They always telling him how good he is. "Out of sight, man, the way you play." "You ought to get out of this little town so somebody can hear you play." Most times, he just smile and don't say nothing, or he just say thanks. But I wonder if he really believe em. I tell him, sometime, that he sound better than lots a them men on records. He give me his little cool smile. But I feel he glad I tell him that.

When his friends come over, we sit round laughing and talking and drinking. Orine like that cause she be playing up to em all and they be telling her what a fine ass she got. They don't tell me nothing like that cause Time be sitting right there, but long as Time telling me, I don't care. It like when we go to the Legion, after Time and German started being with us. We all the time get in free and then get to sit at one a the big front tables. And Orine like that cause it make her think she big-time. But she still her same old picky self; all the time telling me to "sit cool, Martha," and "be cool, girl." Acting like cool the most important thing in the world. I finally just tell her, "Time like me just the way I am, cool or not." And it true; Time always saying that I be myself and I be fine.

Time and his friends, they talk mostly bout music, music and New York City and white people. Sometime I get so sick a listening to em. Always talking bout how they gon put something over on the white man, gon take something way from him, gon do this, gon do that. Ah shit! I tell em. But they don't pay me no mind.

German say, one night, "Man, this white man come asking if I want to play at his house for—"

"What you tell him, man, 'Put money in my purse'?" Time ask. They all crack up. Me and Orine sit there quiet. Orine all swole up cause Time and them running some kind of game and she don't know what going down.

"Hey, man, yo all member that time up in Frisco when we got fired from that gig and wan't none of our old ladies working?" That Brown, he play bass with em.

"Man," Time say, "all I remember is that I stayed high most of the time. But how'd I stay high if ain't nobody had no bread? Somebody was putting something in somebody's purse." He lean back laughing a little. "Verna's mamma must have been sending her some money, till she got a job. Yeah, yeah man, that was it. You remember the first time her mamma sent that money and she gave it all to me to hold?"

"And what she wanna do that for? You went out and gambled half a it away and bought pot with most of the rest." German not laughing much as Time and Brown.

"Man, I was scared to tell her, cause you remember how easy it was for her to get her jaws tight. But she was cool, didn't say nothing. I told her I was going to get food with the rest of the money and asked her what she wanted, and—"

"And she say cigarettes," Brown break in laughing, "and this cat, man, this cat tell her, 'Woman, we ain't wasting this bread on no nonessentials!' " He doubled over laughing. They all laughing. But I don't think it that funny. Any woman can give a man money.

"I thought the babe was gon kill me, her jaws was so tight. But even with her jaws tight, Verna was still cool. She just say, 'Baby, you done fucked up fifty dollars on nonessentials; let me try thirty cents.' "

That really funny to em. They all cracking up but me. Time sit there smiling just a little and shaking his head. Then, he reach out and squeeze my knee and smile at me. And I know it like I say; any woman can give a man money.

German been twitching round in his chair and finally he say, "Yeah, man, this fay dude want me to play at his house for fifty cent." That German always got to hear his self talk. "I tell him take his fifty cent and shove it up his ass—oh scuse me. I forgot that baby was here—but I told him what to do with it. When I play for honkies, I tell him, I don't play for less than two hundred dollars and he so foolish he gon pay it." They all laugh, but I know German lying. Anybody offer him ten cent let lone fifty, he gon play.

"It ain't the money, man," Time say. "They just don't know what the fuck going on." I tell him Larry sitting right there. I know he ain't gon pay me no mind, but I feel if German can respect my baby, Time can too. "Man, they go out to some little school, learn a few chords, and they think they know it all. Then, if you working for a white man, he fire you and hire him. No, man, I can't tie shit from no white man."

"That where you wrong," I tell him. "Somebody you don't like, you supposed to take em for everything they got. Take em and tell em to kiss yo butt."

"That another one of your pictures, I guess," Time say. And they all laugh cause he told em bout that, too, one time when he was mad with me.

"No, no," I say. "Listen, one day I walking downtown and this white man offer me a ride. I say okay and get in the car. He start talking and hinting round and finally he come on out and say it. I give you twenty dollars, he say. I say okay. We in Chinatown by then and at the next stop light he get out his wallet and give me a twenty-dollar bill. 'That what I like bout you colored women,' he say easing all back in his seat just like he already done got some and waiting to get some more. 'Yeah,' he say, 'you all so easy to get.' I put that money in my purse, open the door and tell him, 'Motherfucker, you ain't got shit here,' and slam the door."

"Watch your mouth," Time say, "Larry sitting here." We all crack up.

"What he do then?" Orine ask.

"What could he do? We in Chinatown and all them colored folks walking round. You know they ain't gon let no white man do nothing to me."

Time tell me after we go to bed that night that he kill me if he ever see me with a white man.

I laugh and kiss him. "What I want with a white man when I got you?" We both laugh and get in the bed. I lay stretched out waiting for him to reach for me. It funny, I think, how colored men don't never want no colored women messing with no white mens but the first chance he get, that colored man gon be right there in that white woman's bed. Yeah, colored men sho give colored womens a hard way to go. But I know if Time got to give a hard way to go, it ain't gon be for scaggy fay babe, and I kinda smile to myself.

"Martha—"

"Yeah, Time," I say turning to him.

"How old you—eighteen? What you want to do in life? What you want to be?"

What he mean? "I want to be with you," I tell him.

"No, I mean really. What you want?" Why he want to know, I wonder. Everytime he start talking serious-like, I think he must be hearing his sliding song.

"I don't want to have to ask nobody for nothing. I want to be able to take care of my own self." I won't be no weight on you, Time, I want to tell him. I won't be no trouble to you.

"Then what are you doing on the Welfare?"

"What else I gon do? Go out and scrub somebody else's toilets like my mamma did so Larry can run wild like I did? No. I stay on Welfare awhile, thank you."

"You see what the white man have done to us, is doing to us?"

"White man my ass," I tell him. "That was my no good daddy. If he'd gone out and worked, we woulda been better off."

"How he gon work if the man won't let him?"

"You just let the man turn you out. Yeah, that man got yo mind."

"What you mean?" he ask real quiet. But I don't pay no tention to him.

"You always talking bout music and New York City, New York City and the white man. Why don't you forget all that shit and get a job like other men? I hate that damn piano."

He grab my shoulder real tight. "What you mean, 'got my mind?' What you mean?" And he start shaking me. But I crying and thinking bout he gon leave.

"You laugh cause I say all I got in my mind is pitchers but least they better than some old music. That all you ever think about, Time."

"What you mean? What you mean?"

Finally I scream. "You ain't gon no damn New York City and it ain't the white man what gon keep you. You just using him for a scuse cause you scared. Maybe you can't play." That the only time he ever hit me. And I cry cause I know he gon leave for sho. He hold me and say don't cry, say he sorry, but I can't stop. Orine bamming on the door and Time yelling at her to leave us lone and the babies crying and finally he start to pull away. I say, "Time . . ." He still for a long time, then he say, "Okay, Okay, Martha."

No, it not like he don't want me no more, he—

"Martha. Martha. You ain't been listening to a word I say."

"Mamma." I say it soft cause I don't want to hurt her. "Please leave me lone. You and Orine—and Time too, sometime—yo all treat me like I don't know nothing. But just cause it don't seem like to you that I know what I'm doing, that don't mean nothing. You can't see into my life."

"I see enough to know you just get into one mess after another." She shake her head and her voice come kinda slow. "Martha, I named you after that women in the Bible cause I want you to be like her. Be good in the same way she is. Martha, that woman ain't never stopped believing. She humble and patient and the Lord make a place for her." She lean her hands on the table. Been in them dishes again, hands all wrinkled and shiny wet. "But that was the Bible. You ain't got the time to be patient, to be waiting for Time or no one else to make no place for you. That man ain't no good. I told you—"

Words coming faster and faster. She got the cow by the tail and gon on down shit creek. It don't matter though. She talk and I sit here thinking bout Time. "You feel good . . . You gon be my Black queen? . . . We can make it together . . . You feel good . . ." He be back.

Mississippi Politics:
A Day in the Life
of Ella J. Baker*

Joanne Grant

AUTHOR'S NOTE:

The state convention of the Mississippi Freedom Democratic Party was held on August 6, 1964, in Jackson, Mississippi, as a prelude to the party's challenge to the seating of Mississippi's regular state Democratic delegation at the Democratic Party's national convention held later that month in Atlantic City. The MFDP was challenging the state's exclusion of Negroes from the political process.

The MFDP was an adjunct to the Mississippi Summer Project, in which hundreds of volunteers, mainly young, white, Northern students, joined with the predominantly young, Black staff workers of the Student Nonviolent Coordinating Committee and the Congress of Racial Equality to demonstrate through a summer of work in rural Mississippi that Negroes wanted to participate in politics, that the Mississippi system tried every means at hand to exclude Negroes, and that the nation should take steps to change that system.

* From a forthcoming biography of Ella J. Baker.

The young people worked that summer to establish Freedom Schools, community centers, and an open political party under the severe handicaps of a pervasive fear created through the years by nightriders, brutal police, and the economic stranglehold through which Mississippi whites controlled Mississippi Blacks. At the beginning of the summer, to show these youngsters what they faced, three of the young workers disappeared. As the young people took up their work late in June, they knew the three young men were dead. The bodies were found buried in a dam on August 5, 1964.

The slightly cooling breeze of the Mississippi summer morning and the feebleness of the sun fighting its way through the haze didn't fool anyone into thinking the day would not turn out to be, as always, a scorcher.

Miss Baker in her neat cotton suit and fashionable straw hat walked along Jackson's Lynch Street in front of the Movement office toward a friendly home for an hour's rest before the activities of the day were to begin. She had just arrived from Washington, where she was heading the Mississippi Freedom Democratic Party's capital office.

"I have no place to stay. But they're taking me somewhere for a little while," she said as Howard Zinn relieved her of her suitcase. Her smile belied the weariness she must have felt after her early-morning journey. Her take-it-as-it-comes attitude in place, she went off to "wash my face and change my blouse."

Miss Baker had arrived on the great day—the day of the first state convention of the Mississippi Freedom Democratic Party. She was, as has often happened, the substitute keynote speaker, pinch-hitting for the famous who were unable to attend.

In a reflection of the two currents which prevailed in the Movement, there had been those who had wanted Ralph Bunche to make the convention address. He would draw the press, some argued, and show by such renowned participation that the MFDP was important. There were others who felt that the content of the convention address was more important than the fanfare which would attend a federal official or a personage such as Bunche.

Sandra Hayden of the MFDP staff had called Miss Baker to ask her to determine the availability of Bunche and then, as second choice, the Secretary of Agriculture. Then Bob Moses, the Student Nonviolent Coordinating Committee leader in Mississippi, called and importuned Miss Baker to make the address herself. She declined at first because she said the MFDP perhaps needed someone "on a different level" than herself, but Bob persisted and prevailed. Miss Baker had worked with the people of Mississippi and she knew them. The young people who were helping the Mississippians organize their own political party had faith in her, trusted her, and wanted her.

The year before Miss Baker had spoken in Natchez, Fort Gibson, Vicksburg, and elsewhere to help the MFDP get out the Freedom Vote, its first test of strength and a demonstration of the Mississippi Negro's desire to be in politics if not deliberately prevented.

And in the months just before this convention, she had been at meetings in Jackson where the battle for control of the MFDP's challenge was fought and won by the people of the state. Miss Baker had championed the right of the people to do their own politicking with delegations from other states, to seek support themselves for their right to be seated at the national convention.

The people should speak for themselves, she said. A coalition of national leaders should not do the talking. It was not urbane articulateness that was needed; the people who were suffering could say it better.

And so she arrived that hazy, hot morning, the pinchhitter, hastened not to a cool, clean room for rest and refreshment but, true to form, to a meeting. As she sat listening to the MFDP Steering Committee debate over procedure for the afternoon's convention, she reflected on how much homework the youngsters had done. The footwork they had done in the local areas helping to define the kind of delegates who would best represent the idea of a Mississippi political party open to all.

"I got the impression at this meeting that there were those who said the kids had controlled it too much, but the basis on which they seemed to have been attempting to control it, or to influence it, seemed to me to have been a very sound basis," Miss Baker reflected. "It seems that at the point at which the MFDP's participation in the national Democratic convention loomed as a reality there was quite a rush on the part of some of the more middle-class types to be identified with the delegation."

At the Steering Committee meeting one of the more pompous types rose to nominate a delegate who would be the kind of person needed, one with more formal education, whose credentials included a list of positions held in various organizations. It was Charlie Cobb, one of the young people who had worked for the MFDP in the previous months, who countered the argument. He named delegates who had been nominated in the county meetings who did not have the qualifications of formal training and office-holding; delegates who had worked day and night to get people out to precinct and county meetings in preparation for the state convention.

The result was a "people's delegation" in Atlantic City at the national convention. "This would not have occurred had it not been for the youngsters who saw to it that the little people who had given so much energy were not run over," Miss Baker said.

As the Steering Committee continued to work on plans for the convention, all morning the people who had been helping others to register to vote, canvassing over dusty country roads to urge farmers and housewives to join the MFDP, had been arriving at the Masonic Temple across Lynch Street from the Movement office.

Among them was Hartman Turnbow from Holmes County, a small wiry man of fifty-nine who was the first Black person to attempt to register to vote in Holmes County in a hundred years. Turnbow, a leader in the MFDP, was a symbol of resistance.

"In April I went down to reddish," Turnbow says in his singular vernacular, "and they accused me of being a integration leader. I was writ up in the paper. In May they fire-bombed my house. There was two cocktail bombs in the living room and one in the bedroom. The whole house was in flames." Turnbow ran outside and had a gun battle with the bombers. Since then, Turnbow said, he didn't go anywhere where he would be a target. "I don't go nowhere at night except to meetins," he said.

But Turnbow and others who had had similar experiences who gathered for this—their first political convention—had hope. Turnbow maintained that if "the circus clerk" were pressured enough, people would be able to pass the voter registration test.

Turnbow had four summer volunteers living in his home and a community center was being built by local Movement people and volunteers on his 117-acre farm. Turnbow said there would be a "roof-raisin" of the community center on August 20.

"The students hadn't been there a week when the Uncle Toms said we were going to have niggers dancin' with white girls at the center. So we gonna have a dance." He smiled broadly. "The first round the colored boys 'ul dance with the white girls and the next round the white boys 'ul dance with the colored girls. We gonna let the Uncle Toms in so's they can run and tell."

Turnbow was telling this story in the convention hall, interrupting it from time to time to greet Miz Hamer, the ebullient fighter from Rulesville who had worked tirelessly for the Movement since she was run off a plantation for registering to vote, and Miz Devine, who had run for Congress the previous fall in the MFDP's Freedom Vote.

As more and more delegates arrived the convention took on an aura of excitement. The seats lined up beneath district and county signs began filling up. The young civil rights workers stood around the hall talking excitedly about the turnout.

The hall was decorated with red, white, and blue banners: "One Man, One Vote," one read. Another, "The Freedom Democratic Party will make Mississippi an OPEN Society."

Some of the young workers had stayed up all night checking delegation lists and arrival times and making the signs that lined up the convention hall: First District, Second District, Holmes, Kemper, Tallahatchie. These were the names of the counties that were to be represented, counties where civil rights workers were run off the roads and shot at, where Negroes' homes and churches were bombed and burned. The delegates were people who had never been "in politics" before, as one man from Greenwood expressed it. People who had recently been permitted to register to vote for the first time, people who had been turned away from meetings of Mississippi's lily-white Democratic Party, people who had faced threats and arrests and jail and beatings to travel dark country roads harassed by Klansmen and police to attend precinct meetings of their own party. A party they had built to challenge Mississippi's way of life.

The convention itself was a surprise and just the look of it was exhilarating—to see those lettered signs designating county delegation seats, the jam-packed hall. More than half of the state's eighty-two counties were represented. It looked like and was a real convention.

Aaron Henry, state NAACP president and MFDP chairman, opened the meeting under the glare of television lights, which raised the temperature in the packed hall. True to its pattern, the Mississippi sun had put the mercury at 100 degrees. But the air was hot, too, with excitement.

Washington attorney Joseph Rauh, legal adviser to the MFDP and a member of the credentials committee of the national Democratic convention, rose to speak. The audience setted down to business. Rauh told them that if the MFDP was not seated by the credentials committee an effort would be made to bring the issue to the convention floor. He announced that nine state delegations had adopted resolutions in support of the MFDP. The audience responded with shouts of approval to his announcement of the states that had expressed support: California, Colorado, Massachusetts, Michigan, Minnesota, New York, Oregon, Washington, Wisconsin, the District of Columbia.

In an emotion-filled voice Rauh expressed his admiration, praised the courage of "you people." The emotion was not transmitted. The phrase "you people" hit the audience as if he had said "you nigras." He retired gracefully, unaware.

Then Bob Moses got up. Delegates stood to applaud him as he mounted the platform to introduce Miss Ella Baker.

"We must consider this a demonstration of the people of Mississippi that they are determined to be a part of the body politic of Mississippi," she said. "They are determined to be regarded as men and women—even in the Delta of Mississippi.

"We are here to demonstrate the right of the governed to elect those who govern, *here*, in *this* state." She pointed out that the Southern states function as an oligarchy and that the rest of the country goes along with it. "It has never been true," she said, "that the Negro people were satisfied. It was never true even in the darkest days of slavery." Delegates applauded and shouted, "Freedom! Freedom!"

"True, there has been some accommodation to slavery. But the sit-ins ended the leadership of the accommodating type of leader.

"The symbol of government of this state is that three bodies are lying somewhere in this state. We must make the rest of the country turn its eyes to the fact that there are other bodies lying under the swamps of Mississippi.

"Until the killing of Black mothers' sons is as important as the killing of white mothers' sons, we must keep on."

The audience was now on the heights, ready to soar.

Then she spoke of the coming national Democratic convention. "It is important that you go to the convention whether you are seated or not.

"It is even more important that you develop a political machinery in this state. The Mississippi Freedom Democratic Party will not end at the convention. This is only the beginning.

"You are waging a war against the closed society of Mississippi. You have not let physical fear immobilize you. And there is that other fear—the fear of communism. The red-smear which is part of the effort of the power structure to maintain itself and maintain its strangehold."

Then she added, "But we have sense enough to know who is using us and who is abusing us." The convention shouted and cheered.

Delegates jumped to their feet applauding. The standing ovation lasted minutes. Shouts of "Freedom" rang through the hall. Then delegates began to sing:

"Ain't gonna let nobody turn me round
Turn me round, turn me round
Ain't gonna let nobody turn me round
Gonna keep on a-walkin', keep on a-talkin'
Marchin' up to Freedom Land."

Delegates grabbed county signs and began to march around the hall. For fifteen minutes the singing, clapping demonstration shook the hall. Flashbulbs flashed and TV cameras whirred, even the press corps seemed elated.

The convention had come alive. The MFDP was launched.

Motherhood

Joanna Clark

My first words as I came from under the ether after I had my son were, "I think I made a mistake." Unfortunately, since then, and one more child later, I've had very little reason to change my mind. This is not to say that children cannot be lovable. It's not them, it's all the foolishness that goes on in the name of them. From the beginning, motherhood took on the complexion of a farce.

To begin with, aside from the indignity of being trussed up like some sort of sacrificial pig in order to be delivered, there was the matter of nursing. I chose to brew my own rather than to spend the next few months encumbered by a slew of rattling bottles. At first the hospital staff was rather sweet and condescending about it. They'd bring me the baby, say something like, "Aren't you a good little mother," and then whip those bed curtains around to screen me from my roommate as if a little infant fellatio was the very least that was going to happen inside my hutch.

After the first day, however, someone decided that there was something strange about the color of my child's stool. The pediatrician came in to talk to me. The import of his conversation was that, while it was very rare, occasionally babies were allergic to their mother's milk and he wanted my permission to put the child on a formula. I said if he was allergic to anything it was probably the four-a.m. feeding they slipped him in the nursery. He turned and stomped out and I thought that was that, but the next time I took a walk down the hall to have a look in the nursery, I saw that my baby was in isolation. Since I had never heard of anyone having a contagious allergy, the only reason I could think of was that they felt there must be something inherently wrong with anyone who had a mother freaky enough to breast-feed. But, I must tell the truth, he wasn't just breast-fed—he was also uncircumcised.

I wasn't trying to prove anything. I had thought about it and it seemed to me that I had perfectly good reasons for having an uncircumcised son. I had read somewhere that circumcision lessened sexual pleasure. No one knows exactly how much, but it didn't seem to me that I had the right to start meddling in his sexual life before he could say a word about it. Then, I knew me, and I knew that the last thing I wanted to do was to take him home and have to deal with a gauze-wrapped, bloody, infection-prone little ding-a-ling. Besides soap and water are plentiful enough in this society so that no one need ever lose a penis to smegma.

When I refused to sign a release for the operation, I was visited by a platoon of doctors. They kept saying it would be cleaner and "How will he feel when he grows up and everybody's circumcised but him?" If he wanted to have it done when he was older that would be his business, but for the time being, I said no. One of the doctors snatched up the release and said huffily, "Well, never mind. We'll get your husband to sign it." Sure enough one of them laid in wait during visiting hours and proceeded to harass my husband. My son kept his foreskin and I received my first lesson in motherhood. You are everybody's whipping boy.

I may be more upsettable than most, but during the years I was involved with carriages and strollers and wagons and tricycles, I was always getting bugged. Why wasn't there, even in the children's section of a department store, a high chair so you could deposit your child and spend your money in some sort of comfort? Why did it have to be a major struggle to get a stroller or a shopping cart across a street; would it cost so much to rake the curbs? And why did the entrance to the playground offer the steepest curb of all? Small enough problems, but enough to clue you in to the fact that the last people anyone in charge of planning the city are concerned with are mothers and children.

So I should have been forewarned when I finally locked out my charming, but philandering and non-supporting Peter Pan of a husband. I was working (selling honeymoons in the Poconos and feeling like a hypocrite) when I turned the bolt. But if I didn't get sick, one of the children would, and if the three of us stayed on our feet, the baby sitter was sure to keel over with a gallbladder attack. I finally came up with a really simple solution. I would put the children in one of the city's day-care centers. It would certainly be more reliable and I'd probably save enough money to hire someone to stay with them while I finished my last semester at City College.

I called the Day Care Council to find where the nearest school was. The woman on the other end of the line wanted to know why I needed a nursery. I told her that I had to work. She seemed insulted. "What do you mean, you have to work? In New York City there's no such thing as a mother having to work. You can go on welfare!" I told her that I didn't want to go on welfare. The last thing I wanted to do was sit around all day in my Lower East Side hovel. I wanted to do something to get out of it. I didn't get the address of the nursery, but she did tell me where my nearest friendly welfare office was. On my own I found several nurseries and tried to register my children. If what those schools say about their waiting lists is true, three-quarters of their prospective clients will be through graduate school before there is an opening for them in the four-year-old group.

I hung in there for a while longer, but, besides being sporadic, I have to admit that I wasn't selling honeymoons with total dedication. So I got fired. For a very short while I depended upon Peter Pan, but the next time the rent was due, there I was sitting in the welfare office. I had talked Peter into saying, if anyone asked, that he couldn't support us. It was the truth, but I wasn't sure that he knew it.

Despite what they say, I don't think the welfare department checks too deeply into eligibility. They use a cheaper system. They just keep putting you off and telling you to come back the next day. After a few days of that, if you can scrounge up money anywhere else, you will. On my third day I threw a fit that outdid every crotchety baby in the center. Within fifteen minutes I was a bonafide welfare recipient with a yellow card to prove it.

Anyone who can live on welfare should be courted by Wall Street. He is a financial genius. I paid $40 a month rent and received $69 every 15 days. That included an extra amount for electricity since I lived in a dark apartment. I guess I could have started having more babies and parlayed my allotment into something really terrific, but I didn't and I wasn't a financial genius so I depended upon the occasional kindness of my husband.

I had as an investigator a man extremely gung-ho about filling out forms. He had gold teeth and a glint in his eyes behind his gold-trimmed glasses that made me believe that within a few years he'd probably have a whole section of the welfare office under his supervision. He was on my doorstep so often that I assumed he must have been as tired of looking at me as I was of him. I made him an offer: if he arranged for the city to supply me with a homemaker and carfare for me to finish my last semester of college, within a few months a family of three would be off the welfare rolls at, in the long run, a considerable saving to the city. He almost had apoplexy on my living-room floor. The City of New York does not send mothers to school, and if I came up with the money to do it on my own, I must report it to him immediately so he could throw me off welfare. So much for being aboveboard.

Shortly after this I got a part-time job and found a woman in Queens who would keep the children from Monday morning until Friday night for only a few dollars a week more than the welfare department gave me. I even got a student loan.

I had just about made it. I had spent all my money and I was half dead, but school had ended and I had the promise of a job in a month. I could live on the welfare checks until then. But I hadn't reckoned on the men in my life. The investigator, in the interest of nice up-to-date records, paid a visit to Peter Pan. During the time I was married to the man I could never analyze his rationale so I won't try in retrospect. Whatever his reasoning, he decided to say that he didn't see why his family was on welfare since he was able to care for it.

The first I knew of his new capacity for caring was when I got a letter from the welfare department saying that I was no longer eligible. I was not too happy. I asked Peter Pan for money. He said that he didn't have any at the moment but he was sure he could borrow a couple of dollars for me if I really needed it. I ran to the welfare office and screamed that I didn't care what my husband had said, he wasn't giving me any money and if he was, let him show the receipts to prove it. It doesn't work like that. If he said yes and I said no, even if he couldn't substantiate his claim, the burden of proof was on me. The only thing I could do at this point was to take him to court.

The Support Court does not offer the most cheerful surroundings in which to while away a morning, especially if you are sitting there most nonchalantly ignoring your husband on the opposite bench, fighting a strong desire to hit him over the head with your copy of *Dr. Spock* as he pores soulfully over his collected John Donne. Nor is the urge to mayhem alleviated when a woman steps out of her office and says, "How do you do? I am your probation officer." Apparently, trying to collect money from a recalcitrant husband is a really antisocial act entitling you to parole without benefit of trial.

We went into her office, where, while I sat on my hands, swallowed my spume, counted to ten, and in general saw red, they dickered over what he could afford to pay. No one asked me what I needed to live on. After a while they turned to me and said that my spouse felt that he could, with great difficulty, eke out fifteen dollars a week. I suppose it was then that I began to nut out. "What the hell," I wanted to know, "am I supposed to do with fifteen dollars a week? Move into the Waldorf?" The probation officer interjected with the idea that I did not seem to have the proper attitude. "What attitude am I supposed to have?" I screamed. "I didn't mess up his life by running around telling people I could support him. Well, I can't take care of two children on fifteen dollars a week. Let him do it. He can have them right now." That really brought the probation officer to her feet. "You can't desert your children. That's against the law."

"How can I be deserting them? I'm giving them to their father."

"But you can't do that! You're their mother." People, especially those without children, sometimes have a way of saying "mother" that I find incredible. They manage to pronounce a halo around it. I suppose if you're in the mood you feel like the Virgin Mary. I wasn't in the mood. "Suppose I offer to give him fifteen dollars a week along with the children. Would that be better?" It would not. Apparently if I tried to leave the building without two children she had the right to call the police. I was squelched for the moment. However my avarice got the better of me. If I was supposed to get fifteen dollars a week, where was my fifteen dollars? Peter explained that he had a few debts to clear up first but he felt sure that in a couple of weeks he would be able to make the first payment.

I held myself together long enough to collect the children from the court's nursery. And then, as I pushed them down the street in their stroller, I began to think over my alternatives. I refused to go sit in the welfare office again. I had no intention of just going home when there was no relief in sight. The only really definitive thing I could think of to do under the circumstances was to nut out. I hurried over to St. Vincent's Hospital, which seemed a pleasant enough place as hospitals went to collapse upon.

I must have made quite a racket, which wasn't too difficult considering the mood I was in. All I knew was that I wanted someone to take care of those children while I went off and slept for a couple of weeks. Someone patted me on the back and maneuvered the three of us into a room to wait for a doctor. After a short while, in walked a young, blond, well-raised, right-thinking, white-clad paragon. "What seems to be the trouble?" he said. "I can't go on," I wept. "I'm married to this man who thinks that all you need to live on is a tiny bit of money and love will take care of the rest." He pulled up a chair. "What's wrong with that?" he wanted to know. "Love" is another one of those words like "mother." When my husband said "love," he meant whatever emotion he could generate in you that would sustain you enough to put up for and with him. It was too complicated and paranoid to try to explain, especially to anyone who wore white bucks. I decided to stick to the "I can't go on" thesis. He explained that St. Vincent's just didn't take in people from off the street, but that if I really couldn't go on, Bellevue was the place to go. Anyone can tell from just looking at that hospital that that is no place to go for a nice, peaceful, recuperative nervous breakdown. The drabness alone would finish off your mind. When I shook my head no to that, he told me to wait a minute, left the room, and reappeared shortly bearing aloft a mammoth hypodermic needle. "This is Librium," he said. "It will make you feel better." He gave me a shot in the behind and shoulder-patted me out of the room. Under the soothing effects of Librium, I began to nurture a sincere distrust in the judgment of doctors, and the nearest thing to hallucinations that I have ever known resulted.

After I left the hospital, I passed a waist-high iron fence and I kept seeing myself grabbing my daughter out of the stroller, holding her by the legs, and rattling her against the fence the way you would a baseball bat. I saw a police station ahead and I suppose it brought to mind ice cream cones and wearing the captain's cap. I staggered in and announced that I wanted to leave my children on the desk sergeant's blotter. They didn't take children accompanied by adults, but they did pat me on the shoulder and tell me about the Department of Welfare. Then, from my dealings with the nursery schools, I remembered the Department of Child Welfare. I didn't know what they were good for, but I looked them up in a telephone book and off I careened with my stroller thrust rakishly before me.

Between the tears and the Librium, I never saw a single streetlight. By rights, I should have been hit by a good fifty cars, in addition to being arrested for jaywalking and endangering the life of a minor at least two dozen times. To add to the joy of my escapade, some wizened old man followed me for a few blocks muttering about coming up to see his apartment. I'm not sure if he was after me or the children.

At the Department of Child Welfare, I wasted no time on pleasantries. I parked my stroller in front of the receptionist's desk and screamed at the absolute top of my lungs, "SOMEBODY'S GOT TO TAKE THESE GODDAM CHILDREN!" They believed me. All they wanted to know was if the children had a father, if so, were we married, and then his telephone number so he could come in and sign his consent.

Good old Peter showed up in less than half an hour. But, once the pen was in his hand, he could not bear to dismiss himself of his responsibilities so summarily. The social worker brightened. Perhaps he was willing to help with some money. Unfortunately, at the moment he had only a token with which to get home, and, while under other circumstances he would be more willing to take the children himself, he happened to be living for the time being in diggings to which it would be grossly unfair to expose them. The social worker asked him what his wife was supposed to do at this point. "She's an intelligent woman," he said, "I'm sure she'll think of something."

I remember once a girl friend of mine was found wandering around the streets of Harlem trying to sell subscriptions to the *Jewish Daily Forward,* or if that didn't appeal, a visit to an orgone box she knew about. After she was tucked into Bellevue, I bumped into her husband, from whom she was separated, and asked him what he intended to do about their two children. He had decided that as soon as Karen was released she could have the children back because, no matter what, he still had faith in her as a mother. She got out, got the children back, and lasted two months, which was long enough for him to disappear. The children have spent the last five years in a foster home. But he's kept the faith.

Anyway, I was intelligent enough to tell my husband that I would have to defer for a while the pleasure of raising his children. That they were his children as well as mine and therefore I had just as much right to cop out as he did.

When a marriage is breaking up there is a tendency for onlookers and agency types to behave as if the mother in the case went out behind a barn somewhere and knocked herself up with the nearest twig. A divorced man may be grieved over leaving his children, but he manages to bear up and no one thinks of condemning him unless she's his bitchy ex-wife. Mothers may die, or occasionally run away, but if the father is adamant about keeping his family together, the city will supply him with a homemaker whom he pays on a sliding scale and who stays with him for years if necessary. There are few ways of prying a homemaker loose from the city if you are a woman. The most effective one is to have a husband living in the home, ten children, and a terminal case of cancer. Where is the equity?

I had received the same education as my husband and the same amount of it. I hadn't even tried to excuse myself from gym classes on "those days." All right, I'd been foolish enough to have two children, but then, so had he. So now what kind of a job was I supposed to do on my head so that I could accept doing very little else in the next few years except raising children on the lowest possible terms?

There was nothing to do but go to court the next morning and swear out a deposition stating neither my husband nor I was mentally or financially capable of caring for our children. It was all simple enough after that, if you call never being able to take your children off someone else's property, or never seeing them naked, and having them smell like somebody else, simple.

After my children were in a foster home, I became aware of another inequity. Not only is the city willing to pay a couple to take care of other people's children, but it is willing to foot the bill for private doctors, dentists, and clothes. And the clothes, they encourage, should not be the cheapest, for the foster children should not be stigmatized in any way. You get the feeling that the mortgage on every other house in St. Albans is being paid for by foster children, and that the powers that be think that to provide the same assistance to the blood mothers would break the back of the free-enterprise system.

It's over now, and I have my children back. They have a new father who works. And while we haven't come along so far as to get out there into the park every Sunday with a baseball and bat, we do have a go at it with the frisbee every now and then. It's still very clean living and all-American. But I learned a lot. . . . A friend of mine not too long ago had a vaginal infection and took herself off to a gynecologist. He was good, but he was German. And the lady trembled lest Herr Doktor take one look at her little brown face and decide to practice a bit of "genocide." Black ladies, the last thing we have to worry about is genocide. In fact, we could use a little. Look at what's happened to us in the last hundred years; we've been bravely propagating and all we've gotten are a lot of lumps and a bad name. On the other hand, there are people like Glazer and Moynihan carrying on about our matriarchy and inferring that we've botched up the job long enough and that if we insist on doing something, confine ourselves to standing behind the man of the family and bringing him up to par. On the other hand, there are the brothers (from mother and son to brother and sister—what's so hard about being man and woman?). Anyway, there's the brother nattering away about how we've been lopping off balls long enough, it's time to stand aside. So you stand there looking as pink and white and helpless as is possible under the circumstances and he wants to know what's wrong with you, do you have at least the excuse of being sick or are you just going to stand there like some cow spending up his money?

We don't need it. If we've got to turn our eyes eastward and re-discover our heritage, let's not get hung up on the hairdos and the dashikis. There are more salient aspects of that culture to adopt. No self-respecting African woman would ever get married without a dowry, without something to back her up if the marriage ran into trouble. Admittedly, dowries are not too easy to come by, but the pill is. Let's not worry about what we think the white man thinks about his generosity with his contraceptives. The Jews have never been noted for their sprawling, epic-type families, yet they've man-aged to make themselves a race to be reckoned with. And they didn't do it by Soul.

I realize, or at least I think, that most women have had experiences in childrearing less picaresque than mine. I know some have had more gothic ones—but I relate mine to show what authority I hold for having the opinions I do. I have had a rare opportunity to see husband at bay and the legal system when it pertains to man and wife. Once, when I was safely remarried and could afford to spend a day in court fighting for my rights, I had a set-to with my first husband over the amount he was in arrears with his child support. He owed something like a third of the amount he was supposed to pay. The judge (a man) looked me in the eye and said, "Well Madam, he isn't doing too badly." Jesus Christ, let me try walking up to the man from Consolidated Edison busily turning off my service because I only paid one-eighth of the bill and saying, "Well, I'm not doing too badly."

As mothers, we are worse off than we think we are. In this age of the sit-in and the be-in, it is time for a sit-down. And let's not get up off of it until there's at least social security and unemployment insurance for every mother.

Dear Black Man

Fran Sanders

For years, the white man has projected the theory that all Black people were the same. The outside person may change in size, shape, and, to a certain extent, color. But on the inside was contained an admixture of slyness, laziness, amorality, stupidity, dishonesty, and on top of this was added the ability to shuffle along under the worst of life's circumstances and still remain happy-go-lucky. He was wrapped up in a tight little package and neatly disposed of, thereby eliminating the necessity of dealing with him. But that was light-years ago and I am optimistic. The Black man means to be seen and to be heard. And indeed he is.

But what of the Black woman? What has become of her? How does she feel about the new breed of Black man? How has her relationship to him changed, if at all? For two hundred years it was she who initiated the dialogue between the white world and the Black. When slavery was abolished, she exercised the very dubious prerogative of starving to death or working, for a most minimum wage, for the very people under whom she had previously been a slave. This proved to be a fine arrangement for the whites since they were no longer obliged to provide both her and her family with

inductive reasoning

room and board, but had only to pay her as little as was humanly possible for the privilege of waiting on them hand and foot for sixteen to twenty hours a day. It has changed little by little but only because it is the nature of life to change.

Hollywood helped perpetuate the myth of the satellite Negro by constantly showing the Black man or woman as hovering over some poetic white person, fetching this and that, lifting heavy steel beams from off his bloody but unbowed head and giving him straight, down-home, philosophical talk about how to bear up. "Don't give up now, Mr. Bob. Not after you've come this far." Or "He'll come back, Miss Nellie. Don't worry. Just go in there and put on your prettiest dress and go on down to the ball. Before you know it he'll be back, eating out of your hand." And the relationship, if you could call it that, between the Black man and Black woman was more of mother-boy than mate; she, strong and enduring, standing over the pots in a no-nonsense attitude; he, when not delivering some cornpone homilies, fleeing ghosts or some such and hiding under her skirts. They were not as much people as conversation pieces or interesting oddities—like talking dogs.

In the not too distant past, there has been, on the part of most writers, be they historians, novelists, present-day documentarians, or statisticians, the tendency to villify the Black woman as castrating matriarch. Whether she went about this task with a velvet glove or a steel gauntlet, she produced the same effect—she de-balled the Black man. Now let's face it, it was she who caused the race to survive. And if we are now all finally finding our voices to assert ourselves as a race, let it not be at her expense. Whether she was right or wrong is not particularly relevant at this point. It can only lead to an overreaction on the part of the Black man when it comes to dealing with his woman. And it will produce a lot of unnecessary dialogue that will tend to postpone real communication here and now.

In the first place and in the final analysis, we are women. Perhaps the majority of us are not the hot-house lilies that are depicted in the novels, but we each possess in some degree, at least, a minimum of those things which make us temperamentally different from men. The Black woman is in a unique position at this time. She is suddenly being discovered by the Black man. She has waited on the sidelines for generations while the Black man sought his soul in other things. She was a secondary consideration in his quest for a reality other than that of the pick and hoe. And since his way was blocked more often than not with all of those impediments which have been there since he first stepped foot on these shores, reality usually turned out to be another woman. (What better way to prove that one is a man.) Being expert proponents of the Victorian "theory" (more by natural predilection than by any intellectually conceived ideas), it was deemed natural for him to leave his wife at home with the children, while he went out and did his thing.

Now, it would seem, he can more readily accept the Black woman on her terms. But wait a minute. Did I hear on the bus today, two Black men talking about "no good" Black woman should wear false eyelashes? Surely we are not to the point where female prerogatives are to be thrown out altogether. What could possibly be the point? Certainly there are more important things to think about. Are we to defer the confrontation of the real Black man and woman for another few years? Could it be that we are regressing even farther back into the Victorian age? And is the Black woman to suffer all the bad things that this entails and none of the good? Are we to be told what to do and how to do it, without benefit of being able to sit back and be lovely and feminine and delicate and to be taken care of in the bargain? Or are all these choices to be reserved for the white woman? And while I'm about it, may I also ask what is so different about the Black woman where the Black man is concerned, that what may be taken for a very attractive trait or habit or manner in the white woman is derided in the Black, as if she were copying or trying to emulate her white counterpart? After all, there are certain things in a woman's nature that are universal and transcend the boundaries of race. And although I will be the first to admit that there are habits that the white woman has developed in her relationship with her man that certainly do not bear repeating in a Black frame of reference, if there is to be any progress in the relations between the sexes, I feel that I must point out the fact that certain things found unattractive in the Black woman by the Black man become the very focal point of the attraction between the Black man and the white woman. Black women are taken for granted a great deal in the manner in which they are dealt with by the Black man. Certain fixed notions are uniformly projected onto the Black woman regardless of age, background, personality, education, ability, etc. All of the notions are those which caused women to chafe under the yoke of Victorianism. We must constantly prove ourselves. It is not enough to be good at something or to be capable at our jobs or to have very valid thoughts on any matter at hand. We can all be summarily dismissed by a wave of the hand and the comment that we are only women and so, logically, our thinking leaves something to be desired. This kind of attitude has made even a chance encounter with a Black man a situation to be reckoned with.

For instance: I was walking down the street the other day, when a young Black man who had been standing, talking to a friend, stepped up to me and in a voice filled with hostility said to me, "Hey, soul-sister." Now I have this said to me several times a day. Two-thirds of the time it is said with much warmth. One cannot help but smile. It has the sound of great approval. But there are other times when the man could just as well be saying "Hey, Bitch," or some other little "euphemistic" greeting by which some Black men have traditionally come on with the Black woman. I realize that there has always been among Black men in this country a certain amount of hostility in his approach to his woman. One can readily appreciate why this is so, since at every turn in the outside world he was met by obstacles of every description from icy stares (the nuances of which were honed to devastating sharpness in the North, where it was deemed uncivilized to publicly spit in a man's face), to the Southern version of fun and games with the Black man as the toy, in which version the players would do anything from poking fun at him if they were in a good mood to eviscerating and de-balling him if they weren't feeling so hot. It is almost right and reasonable that the people who loved him most, his women and children, would have to bear the brunt of his frustrations.

But, I am digressing. To return to the original point, I found the incident with this man very disturbing. Mainly, because it did not stop there. He went on to say that if I ever came that way again and didn't speak to him that he would get a gun and shoot me. Now, if he was making a pass at me he failed to get his point across. If he meant, instead, to frighten me or to alienate me, he certainly achieved that. Not able to leave it at that, he turned to his friend and muttered, "And she's got the nerve to have all that stuff on her head . . ." He was referring to my "afro." Given the fact that Black men are acknowledging (and beautifully so) Black women more than they ever have in the past, I would like to know since when does the way a woman wears her hair indicate to a man that she will react any differently than any other woman under similar circumstances, namely, that of passing an unknown man on a street corner who speaks to you in a hostile manner, to which you don't feel obliged to answer. One should hardly have to be called to task on the basis of a racial tie to suffer the indignities and insults that would send other than a Black woman searching frantically for the nearest policeman.

If a percentage of Black men were not as capable as the men of other races of certain acts—robbery, mayhem, murder, and so

on—then there would be no need to exercise restraint in respond-
ing to any kind of remark or greeting. (And if, indeed, he were in-
capable of these things, you'd have to beat women of all races off
with a club to get near the Black man.) But being a human being, he
is heir to all that this implies. So, depending on her level of tolerance and her judgment in these situations, a woman protects herself as best she can. Chances are she will ignore the situation and
keep on walking. From the point of view of the man in this sort of
situation, I should have, presumably, grinned from ear to ear at his
acknowledgment of my existence and at least stopped to have a
chat or perhaps a drink. Victorianism rides again. When I got back
to my office, I called two of my friends to see if I was simply being
paranoid in my reactions. They both assured me that I was not and
that the "Soul Sister" routine was being used at present as the
newest measure to insure recognition from the woman. It is calculated, in these encounters, to exploit any guilt feelings we Black
women may have about not being understanding enough with our
men. Let me assure all Black men right here and now that I, that we,
do indeed love and understand you. But relating is still a one-to-
one situation. I am a woman, and if I get that certain feeling about
a man, he will be the first to know, provided that there is the possibility that he is capable of feeling the same way. But I will hardly feel
that way about every man I pass on the street. And each chance encounter has little likelihood of coming to fruition as a full-blown
love affair.

My friends also suggested that the next time a situation like this
develops, I simply grin and split. Perhaps the fault's in my stars, but
this kind of dealing with life's little realities leaves me very unful-
filled. I feel that I am cheating. Men are not stupid enough to think
that every woman that they make a pass at is going to fall into their
arms. Nor are they likely to expect that they will even be acknowledged by every woman that they speak to. So why, now, is the Black

woman expected to fall into a state of ecstasy at the sidewalk over-tures? There is a kind of come-on that is almost traditional with the Black man. It's a kind of mating dance in three parts. First, "the hard come-on," to let the woman know that he exists; then the "cooling-it," so she can get a good look and see what he's all about; and then the "getting-it-all-together," the real point of communi-cation. If you've got eyes for the man then this can be exciting. If you don't, this can lead to humiliation, since his face-saving tactic is always "She thinks she's cute, shit."

Also along the lines of irrational female prerogatives, I want it to be known that the term "Soul-Sister" leaves a lot to be desired as far as I am concerned. I am not and never have been a sister to any man except my brother, Danny, and I feel that the whole thing is about to go too far. It seems positively incestuous. I mean, how does one make the transition from brother to lover if need be? Do I suddenly see this man who has previously been addressing me as sister as a potential lover? Not hardly! The lines have been too defi-nitely drawn for us to retrace our steps and redefine. The way back is too clogged with past rhetoric to start a dialogue with some per-sonal meaning, and although the transition probably can be made, it will not be easy. Better to see the woman as a woman and treat her accordingly, while at the same time trying to upgrade the quality of the relationship. Me, woman. You, man. So, let's try again. We haven't been at this thing for so long that we've reached the point of no return. We've been too busy trying to survive.

The average white man in his dealing with his woman has de-veloped some very bad habits, among them the substituting of var-ious standard phrases designed to fit any and all occasions where real relating may be necessary. Let's not have that happen to us any more than it has already. We Black women don't want to turn around in a few years to find that you do indeed regard us as sisters and have, accordingly, gone to find your pleasures of the flesh elsewhere, and that all those words of togetherness have turned to saw-dust in our mouths. (A friend of mine slipped one day and told me that he can't seem to have a go at it with a Black woman because she reminds him too much of his mother and sister.) Let us learn by the mistakes that the white man has made and those mistakes made by the middle-class Blacks. In the final analysis, it all starts with a man and a woman. And from there the quality of their relationship re-fines itself in direct proportion to the energy and honesty that each is willing to expend in that direction.

Talk to me like the woman that I am and not to me as that woman who is the inanimate creation of someone's overactive imagination. Look at me with no preconceived notions of how I must act or feel and I will try to do the same with you. No pre-sumption, no assumptions, no banal rhetoric substituted for real person-to-person giving and receiving. Look at my face when you speak to me; look into my eyes and see what they have to say. Think about the answers that you give to my questions. Don't speak to me in ad-agency prose or in the hip jargon of the day. I am a woman and you are a man and I have always known it. If you love me, tell me so. Don't approach me as you would an enemy. I am on your side and have always been. We have survived, and we may just be able to teach the world a lesson.

Final Point

To Whom Will She Cry Rape?*

Abbey Lincoln

Mark Twain said, in effect, that when a country enslaves a people, the first necessary job is to make the world feel that the people to be enslaved are subhuman. The next job is to make his fellow country-men believe that man is inferior, and, then, the unkindest cut of all is to make that man believe himself inferior.

A good job has been done on the Black people in this country, as far as convincing them of their inferiority is concerned. The general white community has told us in a million different ways and in no uncertain terms that "God" and "nature" made a mistake when it came to the fashioning of us and ours. The whole society, having been thoroughly convinced of the stained, threatening, and evil nature of anything unfortunate enough to be, or to be referred to as, black, as an intended matter of courtesy refers to those of African extraction as "colored" or "Negro."

The fact that "negro" is the Spanish word for "black" is hardly

* Reprinted from *Negro Digest*, September 1966.

understood, it would seem; or it would seem that the word "black" may be intimated or suggested, but never simply stated in good English.

Too many Negroes, if described or referred to as "black," take it as an affront; and I was once told by a Canadian Irishman that I'd insulted him by referring to my person as a Black woman. He insisted that, in actuality, I was brown, not black; and I felt obliged to tell him he described himself as "white," and that he wasn't white either.

The fact that white people readily and proudly call themselves "white," glorify all that is white, and whitewash all that is glorified, becomes unnatural and bigoted in its intent only when these same whites deny persons of African heritage who are Black the natural and inalienable right to readily and proudly call themselves "black," glorify all that is black, and blackwash all that is glorified.

Yet, one is forced to conclude that this is not the case at all, that an astonishing proportion of the white population finds it discomforting that Blacks should dare to feel so much glory in being beautifully black. In the face of this kind of "reasoning," the only conclusion one can logically come to is that there is something wrong with this society and its leadership. "The Man's" opinion of God is sorry, to put it nicely, and his opinion of himself is simply vague and hazy. Consider:

Swearing his love and devotion to the Omnipotent One on the one hand, yet defying and cursing him with rank impudence on the other; using the crutch of his "inherently" base and callow nature on the one hand, and claiming his godhood on the other; worshipping a Jew as the Son of God on the one hand, yet persecuting all other Jews as enemies of God on the other; historically placing this same Jew on the African continent on the one hand, and describing him as a European in physical appearance on the other (still, one would suppose that it's tacitly understood by all that "God" couldn't be anything other than "white," no matter where He was born); advocating that the Black man is made of inferior stuff on the one hand, yet defying him not to prove his superiority on the other; naming hurricanes for women on the one hand, yet H is for the heart as pure as gold on the other; giving her pet names such as "whore," "slut," "bitch," etc., on the one hand, yet, put them all together and they spell mother, the word "that means the world to me," on the other.

No wonder the slogan "white is right" could take a whole nation by storm. One could never accuse this society of being rational.

Still, instead of this irrational society warping my delicate little psyche, it only drove me, ultimately, to the conclusion that any Black human being able to survive the horrendous and evil circumstances in which one inevitably finds oneself trapped must be some kind of a giant with great and peculiar abilities, with an armor as resistant as steel yet made of purest gold.

My mother is one of the most courageous people I have ever known, with an uncanny will to survive. When she was a young woman, the white folks were much further in the lead than they are now, and their racist rules gave her every disadvantage; yet, she proved herself a queen among women, any women, and as a result will always be one of the great legends for me.

But strange as it is, I've heard it echoed by too many Black full-grown males that Black womanhood is the downfall of the Black man in that she (the Black woman) is "evil," "hard to get along with," "domineering" "suspicious," and "narrow-minded." In short, a black, ugly, evil you-know-what.

As time progresses I've learned that this description of my mothers, sisters, and partners in crime is used as the basis and excuse for the further shoving, by the Black man, of his own head into the sand of oblivion. Hence, the Black mother, housewife, and all-round girl Thursday is called upon to suffer both physically and emotionally every humiliation a woman can suffer and still function.

Her head is more regularly beaten than any other woman's, and by her own man; she's the scapegoat for Mr. Charlie; she is forced to stark realism and chided if caught dreaming; her aspirations for her and hers are, for sanity's sake, stunted; her physical image has been criminally maligned, assaulted, and negated; she's the first to be called ugly and never yet beautiful, and as a consequence is forced to see her man (an exact copy of her, emotionally and physically), brainwashed and wallowing in self-loathing, pick for his own the physical antithesis of her (the white woman and incubator of his heretofore arch enemy the white man). Then, to add guilt to insult and injury, she (the Black woman) stands accused as the emasculator of the only thing she has ever cared for, her Black man. She is the scapegoat for what white America has made of the "Negro personality."

Raped and denied the right to cry out in her pain, she has been named the culprit and called "loose," "hot-blooded," "wanton," "sultry," and "amoral." She has been used as the white man's sexual outhouse, and shamefully encouraged by her own ego-less man to persist in this function. Wanting, too, to be carried away by her "Prince Charming," she must, in all honesty, admit that he has been robbed of his crown by the very assaulter and assassin who has raped her. Still, she looks upon her man as God's gift to Black womanhood and is further diminished and humiliated and outraged when the feeling is not mutual.

When a white man "likes colored girls," his woman (the white woman) is the last one he wants to know about it. Yet, seemingly, when a Negro "likes white girls," his woman (the Black woman) is the first he wants to know about it. White female rejects and social misfits are fragrantly flaunted in our faces as the ultimate in feminine pulchritude. Our women are encouraged by our own men to strive to look and act as much like the white female image as possible, and only those who approach that "goal" in physical appearance and social behavior are acceptable. At best, we are made to feel that we are poor imitations and excuses for white women.

Evil? Evil, you say? The Black woman is hurt, confused, frustrated, angry, resentful, frightened and evil! Who in this hell dares suggest that she should be otherwise? These attitudes only point up her perception of the situation and her healthy rejection of same.

Maybe if our women get evil enough and angry enough, they'll be moved to some action that will bring our men to their senses. There is one unalterable fact that too many of our men cannot seem to face. And that is, we "black, evil, ugly" women are a perfect and accurate reflection of you "black, evil, ugly" men. Play hide and seek as long as you can and will, but your every rejection and abandonment of us is only a sorry testament of how thoroughly and carefully you have been blinded and brainwashed. And let it further be understood that when we refer to you we mean, ultimately, us. For you are us, and vice versa.

We are the women who were kidnapped and brought to this continent as slaves. We are the women who were raped, are still being raped, and our bastard children snatched from our breasts and scattered to the winds to be lynched, castrated, de-egoed, robbed, burned, and deceived.

We are the women whose strong and beautiful Black bodies were—and are—still being used as a cheap labor force for Miss Anne's kitchen and Mr. Charlie's bed, whose rich, black, and warm milk nurtured—and still nurtures—the heir to the racist and evil slavemaster.

We are the women who dwell in the hell-hole ghettos all over the land. We are the women whose bodies are sacrificed, as living cadavers, to experimental surgery in the white man's hospitals for the sake of white medicine. We are the women who are invisible on the television and movie screens, on the Broadway stage. We are the women who are lusted after, sneered at, leered at, hissed at, yelled at, grabbed at, tracked down by white degenerates in our own pitiable, poverty-stricken, and prideless neighborhoods.

We are the women whose hair is compulsively fried, whose skin is bleached, whose nose is "too big," whose mouth is "too big and loud," whose behind is "too big and broad," whose feet are "too big and flat," whose face is "too black and shiny," and whose suffering and patience is too long and enduring to be believed.

Who're just too damned much for everybody.

We are the women whose bars and recreation halls are invaded by flagrantly disrespectful, bigoted, simpering, amoral, emotionally unstable, outcast, maladjusted, nymphomaniacal, condescending white women . . . in desperate and untiring search of the "frothing-at-the-mouth-for-a-white-woman, strongbacked, sixty-minute hot black." Our men.

We are the women who, upon protesting this invasion of our privacy and sanctity and sanity, are called "jealous," and "evil," and "small-minded," and "prejudiced." We are the women whose husbands and fathers and brothers and sons have been plagiarized, imitated, denied, and robbed of the fruits of their genius, and who consequently we see emasculated, jailed, lynched, driven mad, deprived, enraged, and made suicidal. We are the women whom nobody, seemingly, cares about, who are made to feel inadequate, stupid and backward, and who inevitably have the most colossal inferiority complexes to be found.

And who is spreading the propaganda that "the only free people in this country are the white man and the Black woman?" If this be freedom, then Heaven is Hell.

Who will revere the Black woman? Who will keep our neighborhoods safe for Black innocent womanhood? Black womanhood is outraged and humiliated. Black womanhood cries for dignity and restitution and salvation. Black womanhood wants and needs protection, and keeping, and holding. Who will assuage her indignation? Who will keep her precious and pure? Who will glorify and proclaim her beautiful image? To whom will she cry rape?

The Black Woman as a Woman

Kay Lindsey

As the movement toward the liberation of women grows, the Black woman will find herself, if she is at all sensitive to the issues of feminism, in a serious dilemma. For the Black movement is primarily concerned with the liberation of Blacks as a class and does not promote women's liberation as a priority. Indeed, the movement is for the most part spearheaded by males. The feminist movement, on the other hand, is concerned with the oppression of women as a class, but is almost totally composed of white females. Thus the Black woman finds herself on the outside of both political entities, in spite of the fact that she is the object of both forms of oppression.

Before Abolition, Black people were referred to as "slaves." No other designation was necessary, for our place in society was strictly enforceable. Since Abolition, and now that the institution of slavery has ceased to exist formally, those who define us in this society rec-

→even without slavery, society categorizes and organizes sub groups enforcing a social political difference in status

ognized the need to categorize us in increasingly sophisticated sub-groups, so that we become not only "good niggers," "bad niggers," and "crazy niggers," but "The Black Man" and "The Black Woman."

Classifications and categorizations of groups of people by other groups have always been for the benefit of the group who is doing the classifying and to the detriment of the classified group. The original sin in this context was the separation of the sexes, which on the surface appeared to be merely a division of labor, with respect to each sex's capacity to do certain types of work—the fact of child-bearing and the supposed physical limitations of the female being the rationalization for this division. This theory cannot be supported in light of the many contradictions in different societies where the roles of men and women are the reverse of the ones which we have known and which have been promoted in our own lives. A more realistic theory would be that out of the supremely human frustration of attempting to close the gap between our physical limitations and our boundless imaginations, men attempt to co-opt other human beings in order to extend themselves. The temporary incapacitation of women in pregnancy and childbirth offered men the opportunity to use women as their extensions, and in so doing, devoured the consciousness of women, robbing them of their potential autonomy. From females, men moved on to children; out of this grouping the family evolved. The family and the land on which it lived and cultivated its crops became the man's property, which was protected and defended against all comers. From protection and defense of his property, man moved on to the seizure of the land of others and his prisoners of war became his slaves. Upon this base, the state evolved and empires were created.

a lil hazy or meaning

• • • •

KAY LINDSEY | *The Black Woman as a Woman*

That there are parallels between being a woman and being Black
has not been denied, but that there are parallels between the Black
woman and the white woman has always been resisted, and the
Black woman has been set apart consistently from her white counterpart. We have instead been considered as a special subgroup
within the Black community, which Black men should try to deal
with as their own private extensions. This is an illusion perpetrated
on the Black man in order to deflect him from the task at hand,
which is not to create a domestic niche for his woman, but to
re-create society at large, a task which involves direct conflict with
the white agency, which at the very least would overturn all its institutions, including the family. The family, as a white institution,
has been held up to Blacks as a desirable but somehow unattainable
goal, at least not in the pure forms that whites have created. Witness
the Black middle class or pseudo-escapees into the mainstream.
This group has assumed many of the institutional postures of the
oppressor, including the so-called intact family, but even here we
find a fantastically high divorce rate and the frustration on this domestic level has increased dissension between individual Black
men and women, when it should instead be a signal that something
is radically wrong with the model they have chosen to imitate. A
latter-day effort, and more superficial for all that, on the part of the
white agency is to encourage the acquisition of property among
Blacks via Black Capitalism, which, if the idea took hold, would
probably serve to further intensify the stranglehold on women as
property.

The family has been used by the white agency to perpetuate the
state, and Blacks have been used as extensions of the white family,
as the prisoners of war enslaved, to do the dirty work of the family,
i.e. the state. If the family as an institution were destroyed, the state

would be destroyed. If Black people were destroyed, but the family left intact, the basic structure of the state would allow for rebuilding. If all white institutions with the exception of the family were destroyed, the state could also rise again, but Black rather than white.

To be a Black woman, therefore, is not just to be a Black who happens to be a woman, for one discovers one's sex sometime before one discovers one's racial classification. For it is immediately within the bosom of one's family that one learns to be a female and all that the term implies. Although our families may have taken a somewhat different form from that of whites, the socialization that was necessary to maintain the state was carried out. Our family life may be said to parallel our educational opportunities, in that we only need to finish elementary school or high school to get the kinds of jobs which are open to us, and we need only about twelve years of living within some kind of family situation to learn our sexual roles completely. Our first perception of ourselves is of our physical bodies, which we are then forced to compare with the bodies of those with whom we live, mothers, fathers, grandmothers, aunts, uncles, and whomever. Our clothing and the kinds of play activity we engage in are reflections of the lives of those with whom we live. Treatment at school reinforces our sexuality, so that by the time we reach adolescence, we as Black women have perceived our role, all too clearly.

One discovers what it means to be Black, and all that the term implies, usually outside the family, although this is probably less so than it was as the need to politicize all Blacks, including children, has become so obvious. But until recently, the child had only dim

revelations about her color within the fam
she moved out into the community and the
tion of whites to her gave her insight into her
oppression of Blacks by whites is not softened by t
rationale that the female encounters with the male,
not been taught by her family that to be Black is to be p
experiences extreme frustration and anger as she wades
the racial experience in an attempt to learn what is going on.
women, shackled by the limitations imposed on their behavior
cause of their sex, are afraid to explore their condition much be
yond their school years and go on to fulfill their biological destiny
as determined by the male. Among the jobs open to women of
all colors, it does not take long to realize that Black women are
expected to be primarily mothers, domestics and prostitutes.
Teaching, social work, clerk-typing, and other office work are possibilities only if one has managed to finish high school or college.

An inordinately high proportion of Black women become welfare
mothers, usually without a husband, in the household at least, and
while the white agency outwardly deplores the absence in the
household of a father figure, it does not take long to realize that the
state has created an artificial family, in which it, via the welfare
check, takes the place of the husband and can thus manipulate the
"family" more directly.

Large numbers of Black women earn their living, either part- or
full-time, as prostitutes, the most outrageous and flagrant form of
sexual oppression, in which an individual is forced to sell her body
on the basis of both sex and color, rather than use her mind to survive. Black women who spend their working lives not only as

...et another instance of Black
... forced into roles which are
...here the white woman is the
... welfare and the bearer of
...ite woman is the call girl
...t prostitute; where the
...fford it, a Black woman
...or her. In short, to be
... a physical body with-
...white counterpart. While white
...jects, Black women are sexual laborers.
... are the tokens among women in this society, in that
... have the titles, but not the power, while Black women have
neither—although Black women are frequently described by the
white agency in terms that suggest power, such as "strong," "domineering," "matriarchal," and "emasculating." As was suggested earlier in this article, when we are defined by those other than
ourselves, the qualities ascribed to us are not in our interests, but
rather reflect the nature of the roles which we are intended to play.
But the dominion of the kitchen and the welfare apartment are
hardly powerful vantage points.

What we truly are as women or as Black women or human beings
or groups is an unknown quantity insofar as we have not determined our own destiny. We have an obligation as Black women to
project ourselves into the revolution to destroy these institutions
which not only oppress Blacks but women as well, for if those institutions continue to flourish, they will be used against us in the continuing battle of mind over body.

Double Jeopardy: To Be Black and Female

Frances Beale

In attempting to analyze the situation of the Black woman in America, one crashes abruptly into a solid wall of grave misconceptions, outright distortions of fact, and defensive attitudes on the part of many. The system of capitalism (and its afterbirth—racism) under which we all live has attempted by many devious ways and means to destroy the humanity of all people, and particularly the humanity of Black people. This has meant an outrageous assault on every Black man, woman, and child who reside in the United States.

In keeping with its goal of destroying the Black race's will to resist its subjugation, capitalism found it necessary to create a situation where the Black man found it impossible to find meaningful or productive employment. More often than not, he couldn't find work of any kind. And the Black woman likewise was manipulated by the system, economically exploited and physically assaulted. She could often find work in the white man's kitchen, however, and sometimes became the sole breadwinner of the family. This predicament has led to many psychological problems on the part of both man and woman and has contributed to the turmoil that we find in the Black family structure.

Unfortunately, neither the Black man nor the Black woman understood the true nature of the forces working upon them. Many Black women tended to accept the capitalist evaluation of manhood and womanhood and believed, in fact, that Black men were shiftless and lazy, otherwise they would get a job and support their families as they ought to. Personal relationships between Black men and women were thus torn asunder and one result has been the separation of man from wife, mother from child, etc.

America has defined the roles to which each individual should subscribe. It has defined "manhood" in terms of its own interests and "femininity" likewise. Therefore, an individual who has a good job, makes a lot of money, and drives a Cadillac is a real "man," and conversely, an individual who is lacking in these "qualities" is less of a man. The advertising media in this country continuously inform the American male of his need for indispensable signs of his virility— the brand of cigarettes that cowboys prefer, the whiskey that has a masculine tang, or the label of the jock strap that athletes wear.

The ideal model that is projected for a woman is to be surrounded by hypocritical homage and estranged from all real work, spending idle hours primping and preening, obsessed with conspicuous consumption, and limiting life's functions to simply a sex role. We unqualitatively reject these respective models. A woman who stays at home caring for children and the house often leads an extremely sterile existence. She must lead her entire life as a satellite to her mate. He goes out into society and brings back a little piece of the world for her. His interests and his understanding of the world become her own and she cannot develop herself as an individual having been reduced to only a biological function. This kind of woman leads a parasitic existence that can aptly be described as legalized prostitution.

Furthermore it is idle dreaming to think of Black women simply caring for their homes and children like the middle-class white model. Most Black women have to work to help house, feed, and clothe their families. Black women make up a substantial percentage of the Black working force, and this is true for the poorest Black family as well as the so-called "middle-class" family.

Black women were never afforded any such phony luxuries. Though we have been browbeaten with this white image, the reality of the degrading and dehumanizing jobs that were relegated to us quickly dissipated this mirage of womanhood. The following excerpts from a speech that Sojourner Truth made at a Women's Rights Convention in the nineteenth century show us how misleading and incomplete a life this model represents for us:

... Well, chilern, whar dar is so much racket dar must be something out o' kilter. I tink dat 'twixt de niggers of de Souf and de women at de Norf all a talkin' 'bout rights, de white men will be in a fix pretty soon. But what's all dis here talkin' 'bout? Dat man ober dar say dat women needs to be helped into carriages, and lifted ober ditches, and to have de best place every whar. Nobody ever help me into carriages, or ober mud puddles, or gives me any best places, . . . and arn't I a woman? Look at me! Look at my arm! . . . I have plowed, and planted, and gathered into barns, and no man could head me—and ar'nt I a woman? I could work as much as a man (when I could get it), and bear de lash as well—and ar'nt I a woman? I have borne five chilern and I seen 'em mos' all sold off into slavery, and when I cried out with a mother's grief, none but Jesus heard—and ar'nt I a woman?

Unfortunately, there seems to be some confusion in the Movement today as to who has been oppressing whom. Since the advent of Black power, the Black male has exerted a more prominent leadership role in our struggle for justice in this country. He sees the system for what it really is for the most part, but where he rejects its values and mores on many issues, when it comes to women, he seems to take his guidelines from the pages of the *Ladies' Home Journal*. Certain Black men are maintaining that they have been castrated by society but that Black women somehow escaped this persecution and even contributed to this emasculation.

Let me state here and now that the Black woman in America can justly be described as a "slave of a slave." By reducing the Black man in America to such abject oppression, the Black woman had no protector and was used, and is still being used in some cases, as the scapegoat for the evils that this horrendous system has perpetrated on Black men. Her physical image has been maliciously maligned; she has been sexually molested and abused by the white colonizer; she has suffered the worse kind of economic exploitation, having been forced to serve as the white woman's maid and wet nurse for white offspring while her own children were more often than not starving and neglected. It is the depth of degradation to be socially manipulated, physically raped, used to undermine your own household, and to be powerless to reverse this syndrome.

It is true that our husbands, fathers, brothers, and sons have been emasculated, lynched, and brutalized. They have suffered from the cruelest assault on mankind that the world has ever known. However, it is a gross distortion of fact to state that Black women have oppressed Black men. The capitalist system found it expedient to enslave and oppress them and proceeded to do so without consultation or the signing of any agreements with Black women.

It must also be pointed out at this time that Black women are not resentful of the rise to power of Black men. We welcome it. We see in it the eventual liberation of all Black people from this corrupt system of capitalism. Nevertheless, this does not mean that you have to negate one for the other. This kind of thinking is a product of miseducation; that it's either X or it's Y. It is fallacious reasoning that in order for the Black man to be strong, the Black woman has to be weak.

Those who are exerting their "manhood" by telling Black women to step back into a domestic, submissive role are assuming a counter-revolutionary position. Black women likewise have been abused by the system and we must begin talking about the elimination of all kinds of oppression. If we are talking about building a strong nation, capable of throwing off the yoke of capitalist oppression, then we are talking about the total involvement of every man, woman, and child, each with a highly developed political consciousness. We need our whole army out there dealing with the enemy and not half an army.

There are also some Black women who feel that there is no more productive role in life than having and raising children. This attitude often reflects the conditioning of the society in which we live and is adopted from a bourgeois white model. Some young sisters who have never had to maintain a household and accept the confining role which this entails tend to romanticize (along with the help of a few brothers) this role of housewife and mother. Black women who have had to endure this kind of function are less apt to have these utopian visions.

Those who project in an intellectual manner how great and rewarding this role will be and who feel that the most important thing that they can contribute to the Black nation is children are doing themselves a great injustice. This line of reasoning completely negates the contributions that Black women have historically made to our struggle for liberation. These Black women include Sojourner Truth, Harriet Tubman, Mary McLeod Bethune, and Fannie Lou Hamer, to name but a few.

We live in a highly industrialized society and every member of the Black nation must be as academically and technologically developed as possible. To wage a revolution, we need competent teachers, doctors, nurses, electronics experts, chemists, biologists, physicists, political scientists, and so on and so forth. Black women sitting at home reading bedtime stories to their children are just not going to make it.

Economic Exploitation of Black Women

The economic system of capitalism finds it expedient to reduce women to a state of enslavement. They oftentimes serve as a scapegoat for the evils of this system. Much in the same way that the poor white cracker of the South, who is equally victimized, looks down upon Blacks and contributes to the oppression of Blacks, so, by giving to men a false feeling of superiority (at least in their own home or in their relationships with women), the oppression of women acts as an escape valve for capitalism. Men may be cruelly exploited and subjected to all sorts of dehumanizing tactics on the part of the ruling class, but they have someone who is below them—at least they're not women.

Women also represent a surplus labor supply, the control of which is absolutely necessary to the profitable functioning of capitalism. Women are systematically exploited by the system. They are paid less for the same work that men do, and jobs that are specifically relegated to women are low-paying and without the possibility of advancement. Statistics from the Women's Bureau of the U.S. Department of Labor show that in 1967 the wage scale for white women was even below that of Black men; and the wage scale for non-white women was the lowest of all:

White Males	$6704
Non-White Males	$4277
White Females	$3991
Non-White Females	$2861

Those industries which employ mainly Black women are the most exploitive in the country. Domestic and hospital workers are good examples of this oppression; the garment workers in New York City provide us with another view of this economic slavery. The International Ladies Garment Workers Union (ILGWU), whose overwhelming membership consists of Black and Puerto Rican women, has a leadership that is nearly all lily-white and male. This leadership has been working in collusion with the ruling class and has completely sold its soul to the corporate structure.

To add insult to injury, the ILGWU has invested heavily in business enterprises in racist, apartheid South Africa—with union funds. Not only does this bought-off leadership contribute to our continued exploitation in this country by not truly representing the best interests of its membership, but it audaciously uses funds that Black and Puerto Rican women have provided to support the economy of a vicious government that is engaged in the economic rape and murder of our Black brothers and sisters in our Motherland, Africa.

The entire labor movement in the United States has suffered as a result of the super-exploitation of Black workers and women. The unions have historically been racist and chauvinistic. They have upheld racism in this country and have failed to fight the white skin privileges of white workers. They have failed to fight or even make an issue against the inequities in the hiring and pay of women workers. There has been virtually no struggle against either the racism of the white worker or the economic exploitation of the working woman, two factors which have consistently impeded the advancement of the real struggle against the ruling class.

This racist, chauvinistic, and manipulative use of Black workers and women, especially Black women, has been a severe cancer on the American labor scene. It therefore becomes essential for those who understand the workings of capitalism and imperialism to realize that the exploitation of Black people and women works to everyone's disadvantage and that the liberation of these two groups is a stepping-stone to the liberation of all oppressed people in this country and around the world.

Bedroom Politics

I have briefly discussed the economic and psychological manipulation of Black women, but perhaps the most outlandish act of oppression in modern times is the current campaign to promote sterilization of non-white women in an attempt to maintain the population and power imbalance between the white haves and the non-white have-nots.

These tactics are but another example of the many devious schemes that the ruling-class elite attempt to perpetrate on the Black population in order to keep itself in control. It has recently come to our attention that a massive campaign for so-called "birth control" is presently being promoted not only in the underdeveloped non-white areas of the world, but also in Black communities here in the United States. However, what the authorities in charge of these programs refer to as "birth control" is in fact nothing but a method of outright surgical genocide.

The United States has been sponsoring sterilization clinics in non-white countries, especially in India, where already some three million young men and boys in and around New Delhi have been sterilized in makeshift operating rooms set up by the American Peace Corps workers. Under these circumstances, it is understandable why certain countries view the Peace Corps not as a benevolent project, not as evidence of America's concern for underdeveloped areas, but rather as a threat to their very existence. This program could more aptly be named the Death Corps.

Vasectomy, which is performed on males and takes only six or seven minutes, is a relatively simple operation. The sterilization of a woman, on the other hand, is admittedly major surgery. This operation (salpingectomy)* must be performed in a hospital under general anesthesia. This method of "birth control" is a common procedure in Puerto Rico. Puerto Rico has long been used by the colonialist exploiter, the United States, as a huge experimental laboratory for medical research before allowing certain practices to be imported and used here. When the birth control pill was first being perfected, it was tried out on Puerto Rican women and selected Black women (poor), using them as human guinea pigs, to evaluate its effect and its efficiency.

Salpingectomy has now become the commonest operation in Puerto Rico, commoner than an appendectomy or a tonsillectomy. It is so widespread that it is referred to simply as *la operacion. On the island, 10 percent of the women between the ages of 15 and 45 have already been sterilized.*

And now, as previously occurred with the pill, this method has been imported into the United States. These sterilization clinics are cropping up around the country in the Black and Puerto Rican

---

* Salpingectomy: Through an abdominal incision, the surgeon cuts both fallopian tubes and ties off the separated ends, after which act there is no way for the egg to pass from the ovary to the womb.

communities. These so-called "maternity clinics" specifically out-fitted to purge Black women or men of their reproductive possibil-ities are appearing more and more in hospitals and clinics across the country.

A number of organizations have been formed to popularize the idea of sterilization, such as the Association for Voluntary Ster-ilization and the Human Betterment (!!!?) Association for Volun-tary Sterilization, Inc., which has its headquarters in New York City.

Threatened with the cut-off of relief funds, some Black welfare women have been forced to accept this sterilization procedure in exchange for a continuation of welfare benefits. Black women are often afraid to permit any kind of necessary surgery because they know from bitter experience that they are more likely than not to come out of the hospital without their insides. (Both salpingec-tomies and hysterectomies are performed.)

We condemn this use of the Black woman as a medical testing ground for the white middle class. Reports of the ill effects, includ-ing deaths, from the use of the birth control pill only started to come to light when the white privileged class began to be affected. These outrageous Nazi-like procedures on the part of medical re-searchers are but another manifestation of the totally amoral and dehumanizing brutality that the capitalist system perpetrates on Black women. The sterilization experiments carried on in concen-tration camps some twenty-five years ago have been announced the world over, but no one seems to get upset by the repetition of these same racist tactics today in the United States of America—land of the free and home of the brave. This campaign is as nefari-ous a program as Germany's gas chambers, and in a long-term sense, as effective and with the same objective.

The rigid laws concerning abortions in this country are another vicious means of subjugation and, indirectly, of outright murder.

Rich white women somehow manage to obtain these operations with little or no difficulty. It is the poor Black and Puerto Rican woman who is at the mercy of the local butcher. Statistics show us that the non-white death rate at the hands of the unqualified abortionist is substantially higher than for white women. Nearly half of the childbearing deaths in New York City are attributed to abortion alone and out of these, 79 percent are among non-whites and Puerto Rican women.

We are not saying that Black women should not practice birth control. *Black women have the right and the responsibility to determine when it is in the interest of the struggle to have children or not to have them, and this right must not be relinquished to anyone.* It is also her right and responsibility to determine when it is in her own best interests to have children, how many she will have, and how far apart. The lack of the availability of safe birth-control methods, the forced sterilization practices, and the inability to obtain legal abortions are all symptoms of a decadent society that jeopardizes the health of Black women (and thereby the entire Black race) in its attempts to control the very life processes of human beings. This is a symptom of a society that believes it has the right to bring political factors into the privacy of the bedchamber. The elimination of these horrendous conditions will free Black women for full participation in the revolution, and thereafter, in the building of the new society.

Relationship to White Movement

Much has been written recently about the white women's liberation movement in the United States, and the question arises whether there are any parallels between this struggle and the movement on the part of Black women for total emancipation. While there are certain comparisons that one can make, simply because we both live under the same exploitative system, there are certain differences, some of which are quite basic.

The white women's movement is far from being monolithic. Any white group that does not have an anti-imperialist and anti-racist ideology has absolutely nothing in common with the Black woman's struggle. In fact, some groups come to the incorrect conclusion that their oppression is due simply to male chauvinism. They therefore have an extremely anti-male tone to their dissertations. Black people are engaged in a life-and-death struggle and the main emphasis of Black women must be to combat the capitalist, racist exploitation of Black people. While it is true that male chauvinism has become institutionalized in American society, one must always look for the main enemy—the fundamental cause of the female condition.

Another major differentiation is that the white women's liberation movement is basically middle-class. Very few of these women suffer the extreme economic exploitation that most Black women are subjected to day by day. This is the factor that is most crucial for us. It is not an intellectual persecution alone; it is not an intellectual outburst for us; it is quite real. We as Black women have got to deal with the problems that the Black masses deal with, for our problems in reality are one and the same.

If the white groups do not realize that they are in fact fighting capitalism and racism, we do not have common bonds. If they do not realize that the reasons for their condition lie in the system and not simply that men get a vicarious pleasure out of "consuming their bodies for exploitative reasons" (this kind of reasoning seems to be quite prevalent in certain white women's groups), then we cannot unite with them around common grievances or even discuss these groups in a serious manner because they're completely irrelevant to the Black struggle.

The New World

The Black community and Black women especially must begin raising questions about the kind of society we wish to see established. We must note the ways in which capitalism oppresses us and then move to create institutions that will eliminate these destructive influences.

The new world that we are attempting to create must destroy oppression of any type. The value of this new system will be determined by the status of the person who was low man on the totem pole. Unless women in any enslaved nation are completely liberated, the change cannot really be called a revolution. If the Black woman has to retreat to the position she occupied before the armed struggle, the whole movement and the whole struggle will have retreated in terms of truly freeing the colonized population.

A people's revolution that engages the participation of every member of the community, including man, woman, and child, brings about a certain transformation in the participants as a result of this participation. Once you have caught a glimpse of freedom or experienced a bit of self-determination, you can't go back to old routines that were established under a racist, capitalist regime. We must begin to understand that a revolution entails not only the willingness to lay our lives on the firing line and get killed. In some ways, this is an easy commitment to make. To die for the revolution is a one-shot deal; to live for the revolution means taking on the more difficult commitment of changing our day-to-day life patterns.

This will mean changing the traditional routines that we have established as a result of living in a totally corrupting society. It means changing how you relate to your wife, your husband, your parents, and your co-workers. If we are going to liberate ourselves as a people, it must be recognized that Black women have very specific problems that have to be spoken to. We must be liberated along with the rest of the population. We cannot wait to start working on those problems until that great day in the future when the revolution somehow miraculously is accomplished.

To assign women the role of housekeeper and mother while men go forth into battle is a highly questionable doctrine for a revolutionary to maintain. Each individual must develop a high political consciousness in order to understand how this system enslaves us all and what actions we must take to bring about its total destruction. Those who consider themselves to be revolutionary must begin to deal with other revolutionaries as equals. And so far as I know, revolutionaries are not determined by sex.

Old people, young people, men and women, must take part in the struggle. To relegate women to purely supportive roles or to purely cultural considerations is dangerous doctrine to project. Unless Black men who are preparing themselves for armed struggle understand that the society which we are trying to create is one in which the oppression of *all members* of that society is eliminated, then the revolution will have failed in its avowed purpose.

Given the mutual commitment of Black men and Black women alike to the liberation of our people and other oppressed peoples around the world, the total involvement of each individual is necessary. A revolutionary has the responsibility not only of toppling those that are now in a position of power, but of creating new institutions that will eliminate all forms of oppression. We must begin to rewrite our understanding of traditional personal relationships between man and woman.

All the resources that the Black community can muster up must be channeled into the struggle. Black women must take an active part in bringing about the kind of society where our children, our loved ones, and each citizen can grow up and live as decent human beings, free from the pressures of racism and capitalist exploitation.

On the Issue
of Roles*

Toni Cade

In the last few years I have frequently been asked to speak on the topic of the Black Woman's Role in the Revolution. Invariably I get a little tongue tied at the outset, trying to clarify some of the difficulties I have even coping with the title. What Black woman did you have in mind? Each of us, after all, has particular skills and styles that suit us for particular tasks in the struggle. I'm not altogether sure we agree on the term "revolution" or I wouldn't be having so much difficulty with the phrase "woman's role." I have always, I think, opposed the stereotypic definitions of "masculine" and "feminine," not only because I thought it was a lot of merchandising nonsense, but rather because I always found the either/or implicit in those definitions antithetical to what I was all about—and what revolution for self is all about—the whole person. And I am beginning to see, especially lately, that the usual notions of sexual

* An excerpt from an autobiographical essay, *The Scattered Sopranoes*, delivered as a lecture to the Livingston College Black Woman's Seminar, December 1969.

differentiation in roles is an obstacle to political consciousness, that the way those terms are generally defined and acted upon in this part of the world is a hindrance to full development. And that is a shame, for a revolutionary must be capable of, above all, total self-autonomy.

I don't know if there are any viable models in pre-capitalist, non-white societies. I don't know that I can trust the anthropological studies that attempt to illuminate and interpret just how the sexes operated in so-called primitive societies, or just how the self was viewed. For much of the work I run across is either written by white males steeped in the misogynistic and capitalistic tradition, which means that the material is always slanted to reinforce the myth of male superiority, female inferiority, and separation and antagonism between the sexes; or written by women with axes to grind so that the material is always slanted to "prove" that women in the so-called primitive societies were dominant and warlike. When I am left to my own devices—and I am neither a man nor a woman who wishes to be a man—I tend to find no particularly rigid work assignments based on sex. The pre-capitalist, non-white lifestyle seems to be worth checking out. For it sheds some light on the madness of "masculinity" and "femininity," even though it may not offer us any model at this time in history.

Generally speaking, in a capitalist society a man is expected to be an aggressive, uncompromising, factual, lusty, intelligent provider of goods, and the woman, a retiring, gracious, emotional, intuitive, attractive consumer of goods. The move for centuries has been to render her a subordinate being, a background figure, to regard her as a self-sacrificing mother, a loving wife, a generous sex mate, a passive, retiring, physically delicate, not too bright but oft-times devious and cunning member of the household, teaching profession, or secretary pool; one who needs constant protection and guidance, for she has a lascivious nature that must be curbed;

one who is not capable of major economic, political, or social decisions other than choosing Del Monte over Brand X; one who is not capable of serious artistic or creative contributions other than blowing up like Moby Dick and dropping squalling babies; one who risks mental derangement or at least emotional imbalance or "unfemininity" should she elect a profession that puts her in competition with men or should she be crazy enough to fashion for herself a life as something other than the appendage of some man. If the shamans of this culture, the writers and dramatists, are anything to go by—she is either a marketable virgin or a potential whore, but certainly the enemy of men.

Now, we tend to argue that all that is a lot of honky horseshit. But unfortunately, we have not been immune to the conditioning; we are just as jammed in the rigid confines of those basically oppressive socially contrived roles. For if a woman is tough, she's a rough mamma, a strident bitch, a ballbreaker, a castrator. And if a man is at all sensitive, tender, spiritual, he's a faggot. And there is a dangerous trend observable in some quarters of the Movement to program Sapphire out of her "evil" ways into a cover-up, shut-up, lay-back-and-be-cool obedience role. She is being assigned an unreal role of mute servant that supposedly neutralizes the acidic tension that exists between Black men and Black women. She is being encouraged—in the name of the revolution no less—to cultivate "virtues" that if listed would sound like the personality traits of slaves. In other words, we are still abusing each other, aborting each other's nature—in the teeth of experiences both personal and historical that should alert us to the horror of a situation in which we profess to be about liberation but behave in a constricting manner; we rap about being correct but ignore the danger of having one half of our population regard the other with such condescension and perhaps fear that that half finds it necessary to "reclaim his manhood" by denying her her peoplehood. Perhaps we need to let go of all notions of manhood and femininity and concentrate on Black-hood. We have much, alas, to work against. The job of purging is staggering. It perhaps takes less heart to pick up the gun than to face the task of creating a new identity, a self, perhaps an androgynous self, via commitment to the struggle.

The argument goes that the man is the breadwinner and the subject, the woman the helpmate and the object because that is the nature of the sexes, because that is the way it's always been, and just because. And yet my readings of Africa, Asia, the South Seas, and America (pre-white man)—sporadic at best, sloppy at worst—tells me that cultures have conceived of man/woman in a variety of ways, that "human nature" is a pretty malleable quality. And I am convinced, at least in my readings of African societies, that prior to the European obsession of property as a basis for social organization, and prior to the introduction of Christianity, a religion fraught with male anxiety and villification of women, communities were equalitarian and cooperative. The woman was neither subordinate nor dominant, but a sharer in policymaking and privileges, had mobility and opportunity and dignity. And while it would seem she had certain tasks to perform and he particular duties to attend, there were no hard and fixed assignments based on gender, no rigid and hysterical separation based on sexual taboos. She often accompanied him on hunts and donned warrior gear on the battlefield, and he frequently participated in food gathering and in the education of the young.

There is nothing to indicate that the African woman, who ran the marketplace, who built dams, who engaged in international commerce and diplomacy, who sat on thrones, who donned armor to wage battle against the European invaders and the corrupt chieftains who engaged in the slave trade, who were consulted as equals in the affairs of state—nothing to indicate that they were turning their men into faggots, were victims of penis envy, or any such nonsense. There is nothing to indicate that the Sioux, Seminole, Iroquois or other "Indian" nations felt oppressed or threatened by their women, who had mobility, privileges, a voice in the governing of the commune. There is evidence, however, that the European white was confused and alarmed by the equalitarian system of these societies and did much to wreck it, creating wedges between the men and women. It's anybody's pessimistic guess as to what impact the Yankee mentality will have on the harmonious relationships that have developed among the Vietnamese men and women bound together, under fire, committed to common struggle to liberate their nation: Certainly the huge body of poems and love letters pouring out of that country reveal that men are congratulating their women who shoot guns, bear babies, build bridges, keep the village fires going, plot out strategy, and bury the dead; just as it is obvious the women celebrate their men who dig booby traps, feed the infants and the aged, impale G.I.s, write love poems and the like.

If there is any area that is crucial in the Black Studies or Third World Curriculum it is the study of the destructive and corruptive white presence. We think we know; we feel we've been sensitized long enough to really know. But we really ought to check it out with thoroughness. The cooperative community under the matriarchal system was disrupted when the concept of property was introduced in the Motherland. Property led to class divisions which disrupted the communal society. To guarantee the transmission of property, patrilinear inheritance was adopted. To ensure a clear line of inheritance, the woman's liberty and mobility, especially sexual, was curtailed through monogamy. The nuclear family cut her off from the larger society and turned this homebody into nobody. To keep everything running smoothly, he was taught that it was his natural obligation as a man to support his family, she that it was her natural obligation as a woman to serve the family. Just as the "natives" became the white man's burden, his property, she became the man's burden, his Mrs., and the children became the parents' burden.

To be sure, this is a rather simplistic recap of history, but it is sufficiently sound to launch an argument against "that is the nature of the sexes" and "that's the way it's always been." Of course, Christianity helped to reinforce many of the above pathological conditions. The whole story of Genesis is but one example of the white man's hatred and mistrust of his woman. That Eve should be born of man—stranger yet, that she owes her existence to a spare rib—is typical not only of the white man's attempt to render her Other, but also illustrates his disharmony with the natural. In the drama of the Fall, she plays the villain, the vile creature who doomed us all to sinful lives. She plays the role yet in film after film, instigating crimes, manipulating poor saps who don't really want to rob and murder but who are as helpless against her wiles as poor Adam was. The genocidal bloodbath of centuries and centuries of witch hunts sheds some light on the hysterical attitude white men have regarding their women. Unfortunately, it tainted the relationships of men and women in Africa and in exile. Just as the notions of Heaven and Hell, the elect and the damned, reinforced elitism. And the notion of sainthood through martyrdom, submission, and the embrace of death moved us all further and further from our once harmonious relationship with the self and nature.

All this to say what? To say that we would do well to reclaim the old relationships. Fortunately, remnants of the old way persist on the continent. For example, in the Cameroons, I've been told, every woman of adult age is referred to as Mother. That is the way in a communal society with no hang-ups about "mine." And a friend living there for a while was teased daily for asking, "Which is your child? Which one is your mother?" We're so turned around about Western models, we don't even know how to raise the correct questions. But raise them we must if we are to fashion a natural sense of self, if we are to develop harmonious relationships with each other. What are we talking about when we speak of revolution if not a free society made up of whole individuals? I'm not arguing the denial of manhood or womanhood, but rather a shifting of priorities, a call for Selfhood, Blackhood. When Father Divine launched his program, the Peace Mission Movement, the first thing he insisted upon from the novitiate was a shifting from malehood and femalehood to Angelhood. If that program owed its success to anything, it owed it to the kind of shift in priorities. I don't know what the long-range program was regarding sex, but I tend to agree that celibacy for a time is worth considering, for sex is dirty if all it means is winning a man, conquering a woman, beating someone out of something, abusing each other's dignity in order to prove that I am a man, I am a woman.

We have such a reluctance to talk about things like these for fear of being weird. But if we are serious, we shall have to check out everything that is characteristic of the Black Community and examine it for health or disease.

Now it doesn't take any particular expertise to observe that one of the most characteristic features of our community is the antagonism between our men and our women. The mother, daughter, aunt, and grandma tend to line up against the man and his buddies from the pool hall, the bar, or wherever. There is a whole canon of nasty jokes about the enemy camp; a host of phrases we all tend to learn in our grandmothers' kitchens about hardheaded bitches and jive-ass niggers. Mamma tells junior his father was a no-good bum and then proceeds to groom him to be just like his daddy, an abuser of young girls, but faithful of course to Mamma. Mamma tells daughter that men ain't no damn good and raises such suspicions and fears and paranoia in her heart that she is nasty as hell to men she meets and elicits equally lousy behavior. The few semipermanent relationships that do develop are invariably built on some shaky finance-romance basis, her trying to get into his pockets, him trying to get into her drawers. Our blues singers have chronicled that madness for generations. But only lately has there developed something saner. And it's developed through the Struggle.

We used to think, at least where I grew up, that the pimp and the hustler was a Man—pressed back, fly, easy-spending, exploitive of women, a fancy stud. We also thought of the celebrity and entertainer as a Man—jewelry, frilly shirts, tenor voice, women hanging on his neck and tearing off his clothes, a pretty stud. Then there was the athlete—stupid, brutal, white man's pawn, but graceful and sexy, a muscular stud. But then along came Malcolm and Muhammed Ali and changed all that. And now we tend to think of a Man in terms of his commitment to the Struggle.

We used to think of woman in terms of actresses—pretty, anonymous, whitified, surrounded by glamour. Or in terms of singers—tragic, doomed, mournful, short-lived. But now the young look to and emulate Nina Simone, Abbey Lincoln, Kathleen Cleaver, not because they're gorgeous in that old way, but beautiful in a new Black way. We measure their womanhood in terms of their connection to the Struggle.

Years ago I did a terrible thing. I edited a copy of a young male student's paper, "Reflections on Black Women," so that all references to male and female were changed to "us" and "them." After several months elapsed, I read the paper during one of our after-class beer chats. And sure enough everyone reacted to phrases like "I don't believe in the double standard, but" or "They're trying to take over" and agreed it was the usual racist shit. As a matter of fact, the author of the original piece was even more vitriolic in his condemnation of the bigotry and hypocrisy than anyone else. Of course, he went into a tirade about my ethics when I announced that the paper, his paper, originally was not about Black and White but about Men and Women. But after the smoke cleared, we all sat and talked for hours, sharing such painfully private experiences, such poignant struggles with the rubber stamp of what a girl's supposed to be like and what a boy's supposed to be like, that attendance in the class dropped off drastically and we found it difficult to face each other for weeks. But at least the point had been made: racism and chauvinism are anti-people. And a man cannot be politically correct and a chauvinist too.

Several other things came out of that discussion, though, besides the formation of a woman's workshop (which was subsequently wrecked by the presence of the men who could not quite cope with the women's passionate concern with their oppression). One was that most men are just as eager to get off the how-many-babes-I've-laid-this-week treadmill and get down to the business of love, as women are to give up the whatcha-gonna-do-for-me-nigger and be for real. The other had to do with the handling of the woman's liberation question in those organizations established to further the Movement. It would seem that every organization you can name has had to struggle at one time or another with seemingly mutinous cadres of women getting salty about having to man the telephones or fix the coffee while the men wrote the position papers and decided on policy. Some groups condescendingly allotted two or three slots in the executive order to women. Others encouraged the sisters to form a separate caucus and work out something that wouldn't split the organization. Others got nasty and haughty and forced the women to storm out to organize separate workshops. Over the years, things have sort of been cooled out. But I have yet to hear a coolheaded analysis of just what any particular group's stand is on the question. Invariably I hear from some dude that Black women must be supportive and patient so that Black men can regain their manhood. The notion of womanhood, they argue—and only if pressed to address themselves to the notion do they think of it or argue—is dependent on his defining his manhood. So the shit goes on. Of course there are any number of women around willing to walk ten paces back to give him the illusion of walking ten paces ahead. I happen to love my ole man, and I would be loathe to patronize him in that way. But perhaps that is because I don't have to, for he is not obsessive about his balls. And I wonder if the dudes who keep hollering about their lost balls realize that they probably surrendered them either to Mr. Charlie in the marketplace, trying to get that Eldorado, or to Miss Anne in bed, trying to bang out some sick notion of love and freedom. It seems to me you find your Self in destroying illusions, smashing myths, laundering the head of whitewash, being responsible to some truth, to the struggle. That entails at the very least cracking through the veneer of this sick society's definition of "masculine" and "feminine."

Frantz Fanon in *A Dying Colonialism* devoted much space to the impact the Algerian liberation struggle had on changing traditional relationships and socially defined codes of behavior, releasing people from stultifying role-playing, freeing them to fashion a new sense of self. His chapter on the Algerian family is of particular import, for it clearly demonstrates both the possibility and the necessity for creating new values and new persons. When the son, for example, took a revolutionary position, he could no longer abide by the customary regulation to regard his father's word as law. He did not reject his father, he converted him. And the father, to reestablish a sense of sovereignty, joined his son and invoked the authority of the maquis or cell leader. The daughter, heretofore relegated to a mute existence as a minor in her father's household or a minor in her husband's household, found through involvement with the struggle a new discipline, a world of responsibility. She was no longer simply an item in a marriage contract or business deal but a revolutionary committed to action. And she tended to see men in a new light: not as benevolent protectors or tyrants, but in terms of their preparedness to join the FLN. The mother, to protect her family, had to get involved too, often carrying messages or inventing alibis or following her man to the mountains with bandages and food. She found a new sense of mobility and dignity through responsibility. Marriages were no longer contract arrangements but freely chosen unions of individuals bound to a corporate future of freedom. The "family" was no longer a socially ordained nuclear unit to perpetuate the species or legitimize sexuality, but an extended kinship of cellmates and neighbors linked in the business of actualizing a vision of a liberated society. A new person is born when he finds a value to define an actional self and when he can assume autonomy for that self. Such is the task that faces us.

Revolution begins with the self, in the self. The individual, the basic revolutionary unit, must be purged of poison and lies that assault the ego and threaten the heart, that hazard the next larger unit—the couple or pair, that jeopardize the still larger unit—the family or cell, that put the entire movement in peril. We make many false starts because we have been programmed to depend on white models or white interpretations of non-white models, so we don't even ask the correct questions, much less begin to move in a correct direction. Perhaps we need to face the terrifying and overwhelming possibility that there are no models, that we shall have to create from scratch. Doctrinaire Marxism is basically incompatible with Black nationalism; New Left politics is incompatible with Black nationalism; doctrinaire socialism is incompatible with Black revolution; capitalism, lord knows, is out. We need to reject too the opinions of outside "experts" who love to explain ourselves to ourselves, telling the Black man that the matriarch is his enemy, telling Black women through the mushrooming of b.c. clinics that too many children is the Black family's enemy. So he indulges in lost-balls fantasies and attempts to exact recompense by jumping feet foremost into her chest, and she starts conjuring up abandonment stories and ADC nightmares and leaps at his throat. Now what is that but acting like we were just symbolic personae in some historical melodrama. Keep the big guns on the real enemy. Men have got to develop some heart and some sound analysis to realize that when sisters get passionate about themselves and their direction, it does not mean they're readying up to kick men's ass. They're readying up for honesty. And women have got to develop some heart and some sound analysis so they can resist the temptation of buying peace with their man with self-sacrifice and posturing. The job then regarding "roles" is to submerge all breezy definitions of manhood/womanhood (or reject them out of hand if you're not squeamish about being called "neuter") until realistic definitions emerge through a commitment to Blackhood.

It may be lonely. Certainly painful. It'll take time. We've got time. That of course is an unpopular utterance these days. Instant coffee is the hallmark of current rhetoric. But we do have time. We'd better take the time to fashion revolutionary selves, revolutionary lives, revolutionary relationships. Mouth don't win the war. It don't even win the people. Neither does haste, urgency, and stretch-out-now insistence. Not all speed is movement. Running off to mimeograph a fuck-whitey leaflet, leaving your mate to brood, is not revolutionary. Hopping a plane to rap to someone else's "community" while your son struggles alone with the Junior Scholastic assignment on "The Dark Continent" is not revolutionary. Sitting around murder-mouthing incorrect niggers while your father goes upside your mother's head is not revolutionary. Mapping out a building takeover when your term paper is overdue and your scholarship is under review is not revolutionary. Talking about moving against the Mafia while your nephew takes off old ladies at the subway stop is not revolutionary. If your house ain't in order, you ain't in order. It is so much easier to be out there than right here. The revolution ain't out there. Yet. But it is here. Should be. And arguing that instant-coffee-ten-minutes-to-midnight alibi to justify hasty-headed dealings with your mate is shit. Ain't no such animal as an instant guerrilla.

Black Man, My Man, Listen!

Gail Stokes

I have accepted you, taken you back. Embraced you, empathized with your pitiful plight, because I know how they have used and abused you. I have tried to cease with my lamentations and taking your faults, your shortcomings in stride, made you a part of me. I was glad to have you back, and glad that you wanted to come back. Glad that I could accept you out of my own free choosing.

Here we are, you and me, loving each other in our blackness. Day after day I prod and push you along and I love you more in this, our undertaking. I look up at you, and you are beautiful. You are like the earth sprouting forth its taut boldness in a breath of wind, a shower of rain, a fiery circle of sun. And yet, somehow, some way, disillusions start to seep in after we have eaten together, walked together, and soared in love together.

You are dependent, very dependent, upon my proddings, my ideas, my dreams, and at first I am glad that you need me so. I eagerly and happily feed you from the plate of motivation knowing that it is difficult for you to help yourself. But, then at times you cause my arms to grow weary as I work harder straining myself in order to build you up. Straining myself as I watch you now and again hesitate and then refuse the nourishment.

What is it? Isn't the food good? I carefully prepared it and let it simmer gently all the time you were gone. Perhaps, I have added just a little too much sugar and the sweetness of it grows sickening or maybe it contains too much of my soul. In my mind, I look back and stare and wonder at my preparations; are they to be in vain? My quivering senses detect your apathy. It frightens me and I become very angry!

Is this the man, my man, the Black man whom I so readily welcomed home? I look at you closer every day since you have returned. I watch your majesty turn to quietness, evasiveness, and solitude. Silently you sit and wait and watch while I secure the essential ingredients. While I try to make you a man. And all the while you are content in your waiting.

Black man? my man? I vowed to help sustain you, me, us, but . . . never . . . no not like this. This wasn't the way at all. Dear God . . . Dear Allah . . . help me in his apathy. PLEASE, don't let me be USED again!

Time passes and I gather in new hopes. After all, it is time you need, I say to console myself, that is all—just time. Yet, again that dark foreboding cloud continually hovers overhead, because you have shut out everything, even me. Now the cloud has burst amid loud thunder. Rain pours in huge black drops and I wallow in dark pools of despair. For your hopes and my desires are no longer one.

Where are you, Black man? Spread forth your arms. Lead me. For it is very dark. I need your comfort. I need reassurance that what I am struggling so violently for is real, and that which is not now yours nor mine will be ours soon, in the not too distant future.

Through my helplessness and through my anguish anger swells within me, and fills me as I think of our young Black children. How closely they choose to cling to me bearing witness to my distress. And with round searching faces and small hands they reach out in efforts to lift me up, silently saying, we need you and we love you.

My heart is torn and painfully bleeds as I watch your sons watching me and knowing my tiredness. What can I say now? I prepared them for your homecoming a long time ago. I had hushed their frets and refused to hear any of their whining cries against your return. What can I say to them now. What can I tell them in order to ease their little minds that are wise beyond their years. I told them that you were all new. All changed. I told them that you were now a man! Yes, I told them that you now possessed the strength to command the universe, which is yours now to take and hold and keep. Where is your pride, your blackness, your beauty? What has it all amounted to?

Black man, my man listen! Have we no more in common than before? Have we nothing at all but our name? And even that is not ours.

Is the Black Male Castrated?*

*Jean Carey Bond
and Patricia Peery*

In Black communities all over the country today, intelligent and imaginative people are discussing the political, economic, and cultural aspects of the Black Liberation Struggle. Viable approaches for changing the Afro-American's condition in America are beginning to emerge. Almost without notice, an issue slipped in the back door of these discussions and assumed controversial proportions as soon as its presence was acknowledged. We refer to what has become a burning question in our community, and rightly so: what should be the role of women in the movement? Subdivisions of the lead question are: what have been the traditional relations between Black men and women? What are the factors that have defined or determined those relations? Despite the obvious interest of both men and women in this issue, and despite the inclination of both to

* Originally published as "Has the Black Male Been Castrated?" in *Liberator* magazine, vol. 9, no. 5 (May 1969,) pp. 4–8. Copyright © 1969 by *Liberator* magazine.

comment at length and take rigid positions on the topic, we are appalled at a reigning lack of seriousness and sobriety in the debate. Black publications are full of, on the one hand, hysterical and bitter indictments of the past and present conduct of Black men from the bruised and now twisted consciousnesses of sisters who have been driven to irrational extremes by the conditions of a world they never made. On the other, we find the equally neurotic but voguish creed that women must abandon their "matriarchal" behavior, learn to speak only when they are spoken to, and take up positions three paces (or is it ten) behind their men.* As far as we know, the question as to whether her place is not properly beside, rather than in front of or behind, the Black man has yet to be raised.

For their part, many Black men berate Black women for their faults, faults so numerous and so pronounced that one is hard put to discern in their tirades any ground, short of invisibility, on which Black womanhood may redeem itself. They do this, blind to the age-old implications of such a vociferous rejection of a part of themselves. Others run on about the necessity of subordinating women to their superior and manly will in the planning and execution of revolution with a monumental indisposition to examine their motives for advancing this precept.

We view these superficial and unbalanced attitudes as being

---

* It seems to us that many Black women who give lip service to the latter, male-inspired philosophy have played an interesting psychological trick on themselves. Feeling both guilty and resentful in their relations with Black men, they merely alter the mode of attack to fit the new Black party line. Their aggression now takes the form of patronizing, "understanding" pronouncements about Black male so-called inadequacies. Dripping with self-admonition and promises to act right in the by-and-by, they neatly assuage the guilt but not the resentment, which, to be sure, will rear its ugly head in the near future, as troublesome as ever, never having been honestly confronted by either women or men. In the case of some unmarried sisters, we suspect that sheer opportunism motivates their public approval of this idea. What better way to get a man, they reason, than to proclaim your willingness to be his slave?

predicated on a popular and dangerous fiction: the myth of Black male emasculation and its descendant concept, the myth of the Black female matriarchy. These companion myths are not recent in their origin; however, they have most recently been popularized through the highly publicized and highly touted work *The Negro Family: The Case For National Action,* by Daniel Patrick Moynihan—so successfully popularized that even Blacks have swallowed his assumptions and conclusions hook, line, and sinker. It is ironic that at a time when Blacks are newly perceiving and denouncing the shallowness of white analyses of the Black experience, many members of the avant-garde are still capable of being mesmerized by racist social scientific thought, which has utterly failed to produce in-depth studies of the Afro-American social structure.

The emasculation theory, as interpreted by Blacks, is two-pronged, one version being primarily followed by women, the other commanding the allegiance of both men and women. Version number one alleges that Black men have failed throughout our history to shield their women and families from the scourge of American racism and have failed to produce a foolproof strategy for liberating black people. It is therefore concluded that black men are weak, despicable "niggers" who must be brushed aside and overcome by women in the big push toward freedom. Version number two also arrives at the point that Black men are weak via the route that Black women have castrated them by, among other things, playing their economic ace in the hole. (Moynihan's Black matriarchy proposition is based, incredibly, on the statistic that one-quarter—only one-quarter!—of all Black families are headed by women.) Also linked to this thesis is the woefully misbegotten notion that Black women complied with their rapists and used their bodies to rise on the socio-economic ladder, leaving Black men behind. What this all adds up to is that Black men and women are placing ultimate blame for their subjugation on each other, a propensity which fairly reeks of self-hatred. In other words, Blacks are still crippled by self-doubt and, even in 1969, lean painfully toward the view that Europeans could never have kept us in this bind for so long were it not for our weakness, i.e., inferiority. It is not difficult to understand why we are unable to see the forest for the trees. After all, the cat who sponges off of you, knocks you around every now and then, and maybe leaves you, is Black, not white. By the same token, the chick who tells you this is her money, she made it, and you can just get the hell out, is Black, not white. But we are, in fact, focusing only on the trees when we expend time and energy in this senseless and debilitating family squabble while the real culprits stand laughing in the wings.

What is emasculation? In the broad sense, an emasculated people (cultural group) are a broken people, a people whose spirit, strength, and vigor have been destroyed, who have been reduced to a state of almost total ineffectuality. Specifically applied to a male, emasculation connotes the absence of virility and can mean, though not necessarily, effeminacy. Notwithstanding the colossal suffering which has befallen Black people here and abroad as a result of their colonization by Europeans, with its numerous deleterious effects on the black psyche, do our people truly fit the description given above? And notwithstanding the often literal but more often symbolic castration of hundreds of thousands of Black individuals throughout our sojourn in the wilderness, have Black men really been stripped of their virility? We contend that as a whole people, Afro-Americans lack neither spirit nor strength nor vigor, for it is they who have given to this nation the only culture it has, the only humanity it has.

As for Black men, we must ask the question: If the Black male's castration is a *fait accompli* of long standing, why the frantic need on the part of whites to replay the ritual of castration over and over again in a hundred different ways? The answer is simple: the enduring manhood/humanity of Blacks, burning bright despite all efforts to extinguish it, is the nemesis of Western civilization. Nowhere do we find this point more beautifully made than in Ron Milner's brilliant play *Who's Got His Own*. The memorable character of Shithouse Tim embodies the compelling thesis that no matter to what level of degradation a black man might be reduced, within the solitary confinement of his soul his manhood crackles white-hot, so potent that even from its grotesque cocoon it sends out vibrations to the next generation. From whence comes the militant fury of Tim Jr., which explodes in a near-fatal assault on his white "buddy," if not from the heart and mind of that tomming, wife-beating, evil-tongued, indomitable Shithouse Tim?

Moynihan and his gang postulate that Black society is matriarchal, and that Black women have been the primary castrating force in the demise of Black manhood. The casting of this image of the Black female in sociological bold relief is both consistent and logical in racist terms, for the so-called Black matriarch is a kind of folk character largely fashioned by whites out of half-truths and lies about the involuntary condition of Black women. The matriarchal fairy tale is part of a perennial tendency among whites to employ every available device in *their* ongoing effort to demasculinize the Black male. Movies and radio shows of the 1930's and 1940's invariably peddled the Sapphire image of the Black woman: she is depicted as iron-willed, effectual, treacherous toward and contemptuous of Black men, the latter being portrayed as simpering, ineffectual whipping boys. Certainly, most of us have encountered domineering Black females (and white ones too). Many of them have been unlucky in life and love and seek a bitter haven from their disappointments in fanatical self-sufficiency. Others, out of a tragic fear, brutalize their sons in the child-rearing process, hoping to destroy in them aggressive tendencies which might eventually erupt in assaults against white men and the white system. But it must be emphasized that the white man's Sapphire caricature does not closely resemble the real domineering Black female, much less the majority of her sisters who do not share that classification.

We submit that in reality Black women, domineering or not, have not had the power in this male-dominated culture to effect a coup against anyone's manhood—in spite of their oft-cited economic "advantage" over the Black man. A matriarchal system is one in which power rests firmly in the hands of women. We suggest that whatever economic power may accrue to Black women by way of the few employment escape valves permitted them by the oppressing group for their own insidious reasons, this power is really illusory and should not be taken at face value. American society is patriarchal—white women suffer the slings and arrows of that system, in the first instance. Black women are victimized on two counts: they are women and they are Black, a clear case of double indemnity. For the duration of their lives, many Black women must bear a heavy burden of male frustration and rage through physical abuse, desertions, rejection of their femininity and general appearance. Having a job provides relief for her stomach but not for her soul, for a Black woman's successful coping with the economic problem (and we might throw in the education problem) enhances her rejection by Black men, or else invites acceptance in the form of exploitation. Stymied in his attempt to protect and free the Black woman (and himself), the Black man further degrades her. She, doubly powerless and vengeful, insults his manhood by whatever means at her disposal. Thus are many Black men and women hateful partners in a harrowing dance.

These points have never been lost on white folks, and they continue to bend them to their design of divide and rule. Their past and current success is ensured by the persistent adherence of many Blacks—including most would-be revolutionaries—to the basic premises of the American value system, from whence all definitions of masculinity, femininity, right and wrong proceed. It is the transference of values, which work for the oppressor in the capitalist context, to the milieu of the oppressed, where they are dysfunctional, that has pitted Black man against Black woman and vice versa—a situation which, needless to say, is anathema to the pursuit of self-determination.

The salient point, though, in our effort to debunk the castration theory is that although whites falsify the image of Black women and use the distortion as one of several castrating tools, their attempt is ultimately abortive. For while Mr. Charlie does set Black manhood on the run, it always escapes the pursuer's final lurch and turns up, shaken but together, at the wheel of an Eldorado, in a smoke-filled poker den, in a Black woman's bed or on the side of her jaw. More importantly, it has turned up throughout our history in the form of resistance to oppression. Sojourner Truth and Harriet Tubman notwithstanding, Black men hold the majority among our political (and cultural) heroes: Frederick Douglas, W. E. B. DuBois, Marcus Garvey, Malcolm X, et al. Indeed, the Black man always surfaces with his manhood not only intact, but much more intact than that of his oppressor, which brings us to the question: just who is the emasculated person in this society? Surely, it is the white man, whose dazzling symbols of power—his goods, his technology—have all but consumed his human essence. Yes, he is effective because his power enables him to rule; but he is emasculated in that he has become a mere extension of the things he produces. The contrary is true of Blacks: do any of us doubt that Muhammed Ali is the heavyweight champion of the world? What does it matter that Whitey took his jewel-encrusted belt away?

If we accept the emasculation theory, we must accept a host of outrageous misrepresentations of the Black personality. We must accept the quaint Southern myth that most slaves were "good niggers" who passively accepted their lot, the companion theory being that slavery was not really so bad. We must accept most of the stereotypes that have been paraded before us down through the ages, as, for example, William Styron's Nat Turner. But we cannot accept Styron's Nat Turner, and why? Because any fool knows that eunuchs, figurative or actual, do not lead slave revolts. Eunuchs do not write plays that pulverize the very foundations of American theater. Eunuchs do not refuse to fight in unholy wars, thumbing their noses at trophies and fame, to achieve which some men sell their souls. Eunuchs only do the bidding of the king. Such acts of defiance as these are wrought by men in the name of all Black people.

The Kitchen Crisis

*Verta Mae
Smart-Grosvenor*

AUTHOR'S NOTE:
*i do not consider myself a writer, i am a rapper, therefore do not read
this piece silently . . . rap it aloud.*

there is confusion in the kitchen!
we've got to develop kitchen consciousness or we may very well see
the end of kitchens as we now know them. kitchens are getting
smaller. in some apts the closet is bigger than the kitchen. something that i saw the other day leads me to believe that there may well
be a subversive plot to take kitchens out of the home and put them
in the street. i was sitting in the park knitting my old man a pair of
socks for next winter when a tall well dressed man in his mid thirties sat next to me.
i didn't pay him no mind until he went into his act.
he pulled his irish linen hankie from his lapel, spread it on his lap,
opened his attache case, took out a box, popped a pill, drank from
his thermos jug, and turned and offered the box to me, thank you
no said i. "i never eat with strangers."
that would have been all except that i am curious black and i looked
at the label on the box, then i screamed, the box said INSTANT LUNCH

PILL: (imitation ham and cheese on rye, with diet cola, and apple pie flavor). i sat frozen while he did his next act. he folded his hankie, put it back in his lapel, packed his thermos jug away, and took out a piece of yellow plastic and blew into it, in less than 3 minutes it had turned into a yellow plastic castro convertible couch.

enough is enough i thought to myself. so i dropped the knitting and ran like hell. last i saw of that dude he was stretched out on the couch reading portnoys complaint.

the kitchens that are still left in the home are so instant they might as well be out to lunch.

instant milk, instant coffee, instant tea, instant potatoes, instant old fashioned oatmeal, everything is prepared for the unprepared woman in the kitchen. the chicken is pre cut. the flour is pre measured, the rice is minute, the salt is pre seasoned, and the peas are pre buttered. just goes to show you white folks will do anything for their women. they had to invent instant food because the servant problem got so bad that their women had to get in the kitchen herself with her own two little lily white hands. it is no accident that in the old old south where they had slaves that they was eating fried chicken, coated with batter, biscuits so light they could have flown across the mason dixon line if they had wanted to. they was eating pound cake that had to be beat 800 strokes. who do you think was doing this beating?

it sure wasn't missy. missy was beating the upstairs house nigger for not bringing her mint julep quick enough.

massa was out beating the field niggers for not hoeing the cotton fast enough. meanwhile up in the north country where they didn't have no slaves to speak of they was eating baked beans and so called new england boiled dinner.

it aint no big thing to put everything in one pot and let it cook. missy wasn't about to go through changes and whup no pound cake for 800 strokes.

black men and black women have been whipping up fine food for centuries and outside of black bottom pie and nigger toes there is no reference to our contribution and participation in and to the culinary arts.

when they do mention our food they act like it is some obscure thing that niggers down south made up and don't nobody else in the world eat it.

food aint nothing but food.

food is universal.

everybody eats.

a potato is a patata and not irish as white folks would have you believe. watermelons is prehistoric and eaten all ober de world.

the russians make a watermelon beer. in the orient they dry and roast and salt the seeds. when old chris got here the indians was eating hominy grits. and before he "discovered" this country the greeks and romans were smacking on collard greens. blackeyed peas aint nothing but dried cow peas whose name in sanskrit traces its lineage back to the days before history was recorded. uh ah excuse me boss, means befo you-all was recording history. uh ah i know this is hard for you to believe suh but i got it from one of yo history books and i know you-all wouldnt talk with no forked tongue about history.

the cooking of food is one of the highest of all the human arts. we need to develop food consciousness.

so called enlightened people will rap for hours about jean paul sartre, campus unrest, the feminine mystique, black power, and tania, but mention food and they say, rather proudly too, "i'm a bad cook." some go so far as to boast "i can't even boil water without burning it."

that is a damn shame.

bad cooks got a bad lifestyle.

food is life.

food changes up into blood, blood into cells, cells into energy, energy changes up into the forces which make up your lifestyle.

so if one takes a creative, imaginative, loving, serious attitude toward life everything one does will reflect one attitude hence when one cooks this attitude will be served at the table. and it will be good.

so bad cooks got a bad lifestyle and i don't mean bad like we (blacks) mean bad i mean bad bad.

come on give a damn. anybody can get it together for vacation. change up and daily walk through kitchen life like you was on an endless holiday. aint no use to save yourself for vacation. it's here now.

make every and each moment count, like time was running out. that will cool out that matter of guess who is coming to dinner and make it a fact that DINNER IS SERVED.

one of the best meals i was ever served was at my friend bella's. bella served an elegant meal in her two room cold water tub in kitchen six story walk up flat. she had a round oak table with carved legs, covered with a floor length off white shaker lace tablecloth. in the center was a carved african gourd filled with peanuts, persimmons, lemons and limes. to start off we had fresh squeezed tangerine juice in chilled champagne glasses. then scrambled eggs, sliced red onions marinated in lemon juice and pickapeppa sauce, fried green tomatoes, on cobalt blue china plates. hot buttermilk biscuits with homemade apple jelly on limoges saucers (bella got them from goodwill for 10 cent a piece) and fresh ground bustelo coffee served in mugs that bella made in pottery class at the neighborhood anti poverty pro community cultural workshop for people in low socio economic ethnic groups.

you are what you eat.

i was saying that a long time before the movie came out but it doesn't bother me that they stole my line. white folks are always stealing and borrowing and discovering and making myths. you take terrapins. diamondback terrapins. the so called goremays squeal with epicurean delight at the very mention of the word. there is a mystique surrounding the word. diamondback terrapins. are you ready for the demystification of diamondback terrapins???????? they aint nothing but salt water turtles.

slaves on the eastern shores used to eat them all the time. the slaves was eating so many that a law was passed to making it a crime to feed slaves terrapins more than 3 times a week.

white folks discovered terrapins, ate them all up and now they are all but extinct (terrapins).

oh there are a few left on terrapin reservations but the chances of seeing one in your neighborhood is not likely.

in my old neighborhood (fairfax s.c.) we always talk about how folks in new york will give you something to drink but nothing to eat. after having lived for several years in fun city i understand how the natives got into this.

with the cost of living as high as it is here i understand how you can become paranoid and weird about your food. i understand where they are coming from but i thank the creator that there is still a cultural gap between me and the natives. on the other hand you cant be no fool about it. it dont make sense to take food out your childrens mouths to give to the last lower east side poet who knocks on your door but you can give up a margarine sandwich and a glass of water. cant you? eating is a very personal thing.

some people will sit down and eat with anybody.

that is very uncool. you cant eat with everybody.

you got to have the right vibrations.

if you dont get good vibrations from someone, cancel them out for eating. (other things too.)

that is the only way to keep bad kitchen vibes at a minimum. tell those kind of folks that you will meet them in a luncheonette or a bar.

even at the risk of static from family and friends PROTECT YO KITCH'N. it's hard though. sometimes look like in spite of all you do and as careful as you try to be a rapscallion will slip right in your kitchen. i cant stand rapscallions. among other things they are insensitive. you ask them "may i offer you something" "some coffee tea juice water milk juice or maybe an alcoholic beverage."

they always answer "nah nutin for me" or else they say "i'll have tea if you got tea bags" or "coffee if it is instant i dont want to put you through no trouble." check that out! talking about not going to any trouble. hell they already in your house and that is trouble and personal. what the rapscallions are really saying is dont go to any trouble for me cause i wouldnt go to none for you. rapscallions dont mind taking the alcoholic drink because it is impersonal. nothing of you is in that. all you got to do is pour from a bottle. they dont feel that you have extended yourself for them so they wont have to do no trouble for you in return. in most other cultures when you enter a persons home you and the host share a moment together by partaking of something. rapscallions love to talk about culture but their actions prove they aint got none. they dont understand that it is about more than the coffee tea or drink of water.

it's about extending yourself.

so watch out for rapscallions. they'll mess up your kitchen vibes.

PROTECT YOUR KITCHEN

End Racism in Education: A Concerned Parent Speaks*

Maude White Katz

I am a concerned Black parent of two daughters attending the public schools in New York City. I am an aware parent. I am one of the thousands of parents—transformed by Sputnik, the resurging African nations, the UN, the liberation forces in the Far East, TV, automation, and technological advance and the Space Age. A revolutionary change has taken place in the minds of Black parents. There will be no more resignation and accommodation to the status quo as a way of life for them. Things must change for them and their children. They may not know all the facts about their history, but since Lumumba, Nkrumah, and others, they know they have a history. They have roots. They reject the racist philosophy of supe-

* Reprinted from *Freedomways*, Fall 1968.

rior and inferior peoples. They know that racism is used to justify the exploitation and oppression of a people and whole continents for profit, as was the situation during slavery in the South. The same racist philosophy is still prevalent throughout the nation to justify the studied retardation of Black and Puerto Rican children in the public schools of the nation. Exploitation and oppression of the Black people exist now and the school situation is a part of them.

Education serves the interests of those who own and control the economic resources of the country—the Establishment. They decide the quantity and the quality of the education, who should get it and how much. There was a time when the Establishment was ambivalent toward education. Did it serve their best interests? After all, the founders of the great fortunes of the nation were not educators nor educated. They were enterprisers. Education for the laboring classes was inimical to their interests. It was the newly franchised Black man longing for education for himself who fought for and introduced tax-free public education in the South. It was the labor unions in the North who crusaded for free public schools. The Establishment conceded reluctantly.

The Establishment saw the need for an educated elite. The elite is needed to preside over, manage, and control their vast wealth and resources. Economists, scientists, lawyers, and physicians, as well as educators, politicians, and government officials, are needed to support, promote, and defend the Establishment and the present order of things. The Establishment controls and directs the higher institutions of learning through its representatives on the boards of trustees. It controls public education through the local boards of education and educators who justify and extol the virtues of the status quo. For instance, vocational courses were introduced into the high schools in 1917 to fulfill the needs of business and financial interests.

Education is a profitable business. At this moment politicians and government officials are urging businessmen not yet in the education "industry" to make haste (*New York Times*, 8-13-68). Education is the "growth industry" (ibid.). The outlook is not "lush for quick profit" in an industry with current annual expenditures of $50 billion now—but be not dismayed because by 1975 the expenditures will reach $66 billion. A government official assured businessmen that there was ample room for profitable involvement in the service areas such as "school transportation" or in "administrative areas such as school feeding and maintenance." The Radio Corporation of America, already in the education market, is now definitely committed to the opportunities in the "potentially lucrative" education business through its newly organized RCA Institutes, Inc. (*New York Times*, 8-14-68).

Education opens the door to the job. The higher the learning, the higher the pay. Education is the key to the job. And as more people acquire higher education, the competition for the job becomes keener. Insecurity, joblessness, hunger, and fear haunt the majority of people. Even those with jobs feel insecure and apprehensive about the future where jobs fade away as automation and technology advance.

Add the element of racism to the competition for the job and the Black child is confronted with a formidable foe. Competition for the job is apparent in all professions and all branches of the economy, for that matter. He can meet all the qualifications and still not get the job. Racism is a factor because "the improvement of Negro occupational qualifications depends largely, although not completely, upon the improvement in the quantity and quality of Negro education" (*Transformation of the Negro American*, by Leonard Broom and Norval Glenn).

Since racism is the philosophy of the Establishment and is propagated in the institutions of higher learning and by the mass media which they control through ownership, it is not surprising to observe that "a vast majority of the white population south of the Mason-Dixon Line, and large numbers, probably a majority elsewhere, are firmly of the belief that Negroes are subhuman or only semi-human, despite the positive assertions of biology and anthropology to the contrary" (*The Rich and the Super-Rich,* by Ferdinand Lundberg).

The Black parent knows his child is "educable" in spite of all the funded programs and studies to the contrary. Dishonesty and distortions in intelligence tests are common. The literature on such tests shows that when "two groups of whites differ in their IQ's, the explanation of the difference is immediately sought in schooling, environment, economic position of parents. However, when Blacks and whites differ in precisely the same way the difference is said to be genetic" (*The Study of Race,* by Sherwood L. Washburn). There are other instances which show the prevalence of racism. Trade schools (located in all industrial centers) have a long history of excluding Blacks. However, a Black occasionally slips through the net, after which the net is thoroughly examined to see how it happened. The trustees of these trade schools include the conservative officials of craft unions which exclude Blacks from membership. A classic example involved the Sheet Metal Workers Union Local 28 in New York. There were 3,300 white members in the union, but no Blacks. Apprenticeship was reserved almost exclusively for relatives of members. Finally, the State Commission on Human Rights found the local union guilty, and the union agreed that "henceforth every applicant for membership would be judged solely on an aptitude test administered by the New York Testing and Advisement Center."

Dr. Kenneth Clark established a school in 1965 to tutor candidates for Local 28's test. The results were as follows: one passed in 1965, 13 passed in 1966, and 24 candidates passed in 1967. One of the candidates had a perfect score and nine of the ten highest scorers in the test were Black students from Dr. Clark's course! The tests were planned and supervised by Dr. Wallace Gobetz of New York University, who has a background of twenty years' experience in the testing field. No outsider could "rig" the test. Yet the President of Local 28 attributed the high scores to "some nefarious means." Prof. Gobetz had never witnessed such a wide range of "near perfect scores" and any tutoring school producing such results should "be reported for history in the educational journals."

Passing those tests was a confrontation. Those responsible for producing such results must be punished. In a summary procedure the Office of Economic Opportunity could no longer afford to finance the training program. The Sheet Metal Workers Union refused to accept the results of the test. Lastly, Professor Wallace Gobetz asserted the scores were so "phenomenally high" as to be unreliable. The teacher who tutored these Black candidates was a dedicated white teacher, Dennis Derryck, who had left the Gordon High School in Yonkers "because of the attitude the other teachers had toward these kids," who were Black and Puerto Rican.

Richard Joseph was a 1961 graduate of Boys High who was not considered college material according to the standard Iowa Tests. First he won a scholarship to Dartmouth. Then followed a Fulbright scholarship. He has recently been named a Rhodes Scholar (*Amsterdam News*, 1-22-66).

Black parents know their children can learn if the teacher has the right attitude and will teach them. There is enough available literature on hand to confirm this. Yet more than a decade after the historic Supreme Court decision on school desegregation in 1954, the educational situation for the Black has worsened. Black parents began to understand that their children were being rejected as human beings. A racist attitude is demonstrated in what is said to them, what is done to them, and what is said about them. They see the awful effects of trying to "break a child down, especially the Black boy." A white teacher, a mother of a teenage son in a private school, admitted to me in a private conversation that educational administrators would not tolerate the same behavior from a Black boy that is acceptable in a white boy. And Black parents know it from experience. What is normal behavior for a white boy is considered abnormal behavior in a Black boy. They want the Black boy to learn at an early age "to stay in his place."

It is not an accident that children in the highly segregated Black and Puerto Rican schools register an intelligence score of only 70–84. But all of the white segregated schools had intelligence scores of 100 or more (*Pupils and Schools in New York City*, by E. B. Sheldon and R. A. Glazier). We contend our children will learn if exposed to the same classroom material. The intelligence tests require that certain conditions be met—motivation, practice, and guidance. How can a Black or Puerto Rican child excel in a test where conditions for passing are absent? The educational hierarchy says they are not educable. Accordingly, they are not taught the subjects or acquainted with the material—if taught they have insufficient practice, and inferior guidance or none by guidance experts. They are not exposed to the same guidance in quality or quantity. As a matter of fact, many Black parents have justifiably a low opinion of all guidance personnel.

Why should Black parents be satisfied when they know one teacher can cripple the mind and crush the spirit of at least thirty children a year? From kindergarten to sixth grade that one teacher has "murdered the soul" of at least two hundred children? Why should Black parents accommodate an educational system where the quality of teaching in New York's Benjamin Franklin High School has reached the level where only 300 students achieve diplomas out of a total enrollment of 3,000 pupils? Where is the "professionalism" of a teaching staff that permits the highest-scoring basketball player in the history of the high school to spend four years at the school, give him a diploma, and he cannot read (*New York Post*)?

These are a few of the many reasons for the school boycott at Public School 125 in New York City, which began March 13, 1967, and lasted for nine days. The ethnic composition was about 83 percent Black and Puerto Rican. In all such schools in New York City the white children are given "preferential treatment" and Black parents are expected to like it.

There is another important fact that the nation should know about Public School 125. This school, Black parents learned in the spring of 1966, was a Campus School of Columbia Teachers College and had been so for ten years. Student teachers came to this school for training and experience.

What did this venerable institution do to help Black children? One needs a sense of history to understand the record of the Columbia Establishment toward the Blacks in general and the Harlem community in particular. When the Columbia Establishment asserts (as it did recently in a *New York Times* article) that it wants to help develop the Harlem community, one can only imagine the result would be the destruction of Harlem, the snatching of its social and cultural institutions, hospitals, clinics, Schomburg Collection, grabbing the land, and restricting it "for whites only."

The racist attitude of the Columbia Establishment toward Blacks began in 1870 on the eve of Reconstruction in the South. The national movement to discredit Blacks and falsify history began at Columbia University "with the advent of John W. Burgess from Tennessee and William A. Dunning of New Jersey, as professors of Political Science and History" (*Black Reconstruction,* by W. E. B. Du Bois). They were both pro-slavery and anti-Black in thought. Burgess believed in Nordic supremacy and the right of the United States to impose its rule "upon civilized, or half civilized, or not fully civilized, races anywhere and everywhere in the world."

Dunning as professor of history was no less racist in thought, but perhaps not as honest. As a matter of fact the Columbia School of Historians and Social Investigators had issued sixteen studies of Reconstruction between 1895 and 1935—all sympathetic to the South and its racism. The most recent racist professor of the Columbia Establishment is a psychologist, Henry E. Garrett, who has been designated Professor Emeritus. He reigned at Columbia for thirty-three years, from 1923 to 1956, when he retired. He has since written a book entitled *How Classroom Desegregation Will Work* in which he cites unscientific data in an attempt to prove Black children are inferior to white children in intelligence, attitude, and achievement. Just consider the thousands of students, now professors, educators, and teachers, influenced by the racist philosophy of this professor and now working for its implementation. Can anyone wonder why in the two-hundred-year history of the Columbia Establishment there was never a course in Negro history?

Black parents want community control of their public schools in order to determine the destiny of their children. Community control has always flourished in white middle-class suburbs and in the white middle-class neighborhoods. Consequently, the children in these schools show a high performance in intelligence and reading tests. For example, the reading tests in twelve schools located in Riverdale, Bronx, and Queens revealed fifth-graders reading at ninth-grade level. In addition, at Public School 6, at Madison Avenue and 81st Street, the "silk stocking" school, one-half of the fifth graders were "two years or more ahead of the grade level in reading" (*New York Times*, 12-23-66). These schools are in neighborhoods where the parents would not tolerate a teaching staff who could not show results at the end of the school term.

Black parents will not support a union whose hierarchy presents demands inimical to the interests of their children. The union's position on suspension, disruptive children, and preparation periods is meant to intimidate Black parents. Teachers intend to perpetuate their jobs by not educating Black and Puerto Rican children. The union is at the service of the Establishment, which does not want educated Black masses. They are closer to the police than they are to the Black community and their children.

Furthermore, Black parents observe the contempt reserved for Black personnel-teachers and supervisors—by their white colleagues and subordinates. They sense the insecurity felt by Black personnel in the educational system, although some will deny it. And Black children know it, too. A teaching staff that does not relate to Black children is not likely to relate to a Black colleague.

Besides, it is not a wholesome situation to contemplate when over half of more than a million school enrollment is non-white, and of a teaching staff of 60,000 there are a mere token 6,000–6,500 Black teachers, only 200 Black supervisors, and one (just appointed) Black high school principal. Black parents are not going to resign themselves to or accommodate such conditions—neither will their children.

Black parents see now what the Establishment and the educational hierarchy have done to their children. It is unimportant to recognize that at the moment all do not see it clearly. The Establishment has its informers—the "Negroes" who are willing to barter their heritage for a fee. Black teachers had better remember their insecurity and begin to relate to that Black parent who has nothing to lose but her poverty. The Black professionals are accepted reluctantly as a concession to the dissatisfied Black masses. But once the dissatisfaction is suppressed, the token jobs will vanish—whether they be judges, political appointees, even elected officials, Powell and others, will disappear. It did happen during Reconstruction. It can happen again.

You better believe that the Black child who finishes the elementary school today unable to read will remember the struggle for community control of the public schools as the struggle for his survival. He can and does read Fanon, Malcolm X, and knows a lot about the Nazi concentration camps. He sees the Establishment in his community pushing dope to enslave him as the English and French pushed opium to enslave the Chinese people for money. The Black youth will survive; without him no one will survive.

As a fitting close to the celebration of the centenary of the birth of Dr. W. E. B. Du Bois, what greater tribute can we give him than to inspire and motivate the Black child (and white) with the contribution of the freed Black slaves to free public education by the publication of "Founding the Public School, and The Propaganda of History," from his book *Black Reconstruction.* Let the Black child know that in Arkansas, where he was mobbed seeking an education, his Black ancestors "established the first free schools."

They did this in Little Rock, where after paying tuition for a short time, they formed themselves into an educational association, paid by subscription the salaries of teachers, and made the schools free.

In the words of W. E. B. Du Bois in *Black Reconstruction:*

"How the facts of American history have in the last half century been falsified because the nation was ashamed. The South was ashamed because it fought to perpetuate human slavery. The North was ashamed because it had to call in the Black men to save the Union, abolish slavery and establish democracy."

I Fell Off the
Roof One Day
(A View of the
Black University)*

Nikki Giovanni

Up in baby land playing house one day I fell off the roof and into my earth mother's lap. I didn't have anything else to do nor any other place to go so I decided to stay here and see what the game was. As I think about it, I would have liked to go back to baby land where my friends and true family lived, but I didn't know how. So we both began to try to make the best of it. Not that my earth mother was all that cruel; sometimes I even heard her say it hurt her more than it hurt me when she had to discipline me; but we both know, or at least I learned to accept her version of it, that I needed discipline—for my own good. I think a lot of people all over the world are being disciplined "for their own good." Many

* Copyright © 1969 by Nikki Giovanni

many people have fallen from baby land into new families. I guess that's the hard part of being an adult—you not only have to discipline yourself but other people. I would imagine "responsibility" would be the best word.

I've often wondered who should be responsible. In the big white book there is a question: "Am I my brother's keeper?" I think if Black people had written it it would have said, "Am I not my brother's keeper?" I think we understand brotherhood better than the average responsible adult. Responsibility is one of those ten-dollar words tossed around as lightly as love and free sex. Think about that—free sex! Nothing is free these days and certainly not sex. Funny how white folks use words. I have always liked words—they seem like a good way to tell people what you want and what you don't want. There are other ways, but I just have this weakness for words. I never understood why a soldier was not called a murderer, though; or why science is not considered antisocial; or why bail isn't called ransom; or why Clairol doesn't ask, "Is she or isn't she"? I never understood why. I think school is important.

My grandmother lived in the South. They never spoke of neighborhood schools in the South 'cause all kinds of people could live in one neighborhood. In the North they did, however. The whole concept makes a lot of sense to me 'cause you just wouldn't want your little five-year-old running all across town to a school. In the South they just said plainly, "We don't want no niggers in these schools." And all you could really say was "*Any* niggers . . . it's *any* niggers . . . a double negative makes a positive." That's all you could really say, logically speaking. But in the North they said, "We want all people to attend schools in their neighborhoods." Which meant they didn't want no niggers in their schools. That's called de facto segregation. What the trick is, we are finding out twelve years too late, is not who you attend school with but who controls the school you attend. The Black CCNY students believe in neighborhood schools and they want their neighbors to attend it. That's called racism in reverse. When the honkies tell you something and you say all right I'll do it your way, they call it racism in reverse. White people are certainly strange.

Like, almost all the schools across the United States are white-run and most have an overwhelmingly white student body and faculty make-up. Yet when we say a simple little thing like "Mr. White Folks we do not wish to trouble you with our presence and we will therefore start a Black University," white folks call that racism in reverse. Which is like saying they have racism in forward. And Roy Wilkins will call us dangerous and Bayard Rustin will say something, though he's hard to understand because of his lisp (wonder how he got it?), and Whitney Young will just go back to acting out his part as he understood it from "Pinktoes." That's the value of tradition. Once you know who you are, you don't have to worry anymore. Not to digress, but we do recommend "Pinktoes" as the best history yet written of the Urban League—NAACP movement. Histories are important 'cause they point the direction of traditions.

White people would like to think the only history Black people have is of being colonized by them or enslaved by them but most definitely, in whatever language, being controlled by them. There really have been long periods of time when Black people didn't even know that white people existed. And I really think it's such a shame, that the minute we could conceptualize a thing as a white person, ancestorally speaking, honkies showed themselves to be such beasts. That's like inviting a Muslim to dinner a whole month in advance—he pictures lamb and you serve center-cut pork chops. Can you imagine the disappointment? But that's something we must adjust to. They are and we aren't. So there? Elijah has defined heaven and hell; God and the devil. We must move on our realities. He has warned us against pigs. We must recognize that all pig isn't greasy. Nor is it taken internally. Lots of ways pig can man-

ifest itself. Circumcise a pig and he's just a pig circumcised. Kosher
pork is running Israel and quite a few of our newer institutions
here in the United States. You got to have an eye, ear, and nose for
pork if you gonna stay clean.

It's obvious that we need a Black university. Someone asked a
Cornell student why the Black women wanted to live apart from
the white girls. She answered that one night a sister was straightening her hair and a white girl reported the sister for smoking pot.
The straightening comb is a drug but not marijuana. We need to
get away from them. It would appear to some that a Black university is already in existence. Wherever Black people gather, feeling
and information are being transmitted. That's all a school does.
What some are asking for is a way to certify that feeling and knowledge. It's for us to follow our traditions. Ever try to organize in a
Black neighborhood? The first thing that must be done is that you
must live there, as the residents live there. You must know the language and lifestyle of the people. You must, if you are to be successful, be the people. Walking into a strange neighborhood is like
applying for a job. The first thing the residents want to know is how
long you been here; how long you gonna stay? That's asking you for
certification. When you want to join church they ask, when did you
find Jesus? They ask you to certify yourself. When you join the Nation you must learn lessons which if successfully completed will
certify you to become a member. No one asks the mayor, the gover-
nor, or the local presiding Mafia official for permission to take care
of this level of business. Yet we somehow assume that we aren't
qualified to run our schools, own and operate our own apartment
buildings, run our health and educational programs. It is for us to
certify ourselves. 'Course it's no big thing. Logically speaking we
are the only people who want it done correctly for us anyway. It's
bound to be better if it's Black. Maybe we'll put a big poster up in
Harlem and train lights on it a thousand times brighter than those

advertising *Hair* saying IT'S BOUND TO BE BETTER—IF IT'S BLACK. That should be the first lesson taught at any Black institute.

The questions raised about the Black university center around things like should we try to build buildings or should we function in any way we can. In Harlem, I'm told there are five hundred churches and three hundred bars. To me that makes eight hundred school buildings—to be used as we see fit. It would be a beautiful sight to see a sign hanging from Small's Paradise Lounge, AFRO-AMERICAN HISTORY FROM 1664 TO 1886. 8 A.M. TO 4 P.M. DAILY. PROFESSOR LERONE BENNET GUEST LECTURER THIS WEEK. Or to pass Abbyssinia Baptist Church's sign: 11:50-3:35 DR. MATTHEW WALKER LECTURING ON THE ALIMENTARY CANAL AS IT RESPONDS TO THE LIVER DURING EMOTIONAL CRISIS. Or Andre's, where we learn that FRIDAY AND SATURDAY ONLY LEWIS ALCINDOR WILL GIVE DEMONSTRATIONS OF DEFENSIVE PLAYING DURING THE LAST THREE MINUTES OF A TIGHT GAME. Or at the Apollo, REVEREND JAMES CLEVELAND IN DEMONSTRATION LECTURE OF WHAT MUSIC HAS MEANT TO HIM. There will be three classes daily. Register now. Yeah, that's the Black University, and we ought to be putting it in motion. We can do it all over the nation; we can move people around that need to be moved around and have the people in local positions who can function. We can set our standards and give our own degrees—if we want to deal with that kind of thing. A piece of sheepskin is no more and quite a lot less than lambswool. A few words written in a dead language, either English or Latin, never said that you know only what someone tried to teach you. Qualification is based on action and functioning—nothing else. We need and will continue to need a strong apprentice program. We will have to take our pupils with us teaching as well as learning. The people will always decide the relevancy of what we're doing. When we hear complaints we will listen and update. Where there is no response we will replace. And we will have our university. Which will be a total involvement with a total community—wherever these communities are found. There's no need to worry that we haven't invented a bomb; we will learn that we must control the mentalities that do. It doesn't matter that we aren't transplating hearts; our medicine will bring babies into the world, keep them well, and let the sick and dying die in dignity. It certainly doesn't matter that we don't own IBM or something that inane; our computations will come back to earth for earth people and earth people will be able to compute. The Black University already exists; it's for us to recognize it, not create it. And this is good. Our work is crystal-clear. The question is, are we teachers ready to learn—are we leaders ready to follow?

Black Romanticism

Joyce Green

The identities of Blacks in America have been created and perpetu-
ated in a mythology which expounds "White superiority" and
"Black exotic subservience" to such an extent that it is difficult to
determine the degree to which the myth has been internalized. Are
the super-liberals and the ultra-militants Siamese twins, fused together by the fibers of this Black/White myth, declaring independence while owing their existence to this very linkage? Are not these
two personalities, by dealing in the realms of grandness, heighten-
ing and creating merely a more sophisticated mythology?

When one confronts a super-sharp, ultra-hip, Black more-
militant-than-thou militant one wonders just whom he is trying to
convince. For if he has succeeded in destroying the Negro stereo-
type, why must he mourn its death twenty-four hours a day? Why
must he be so occupied with sloganeering and Negro baiting? The
answer might be that his new role is so shaky that it can only be
maintained by constantly attacking the old; however, in doing so,
he is keeping the old alive. If one believes that Black is beautiful,
then it is not necessary to verbally articulate it to every passerby.
Too much energy is expended in this flexing of egotism, for there is

a point at which exhibitionism stops and education begins. But it is difficult to find that divisive line because one problem of the Black liberation movement has been romanticism.

A large part of the movement has been laboring under the guise of revolution personified, while the white power elite continues to parcel out land in Africa, build nuclear weapons in America, and increase tactical police forces in the ghettoes. The reality is that the "man, the honkie, the pig" cannot be destroyed by quoting Mao or by a Harlem riot. In fact, these steps are insurance policies for the maintenance of the status quo. The American society has absorbed these threats. Movies on the riots and on Che are being made to wind up on middle-class America's TV screen, to lull them to sleep on Saturday night. Whites who politically and economically control America are not annihilated by a riot that burns down three Black homes for every one white store.

Romantic stances, postures, ideologies stabilize this society; they exalt masochism and self-inflicted genocide, calling it salvation. It tries to silence the realist by labeling him noncommitted or negative. It thereby becomes a Black handmaiden madam to white oppressiveness. It keeps the various factions of Blacks in conflict; however, most important, it aggravates the friction between the Black man and the Black woman.

The Black woman is being forced into a position of not daring to voice her criticism in the struggle when she sees certain discrepancies, for she wants so not to emasculate the Black man. She wants not to further the Black/White myth of her as the overpowerful partner. But what is she to do when she sees her lover, her husband, and her children slaughtered in actions which are futile, poorly planned, romantic? Many sisters are hard on digging brothers who in a year will be blown away on some dubious conspiracy to conspire, based on the distant tactics of the Cuban revolution. Can the Black woman afford to be silent at the price of being left husbandless and childless? Brothers will argue that her hesitations, criticisms, overconcern for his safety make her an active accomplice of the white man, for it holds the brother back, castrates him.

The problem seems to be that the Black woman's strength has been blown out of proportion, so that now even the slightest degree of aggressiveness or non-dependency is regarded as threatening. Brothers might argue that it was this "over-bearing strength" which turned them toward white women, which forced them into the arms of the peroxide plantation blondes. I suggest that the real problem seems to be that the Black super-militant has not really accepted the Black women because he has not yet accepted himself.

Within the Black women's criticism of his method of being a "man" there is truth and love, for it arises out of a desire to help, not hinder. However, some brothers are so busy being masterful that they have no time for a tender concept like love. They say that what they need is a helpmate in the revolution. They say, look at how the white woman helps her man. Again, the white woman model is held up. But sisters don't have no time to be dumb afros as opposed to dumb blondes.

The allure of the white women was propagated, with the help of the southern "Lady," as being the epitome of freedom for the Black man. The white man devising this scheme proved that he was inhuman, that he would use even his own women as bait, as a diversion from Black liberation.

Eldridge Cleaver in *Soul on Ice* deals with the symbolism of white womanhood. His protagonist in "The Allegory of the Black Eunuchs" states, "I know that the white man made the black woman the symbol of slavery and the white woman the symbol of freedom." However, even though he is conscious of the White man's manipulation of his psyche, he finds it difficult to transcend the conditioning. He later states that if a Negro leader wanted to unite Blacks he had only to offer every Black man a white woman.

Therefore, the white woman becomes the unifying bond, the way out of oppression; she becomes the reincarnation of the Virgin Mary, and the Black man becomes the sacrificial lamb.

Cleaver points up this analogy when his protagonist states, "He who worships the Virgin Mary will lust for the beautiful dumb blonde. And she who yearns to be rocked in the arms of Jesus will burn for the blue eyes of and white arms of the all American boy." What better way to brainwash the Blacks than through religion. It is clear that through religion, the white man hit at the very vitals of the Black man.

However, the white manipulator is not as infallible as he might think. Because while he endeavors to keep the Black man chained to a religion which exalts whiteness, he continues to secularize his society. He creates the contradictions to his own theology, and thereby implants the seeds of his own destruction. American society has created a technology which by its very existence denounces any divine being, and the Black man has come to realize that He Who Never Prays Has the Power. Therefore, increasingly, with each generation of Blacks, atheism is becoming the creed. However, because the Black man is innately spiritual, with religion rooted in his lifestyle, it becomes a constant task to renounce it.

Richard Wright, in *Native Son*, exposes Bigger Thomas, the prototype of the Black man in conflict with himself. He refuses to embrace the Black traditions of family ties and faith in God on one hand, while on the other hand, he employs the old Tomming mask when around whites. Bigger endeavors to be his own man, to stand independently, giving allegiance only to himself. But he is a man in transition, and at this point he is as vulnerable as his old self. His movements are still controlled externally; he worries about reacting to the white world, so he is still caught in a trick.

Bigger is the transformation of Cleaver's worshipper of the Virgin Mary turned into her crucifier. Both characters still want white female flesh, differing in what they want to make of it. Bigger Thomas is placed in a situation in which he accidentally kills a white girl to keep silent the fact that he was in her room. However, what he really wants to silence is his growing awareness of the desire that he feels for her. Therefore, in killing her he is also trying to murder himself—a negative move, because such a dual murder only immortalizes the white women/Black man mythology. After the killing, Bigger finds that his victim is constantly on his mind. She has metamorphosed into his mind.

The problem is that Bigger's passion to be independent is blind, without direction. He never reached the point of asking himself: independent of what and dependent on whom? Bigger is in the embryonic stage of Black awareness. He has not looked within himself for the stable things which will help him to struggle; he was so caught up in the negativism of Blacks that he was unable to extract and use positive aspects of Black life.

Nevertheless, Bigger is a hero, not because he murdered or because we allow ourselves to be anesthetized in sentimentality, but because his errors are a lesson to Black men which may allow them to avoid the same fall. Black men must learn that they don't have to commit dual murders in order to be free.

Clay, in LeRoi Jones's *Dutchman,* is an example of a Black man who succeeded in destroying his attraction for a white woman without taking off himself. He is the third stage in the evolution from Cleaver's and Wright's protagonist; unlike them, he forges his attack on white society by using his intellect, in fact, Western logic. He cannot be dismissed by the argument of emotionalism. He has analyzed the culture of white men and discovered that they are doomed. He takes into account their inhuman acts and concludes that they are the damned. More importantly, however, he looks upon Blacks as the noncontaminated, who if forced to assimilate into Anglo-Saxonism will assimilate to the point of eradicating their models. He states, "With no more blues, except the very old ones, and not a watermelon in sight, the great missionary hearts will have triumphed and all the ex-coons will be stand-up Western men, with eyes for clear hard useful lives, sober, pious and sane, and they'll murder you." By his ability to see into the souls of whites, he has become aware that they are not desirable at all, that they are carnivores who live off each other and off the Black man. Clay's statements have another connotation for Blacks; besides telling them that the time is coming, it delves into the Black life, searching at the roots for a new system of values. Clay is telling Blacks that they must create a new aesthetic, based on their Blackness. For if they have a body of values which arise out of Black experiences, then they can no longer be intimidated by the white man or lured by the white women. Black men will be able to expose white women that try to seduce them, as Clay did, as being magnolia and mint julip ladies of the old South stripped of their gentility, standing in their whorishness. Clay turns himself into a mirror into which she can see herself decay.

Jones's character is very canny about American culture, making him an excellent critic, making him a force that whites cannot deal with, if he will continue to make use of his own aesthetic. He must continue to judge things based not on their form, but on their content. He must not turn into a weakly trimmed afro, who gesticulates at Black political meetings, calling all opposition to his statements "intellectual diarrhea." Although these types of "leaders" cannot be entirely blamed, because they give the self-appointed revolutionary vanguard what they clamor for: a show, a performance. One can see it happen over and over again at meetings; a non-flamboyant brother, even meek, which is a virtue today, will make a statement and his "loving" brothers and sisters will put him down. The next second a "revolutionary" brother will stand up, say a simple sentence filled with verbs, shoot, burn, boom—

and the puppets will yell "Right on," never bothering to *think* about what he is saying.

Blacks have more potential now than ever before, if we don't allow ourselves to be snowed, wasting our energy in facades, games, masquerades. Black men don't have to be the baddest nigger alive in order to be important. There are many levels of the struggle for Black liberation on which he can fight. A thousand demolitionists are not needed now. Black men must do some soul-searching, must be honest with themselves, must expose their shortcomings even when it hurts; they must internally, first, define their identities. And if Black men do this they will be free of the Black/White myth. Sisters will not be confined to playing a role based on some abstract concept of femininity. Brothers will look upon her first as a person, secondly as a Black woman. And, hopefully, once the gaming is seen as a gaming, brothers will say: Why should we want a Nordic snow queen when we can have mango-colored sun goddesses who reflect our rays when allowed to blossom in our presence, freely as they will.

Black People and the Victorian Ethos

Gwen Patton

For the past two years women who are involved in the human rights and/or the anti-war movement have been trying to define their role, their function, and their contribution for the making of the Revolution. At most left conferences women would plan or after repeated failures in communicating with the men would have separate workshops to discuss programs around first aid, education, children, sewing and other activities that are associated with the Victorian Philosophy of womanhood. But there were always those women who questioned the relationship among sister women and among brother men. The results would be a shambles of "why are we shunted into this workshop?" And no easy answer is forthcoming.

This phenomenon was not limited to Black women, because white women were raising the same question, perhaps on a different plane, which caused confusion, but nevertheless, the problem was the hypocrisy of the Victorian Philosophy that made communications between man and women impossible and undesirable.

Then the politics of Black Power further complicated communications between the exploited (white people) and the colonized (Black people).

Black Power forced us to deal with ourselves, but because no one analyzed the Victorian Philosophy that is imposed on white and Black people alike everything was obscured and some of us were in a confused and chaotic state fighting something we knew was hampering communications, but we did not know the name of the unknown nor its manner of action and reaction.

It seems that Black women were fighting against the concept of "castration" and wanted to be more subjugated to their men to create harmony between the Black sexes. In so doing this communication was not only hampered, but was actually forfeited, and it was assumed that everyone was at a psychological peace until the women met in their own workshops. White women were fighting against "male chauvinism" and the psychological peace was turbulently broken, especially when the white women would not allow men in their workshops. On the surface it appeared that Black women and white women were at odds with one another, operating from extreme ends of the pole, and no happy medium would ever be found. No one could see that the women were fighting against the Victorian Philosophy using different means to open the road of communications with their partners.

Young white women began to vigorously attack the concept of "ladyhood" because they knew ladyhood meant bondage and oppression. Living in a society which envelops sex and capitalism as the two most important tenets in American democracy, they used "the pill" and "abortion" as weapons.

These young white women presented an assault to the Victorian Philosophy, but they only received a deaf-ear retort of "pussy power" by their counterparts, which is a systematic, correct reaction by any advocate of the virginal, lily-white, Anglo-Saxon way of life whose women have gotten out of line or had a little too much freedom for their own good. What the young white males forgot was that the Victorian Philosophy is part, if not all (i.e., if you wish to view oppression as the white man's penis hang-up), of the reason for capitalism, Christianity, and the supremacy of the caucasoids wherever they exist. The raping, pillaging, and exploiting of other peoples and lands have always been done in the name of white "ladyhood": to please them more with jewels, money, etc. This same raping and pillaging has been done in the name of preserving white "ladyhood" and protecting her from the savage beasts who were all born with the desire to sexually rape any and all white women they see.

So indeed, for white women to rise up against the sacred Victorian Philosophy is revolutionary and should be embraced by white men. White men should encourage discussions in this direction and open the way for communications which is the very human thing needed for any revolution.

On the other hand, young white women failed to realize that their counterparts are oppressed and exploited and like a Pavlovian condition they automatically oppress the women in order to forget their own oppression. To take away the illusion of "male chauvinism" is synonymous to taking away manhood. The only rationale the system gives people is that the man carries the "big stick" and this is the way it should be.

The young white women are asking, demanding that the white men will destroy the pedestal ideology of "ladyhood" and all of the myths of protecting women by isolating them:

> Peter, Peter, pumpkin eater
> Had a wife and couldn't keep her.
> Then he put her in a pumpkin shell
> And there he kept her very well.

The white women are saying that the belief in the Victorian Philosophy makes you a faggot and that the men should begin to protect themselves by ridding themselves of the Victorian Philosophy, which will open the way to communications between sexes which will destroy one facet of this barbaric society.

Unfortunately, we have some Black men who have a stake in the Victorian Philosophy. Black women, according to the Victorian Philosophy, have de-balled and "castrated" their men. Previously, Black women were a necessary and functional part of the struggle and according to skills were given various tasks to perform. It is true that black people were incorrectly engaged with the illusion of getting freedom through a civil rights program, but it was necessary for the transition to the human rights struggle which will inevitably lead us to the Revolution. The mistakes would have been made whether women were in the leadership or not.

Daniel Moynihan (*The Negro Family: The Case for National Action*) was partly responsible for dividing black men and women. (And the correct thing for the oppressor to do was to create havoc and discord among the colonized, particularly in internal and family relationships because of the sensitivity.) Black men and women were a unifying force that would march side by side, drawing strength from each other, in order to combat racism. Black men moved to protect their women when the brutal cops began to swing their "superficial sticks." Moynihan stopped that force and Black men began to look upon their women as a strange breed who were against them and trying to make them weak.

Black men failed to realize that it is the belief in the Victorian Philosophy that makes you faggots. They failed to realize that a capitalist system will resort to this technique time and time again. The system will not only employ the technique for the colonized, but will also manipulate the technique to apply to the exploited in order to maintain the capitalist system. By keeping communications to a nil or causing turmoil if communications are sought, the colonized and the exploited will have less time to deal with their own oppression, exploit profits, and wars.

Contrary to Moynihan's report, the Victorian Philosophy has always existed in the Black family, and because the Philosophy prevails it has caused many problems and contradictions. The women can work as nannies, cooks, or maids and their pride and/or femininity will not be in jeopardy. However, Black men cannot be janitors or porters for fear of losing pride and a large dose of masculinity. Consequently, the women economically controlled the family and inadvertently according to the Victorian Philosophy Black males were not men because they were not breadwinners. Some men ran to the church to be deacons and preachers to "regain" masculinity. Others ran to the streets to be con men, dope pushers, or pimps to gain pride and prestige with the almighty dollar, which is the strictest equalizer of the capitalist system. But the masses of Black men became the lumpenproletariat who were candidates for dope or alcohol.

Meanwhile, Black women became cold, dull, ugly Amazons who were desired in an animalistic way because of their firm voluptuousness and not because of their femininity because they indeed lack fragility and helplessness in a cold world as breadwinners. According to the Victorian Philosophy Black women became the rapers of Black manhood.

Black men on the other hand were "boys" who did not know what to do with their penises, but only to use them to keep their women in line. Again, the Victorian Philosophy of the "big stick."

BLACK POWER!!! If Moynihan introduced and made people aware of the "castration," then BLACK POWER with its so-called African manifestations will move to correct the situation. Moynihan's report was very successful because it invisibly became the guideline under the guise of Black Power for the Black family.

It is true that Black Power shook many Black men and for the Movement this was a necessary and vitalizing force. Black men could respond positively toward Black Power and could assert their leadership, which included a strengthening of their masculinity and, unfortunately, an airing of their egos. Black women will now take the back position, and in so doing, Moynihan was justified in his observations. Women do have definite, subordinate roles and to deviate is an infamous assault on manhood.

Poppycock. And a contradiction for the making of the Revolution and a victory for the capitalistic system! Black men are now involved with keeping their women in line by oppressing them more, which means that Black men do not have much time to think about their own oppression. The camp of potential revolutionaries has been divided.

For almost two years Black women have been cagey about their comments and their contributions to the Movement for fear of de-balling the needed and well-loved new leaders. Black women have crouched in fear trying to do their thing in a passive form, which needs overt action. Meanwhile, white women have resorted to overt actions like guerrilla theater for massive measures like trying to open the road to more communications with their mates. Women, Black and white, have monopolies on typewriters and children while men have monopolies on revolutionary planning, decision-making, and guns. And this too is within the framework of the Victorian-capitalist Philosophy. Monopolies control certain enterprises. More contradictions for the making of the Revolution.

True, Black people must go back to the roots of African culture, and they will find that the African family acted as a unit with each member contributing productively: while the warrior went hunting for food, the mother and the children would fight off invaders and enemies; and, while the mother tilled the earth, the father would tend the children.

The only way to regain happiness is to make preparations for the Revolution. To do this we must destroy the Victorian Philosophy that plagues our sexual and social life and makes impossible any meaningful togetherness. We must try to realize that we are building a whole and complete army. We have yet to know about a Revolution that was waged by men only. In fact, we have yet to know about rebellions when only the men threw bricks at the cops. We are talking about a People's Army which includes men, women, and children who are fanatics about their freedom.

It is time to give up the Victorian Philosophy of men on top, women on bottom. With the hypocrisy out of the way, we can begin to communicate with each other. And this will lead to the love of humanity which is the main ingredient for the making of the Revolution.

Black Pride? Some Contradictions*

Ann Cook

I have listened with excitement to plans that have been sketched by some very bright and dedicated Black minds for an all-encompassing Black (not Black-front) communications network. The prospects of having a powerful Black multi-media that transmits another set of values and the *TRUTH* of what is happening and what must happen is encouraging. After all, we cannot really expect the man who is the enemy to provide us with the tools that will spell his doom. Yet, to get such a vast project into full operation will take many years. In the meantime, we need to take stock of our present predicament. How far, if at all, have we moved psychologically and intellectually since the new "Black awareness" began? What values do we hold? What values should we begin to embrace?

Many experts, Black and white, are using newspapers and the airwaves to assess the plight of Africans† in this country and to di-

* Copyright © 1969 by Ann Cook.

† "Africans" will refer, in this essay, to all people of Africa whether in Africa or the Western Hemisphere. For clarity, the geographical location of the particular African will be given.

rect us down the proper path to liberation. I do not claim to be an expert. Mine will be a layman's opinion. But then, I do believe that it is the layman African's opinion that must be listened to more often by those who would liberate us.

For this evaluation, two areas need comment. The first area might be called "White Values in Black Face." A most blatant and vulgar example of this was beamed to television viewers on *Like It Is* on Sunday, August 31, 1969, on a show featuring Black models and Black fashions. I shall ignore the fact that most of the Black models preferred to sell their Blackness to white agencies. That is another essay. What really pained me was the elaborate fashion show of clothing in African prints and styles. Now, I would be the first to admit that there is nothing sacred about most African cloth itself. Indeed, much of what is pawned off to us as African prints has never seen Africa. But our turn to Africa should, hopefully, be for the richness of its culture, an awareness of which can enable us to smooth out the rough spots of what we have stubbornly held on to. We would look to the heart of Africa for a purge of decadent Western values, for a new philosophical and spiritual base, in short, for regeneration.

But what did these "proud" American African designers show us? Directly inspired by Africa—there was even a West African model making it all very African—models slithered pass the cameras in African-print bikinis; they wiggled by in hip-hugging African-print bell-bottoms miraculously held up by the model's pelvic bones; and, if enough Western-style sex was not marketed with those, there were the Moslem long dresses and coats that were transparent! (Such irony! Recall the Islamic codes for women.) Caucasians, especially the United States variety, are noted for their ruthless destruction of the cultures of others—whatever parts they can reach—and their vulgarization of what remains. Are we so suicidal that we must destroy ourselves? And for what?

The other examples to be mentioned of white values in black face are not as damnable and will probably sort themselves out in time. Both have to do with the tendency now to break away from white activities and organize our own, modeling the affair after that of the whites. In other words, it is the tendency simply to counter white activities instead of creating Black ones. As a response to the winter Olympics a few years ago, for example, a group in New York organized Black Snow. We also have Black beauty contests, but the format of the competition is haunted to the bone by Atlantic City, tiered crowns, queenly robes (do African queens wear robes?) and all. There are those who would argue that an abrupt departure from the American way would cost us converts. Perhaps so. I will not argue that point here. Let us just hope that all who organize and participate in the contests, whether actively or passively, understand the carbon-copy nature of most of our Black-awareness activities. As for the "African" fashions, the first and by far the most treacherous of the white values discussed, I cannot be charitable at all. The Black designers selling "Blackness" so cheaply must be loudly and roundly condemned!

The second area that seems to need attention is one so pervasive that to attempt to localize or isolate examples leads to a certain amount of distortion. Properly, we can label the area "anti-Blackness" or "The Subtle Self-Hatred of 'Aware' Africans."

A not so subtle example of this anti-Blackness juts out at us from the words and actions of our latest crop of "vanguard" liberators. Once again, as if history has taught us nothing, we have become Black fronts taking money and orders from our great white fathers, who amply reward us by giving us all the publicity we think we need as they make us sound tough and affectionately call our/their new leader a "quintessential" American. Old Uncle Tom has come back as a city slicker.

Again, we are being duped by people who tell us that the anti-

Africanism—and I deliberately say anti-Africanism here and not anti-Blackness—that runs rampant throughout this world, its poisonous fangs pricking even the most well meaning souls, this problem of anti-Africanism, we are told must take a back seat to Karl Marx's priorities. It is far easier to deal in that nebulous world than to turn inward and unite and build ourselves. I will dare to go further. Even though I identify with the other colored peoples of this world, since we all share a common exploiter, and I know that being the majority of the world's population, we should unite to defeat this man, I still have the sneaking suspicion that much of the Third World embrace is yet another unconscious desire not to deal with Africa itself and with ourselves as we finally must. I heard a very passionate denouncement of the United States for its involvement in Latin America by an American African. When asked his feelings about U.S. involvement in Africa, his face showed bewilderment. What involvement?

The most fantastic irony that comes out of this "new" Third World thrust is that again we are seeing more and more distinctly African young people walking around wearing Indian headbands, especially in New York. Remember the pre-Black-awareness days? "Me? I'm part Indian!"

Another more subtle anti-Africanistic tendency is becoming apparent in the bush afro. We do not mind wearing an afro if we have the "kind" of hair that can make a bush or if our straightening comb can help us out. So again, it is "good hair" afros. That is really what Afro-Sheen, Raveen, and all the other complex kits of sprays are all about—getting the kinks out.

Admittedly, there is grave danger in bringing up the question of hair and skin color when we need more than anything else to become united and are finally moving in that direction. And we also, rightly, fear that emphasizing this color contradiction will lead to a rejection of all but the most jet-black and the kinkiest-headed as the beauty symbols. A reversal. There is a clear and present danger that frank discussion of this contradiction can in fact be divisive. But we cannot become truly unified until we sift out this problem. Although I do not subscribe to the belief that slavery and colonialism left us dehumanized (far from it!), I do believe, however, that in the area of color-consciousness, we have been brutally scarred.

As I traveled through Latin America during the summer of 1968, the enormity of the anti-African complex was dramatized. I saw so many parallels to the self-hatred tendencies we know so well here. Somehow, although intellectually we know better, we suppose that language will make us different. We assume that those Africans in this hemisphere who were enslaved by the French or the Dutch or the Spanish or the Portuguese would have been impressed with a different mentality from ours. At least, we feel, they would certainly not have directly translatable phrases like those that are so much a part of our culture. But no matter whether the language of the countries I visited was English, French, Spanish, Dutch, or Portuguese, there were phrases for "good hair" and for "marrying light to *improve* the race" as well as others we would immediately recognize here. I noticed the same phenomenon in the speech of educated Africans during my two years in Africa. "Your hair is your crowning glory," a dear friend always warned me. In Panama, a very prominent Black man told me of his heartbreak when the mother of the girl he wanted to marry prohibited the arrangement, chiding the girl for not having any "ambition." He was not a bum. He was too dark.

Euro-Brazilians, like many other Caucasian Latin Americans who claim to be colorblind, have intricate gauges to see just how African one's features really are. There, it is quite all right to have African blood if it does not show. The more Caucasian the person looks, the more readily he will boast to a black foreigner of his "Negro blood."

I had one of the most amusing experiences of my life when I visited a prominent Brazilian scholar and his wife in their home, along with a white American couple. In the course of that inevitable discussion about the race problem in this country, the Brazilian turned to me with his face beaming with pride. "Ann," he said. "I'm going to tell you something that will surprise you." I waited. "My grandmother was a Negro!" His face and gestures were saying to me, "Now what do you think of that!" I looked at him warmly and said, "Oh, that doesn't surprise me at all. It shows in your features." He panicked! "No, no, no!" he shouted, shaking his head furiously. "I don't have a single Negro feature." By now his entire body was in contortions. Shaking his finger in rhythm with the other movements, he assured me, "Not one!" And, of course, he had measured his skull and his nose and his lips as so many in the twilight zone do. He hurriedly began to pull up his sleeves as he said, "Of course, we Latins—the sun—you know—we get tanned." I never said a word. The house fell absolutely silent in their white embarrassment. I laughed like a son of a gun.

Because these countless categories are set to label each African, men in the twilight zone put Vaseline on their hair and brush it to make it lie down. One man in Recife whom I would have sworn was just a plain white man told me of the care he has to take with his hair, Vaselining it down. The more African the man or boy, the shorter the haircut. The desire is to try to score plus marks in some category. If the hair does not pass the test, maybe the skin will, or the nose, or the skull shape, and hopefully, always, the lips. One successful mulatto businessman from Surinam lamented, "African blood is so strong. It just seems to come through anyway. It's stronger than any other blood!" In his case, he pointed out, he was only part African. Yet look at his features, he moaned.

And in Belem, Brazil, one hears of a brilliant young female economist whose skin is very black. My informant said that the young lady was sorry her hair would not bouffant. She is, by the way, single, in that land where marrying light to improve the race is indeed a seriously practiced doctrine. This bright economist went shopping for a car and ordered one that was completely white, inside and out, including sidewalled tires. She threw a tantrum when the car arrived not conforming to her specifications. For four months, she lay in the hospital after she seriously burned her skin trying to bleach herself with a soda solution. She now walks around with white powder on her face and a blond wig on.

But many Brazilian African women would not have tried to be "beautiful," since women as obviously African as that economist would normally have known that they did not stand a chance. Most would have resigned themselves to being very bright. Brazilians readily admit that the Africans in Brazil are by far the most intelligent members of the citizenry.

But can this young woman who tortured herself so completely to become white simply be dismissed as a mental case? Is she really exceptional; or is it that her *manifestations* of her anti-Africanism are the exception? Surely we are torturing ourselves here just as hazardously. We sing, "I'm Black and I'm proud," but we are far from convincing. To be sure, the healthiest African minds I have met in this hemisphere belong to the so-called "Bush Negroes" of the interior of Surinam. Some Africans in Paramaribo, the capital city (Creoles, they are called), feel the Bush Negroes would be helped if they were referred to as the Bush "Creoles," thus making them a group mixed with that sought-after European blood. The Djukas, one of the Bush Negro tribes in the interior, would not have been flattered at all by the offer from "Bukra slaaf" (the white man's slave). When the Djukas saw me in their villages, invariably they pointed to my afro and praised it lavishly. Most of the Djukas were without Western education until recently because most villages refused to allow missionaries entry. Relatively isolated, they have kept their values pretty free of Western influences. And, unlike the Brazilian African who has also retained much of the obvious traits of African culture, the Bush Negro is very strongly attracted to Africa and Africans. I was warmly received everywhere. A Ghanian was given a thunderous reception when she visited there. Mothers tried to give her their babies to take back to Africa, a gesture not to be taken lightly, since children are adored in their society. It would have been an honor for the child. One mother at Stolemaneisland became very attracted to me, as I became to her and her child. Upon my departure, she tried to give me her son. The child was without a doubt far better off there. Besides, her symbols were a bit mixed up. America is not Africa. I was honored, as I was to be often throughout the trip, by such warmth. But I must sound an ominous note. I must report that cutouts of white models from the European and Brazilian magazines that flood Latin America can now be found on the walls of a new Djuka school.

Everywhere else except in the interior of Surinam, even in urban Africa, we are having to convince ourselves that thick lips, broad noses, and kinky hair accompanying that now acceptable black skin can be beautiful. Harry Belafonte and Lena Horne have hastily been painted black and afros have been put on their heads. The stereotypical "Aunt Jemima" still goes the way of the Brazilian economist. It is even argued, and with much validity, that African men are embracing the Third World concept not only for ideological reasons, nor to avoid the concrete task of organizing Black people; the suggestion is that Third Worldism provides a wider field for getting to a Miss Anne type without the Caucasian-worshipping African's real motive being detected.

This next and final point in the area of anti-Africanisms is, admittedly, a very ticklish one. It has to do with the practice of Islam. I speak of it very reluctantly because, first of all, some of the Africans in this country whom I admire and respect tremendously are converting to Islam. Secondly, racist historians have through the centuries tried to change the map of Africa, making North Africa an extension of Europe and therefore of the "civilized" world. That Africans south of the Sahara were instrumental in the development and perpetuation of the North African civilizations there can be no doubt. Yet, these same Africans, in their often small kingdoms south of the Sahara, when they did accept Islam and other aspects of North-African culture, syncretized it with indigenous religious beliefs, as, of course, they still do.

My question is, why really do we embrace Islam? As a reaction to Christianity? Because of the religious tenets? These things I can accept. Because it can unify Africans? I seriously question that, if we mean also to include Africans of Africa in this unity drive. I wonder if in addition to our choosing Islam as a rejection of Christianity and for its tenets, we are not also accepting it because of its legitimacy. By the same token, I wonder why we spend so much of our discourse about Africa emphasizing the great kingdoms of Songhai, Bornu, Ghana, and Mali. Could it be because these kingdoms were similar in structure and size to European ones and serve as reassurance to us that we had the same thing they had, even if, like Islam, these kingdoms were not the norm?

My point is that we still cannot deal with Black Africa, with "pagan" Africa, from where most of us came. Somehow, we suspect that what they have taught us so well about Black Africa is really sound. After all, these Africans did not have a writing system, except for the Moslems, who were not the majority; they worshipped "fetishes"; they were organized, by and large, into small societal bodies. It is easier to embrace Islam than to begin to look seriously at traditional African religions to find what those concepts are and which ones attract us and are in fact malleable for our situation here. Again, it appears, we have been reluctant to look closely at ourselves.

We are also too lazy often to take close looks. I have heard revolutionary music and read revolutionary plays with what was represented as African languages in the text; but it was simply mumbo-jumbo just like Hollywood would do it. Not even one word or phrase was authentic. Harsh echoes of Tarzan and the westerns with the injun talk are reverberating.

As I conclude by offering some suggestions, I will admit that my criticism touches various thrusts of black liberation efforts. Already, one reader of a draft of this has accused me of moving in the direction of advocating "antiquity cults." I admit that I could not deal with his comments because when I hear the words "cult" and "dialect," in the racist way they are usually employed, various kinds of bells and buzzers automatically go off in my head, effectively impairing my power of reason—"African cults," "African dialects," "Black power cults," "Negro dialect or patois" (as though the standard language form is not also a dialect). But aside from that, the question of whether or not I want Africans here to transfer from Africa, lock, stock, and barrell, all of its culture, I can clearly respond to. Black Africa has cosmological beliefs that are very similar, just as the lifestyles, the dress patterns, the languages all share a common mold. Yet, in this unity, there is diversity in terms of specific rendering of the cultural patterns. I am suggesting that we try to get to the essence of African culture. The trappings are not as important.

And I am suggesting more. There is absolutely no substitute for hard organizing. We cannot escape it. I have been convinced of that by my observations of the ASCRIA movement in Guyana and of the movement's president, Eusi Kwayana, a giant of a man. Various dramatic programs such as the black manifesto on reparations certainly educate us by exposing the contradictions we did not know were there. But whatever hard cash we need, for psychological reasons, must come from us. We must be organized to think in terms of relying on ourselves. We must think in terms of building and sustaining our own institutions—a herculean task for organizers. It requires a discipline we momentarily lack and an orientation too few of us have. Our leaders are still looking for easy ways out.

We will hardly get the orientation that is necessary unless we can take that long look at ourselves, as has been suggested over and over in this essay. In the absence of a powerful media to be our mirror, there seems little substitute for travel. To get out of this territory is to get a breath of clean air and to put everything into perspective. But more. We must see that there is a circular link of Africans. Little here gives us even an inkling of that fact. The West is aware of the vast potential we have as a people. It is for that reason that we have been kept so cleverly fragmented. The publicized enmity between American Africans and West Indian Africans and between the Western Hemisphere Africans and the Africans of our motherland has certainly been a vast and successful propaganda ploy. We have been so demoralized by this trickery that all of us move timidly with each other. The African visiting from Africa is very cautious. When we visit Africa or Latin America, we build a wall with the same caution.

From all indications, the ploy has worked more on us than on any other African. We have no real idea what affection our brothers and sisters all over feel for us here; we are not told in any of the media of the various ways they move to demonstrate their support and affection. This news is effectively blotted out to keep us feeling isolated.

Nor do we realize how much small, hardworking, well-organized groups are doing in many countries to strengthen black people and build solidarity amongst us all. Assuming that we are the "baddest," we spend little time in healthy interchange with groups that could teach us so much as we give them insights. All Africans would readily acknowledge, however, that in a real sense we here are the baddest since we are, to be sure, at the vulture's beak.

In many ways, we have fortunately protected ourselves from America's hang-ups. In one crucial way, we have not and must immediately purge ourselves: When we travel, it must be *American*-style with a maximum of material comfort. This means that we live in luxury hotels and become "tourists," since that luxury hotel environment dooms us psychologically and cuts us off, in actual fact, from all but Caucasians or their types.

But we do have problems. There is the problem of heat, insects, bad water, strange food, and language barriers. To deal with the last obstacle to our non-touristy travel first, language, is probably wise. Language is not as much a barrier as we fear if we really want to communicate. You will find nothing but goodwill on the part of our brothers who will go to all ends to try to understand us. A Djuka boy in Surinam just could not understand how both of us could look alike and not be able to understand each other. He set in to try to teach me Djuka. He would never have tried so tirelessly with a Caucasian. Even when I have insisted that I just did not understand and was ready to give up, there has always been that brave soul in every country who would not let me be so cowardly.

I am not suggesting that we should deliberately move about without knowing the languages of the countries we plan to visit. There should be some knowledge of the languages if it is possible. I have not meant to imply that everything will run as smoothly if you do not speak the language as it will if you do. In nine weeks in Latin America, I gathered far more vital information than many of the white researchers I met there who were studying us. Yet, I missed so much that I would have gained had I spoken the language of the people. As was indicated above, there are times that your nerves fail or you become so frustrated that you want to retreat. But I have learned far more on what for me have been informal trips and have met far more beautiful people than I ever would have had I lived in big hotels and not ventured out, language or no.

The other problems for the American African are far more grave than the language barrier: they center around the need for material comfort. America has made us so soft that many of us honestly cannot survive outside an American-type environment. (Notice how we always come back to this place.) We honestly do need air conditioning. We cannot survive the greedy mosquitoes and other worrisome insects. The latest trend is to move about from our air-conditioned living rooms and bedrooms to our air-conditioned cars to air-conditioned offices. The new genocide will not be a very expensive operation for the man. He will not need to fire a single bullet nor to populate a single camp. Why, he will only need to blow his hot breath on us and watch us as we, affected by the heat from his mouth, melt and die before his eyes. We need comfortable beds. We could never sleep on benches as many of the nation-builders in Guyana have accustomed themselves to doing, enabling them to sleep anywhere. (I hasten to say that I am not suggesting that we sleep on benches, before I lose all readers forthwith! But I have good reason to believe that many students are now not so frightened by the prospect.) We expect room service and are happiest with European food, especially hot dogs and hamburgers.

Therefore, perhaps some intermediate stops before leaving this territory will help toughen us for profitable travel abroad. I propose trips to the rural South first. Bypass Atlanta and that fabulous hotel. Go to "the country," to little towns like my hometown, Buena Vista, Georgia. Someone has suggested getting Northerners down to rural areas and having them pick cotton, shake peanuts, pick peaches, etc. with our brothers and sisters there. It is a good idea. It would certainly force us into another physical environment. And just as travel abroad will solidify us with our brothers, so would close communication with the rural Southerner. It would probably help some of us to begin, for the very first time in our lives, to get the sense of community so pitifully artificial, no matter the efforts, in Northern cities.

Still another obstacle keeps the American African from traveling abroad modestly and so meeting more local people. Just as the fashions we ape are those that New York, Paris, and London sell to us by way of Madison Avenue, so are the aspirations and tastes we struggle to acquire those that are made glamorous to us by the powerful multi-media. We want, when we finally are able to travel, to travel "executive" fashion. First class all the way! Because these trappings have been dangled in our faces for so long, more than anything in the world, we want to experience them.

An acquaintance recently told of his thrill at finally being able to take a taxi in from an airport. He has a list of other experiences he must have, he feels, to prepare himself for the day when he moves into the social class where these accouterments will come naturally. An earthshaking priority is to fly first-class; next to it is his desire to eat at an expensive restaurant. Surely, many of us do have to experience these "thrills" before we can reject them since we have been made for so long to drool for them. But if we must satisfy our curiosity, we should do so right here in this country where harm to ourselves will be minimal. But abroad, we must not be in that bag at all.

We should work hard on ourselves also to extricate ourselves from our feelings of superiority. We exist in a country that is highly technical but there is absolutely nothing superior about us. Nothing. It will be difficult not to feel superior at times when a certain amount of adulation and wonderment is being heaped upon you by those who see the United States as the most wonderful place in the universe, a portrayal beamed to all the world by U.S. multimedia and reinforced by those "been-to's" who have come here to visit or reside and need to enhance their prestige upon their return to their homes. This is why we must work on our ego needs as much as possible before departing. Many people will simply welcome us because we are their brothers—not cousins as Mboya suggested—and because we are involved in a liberation movement. This group will be able to detect those unwarranted superior feelings immediately and, while they may or may not react directly to them, they will nevertheless shift to a "white" relationship with us. But the same will be so when we go to the rural South. The same currents will be present. This is why the South provides such an excellent dry run for Latin America and Africa.

Until now, the word "revolution" has not been used in this essay. Do we have Black pride? Before we can begin to think that a revolution is near, that question must be answered affirmatively. The answer cannot be affirmative when we have only begun the discussion of values and have no machinery for transmitting them. It cannot be an affirmative answer when we are spending more time with theatrics than with hard unglamorous organizing. It cannot be said that we have Black pride or that a revolution is near when we are still, no matter the elaborate disguises, trying to be white. To have Black pride will mean redefining blackness. To redefine Blackness necessitates examining what we are and sorting it out, deciding what should be retained and strengthened and what should be cast aside.

Redefining Blackness necessitates removing the artificial boundaries that now exist among all Africans by thrashing out the contradictions that created them. We would, then, rip down the artificial boundaries of class, complexion, age—the latest hang-up—and territorial limits to see that we do have resources and that these resources do not in any way need to be legitimized by the non-African world. We need only one stamp—our own. With our solidarity assured, we can move as a strong force instead of our usual role of junior partner, flunky, and the other recognizable slots, joining forces with whatever people we choose.

The Pill: Genocide or Liberation?*

Toni Cade

After a while meetings tend to fade, merge, blur. But one remains distinct, at least pieces do, mainly because of the man-woman pill hassle. I don't recall who called the meeting or what organizations were present. But I do remember that one speaker, in mapping out what should be done to make the Summer of Support G.I. coffee-house venture effective—it was a mere idea then—said that we should stock the coffee shops with items guaranteed to attract our Brothers in khaki so that re-education could begin. He began the list of *things* to be sent to the off-base radical projects: "Packages containing homecooked soul food, blues and jazz records, Black journals, foxy Sisters who can rap, revolutionary pamphlets, films that . . ." My gut cramped on the "Sisters." Talk about being regarded as objects, commodities. Not one to sit on my hands, I raised a few questions about the insensitivity of that cataloguing and about the agenda in general, which nicely managed to skirt any

* Reprinted from *Onyx* magazine, August 1969.

issue of the woman's struggle or man-woman relationships. These remarks triggered off all around me very righteous remarks from equally "overly sensitive, salty bitches trying to disrupt our meeting with that feminist horseshit."

During the break before the workshops began, the chairman invited us all to the refreshment table and urged the Sisters to help out in the kitchen. This would not have been so bad except that during the formation of work committees, the Sisters were arbitrarily assigned to man the phones and the typewriters and the coffeepots. And when a few toughminded, no-messin'-around politico Sisters began pushing for the right to participate in policy-making the right to help compose position papers for the emerging organization, the group leader would drop his voice into that mellow register specially reserved for the retarded, the incontinent, the lunatic, and say something about the need to be feminine and supportive and blah, blah, blah. Unfortunately quite a few of the ladies have been so browbeaten in the past with the Black Matriarch stick that they tend to run, leap, fly to the pots and pans, the back rows, the shadows, eager to justify themselves in terms of ass, breasts, collard greens just to prove that they are not the evil, ugly, domineering monsters of tradition.

When we got back into a large group again, we were offered a medley of speakers dipping out of a variety of bags, each advocating his thing as the thing. One woman, the only female speaker out of twelve speakers, six group leaders, two chairmen, and three moderators, spoke very passionately about the education of our children. She was introduced as so-and-so's wife. Others were for blowing up the Empire State, the Statue of Liberty, the Pentagon. A few more immediate-oriented types were for blowing the locks off the schools if the strike ever came to pass. Finally, one tall, lean dude went into deep knee bends as he castigated the Sisters to throw away the pill and hop to the mattresses and breed revolutionaries and mess up the man's genocidal program. A slightly drunk and very hot lady from the back row kept interrupting with, for the most part, incoherent and undecipherable remarks. But she was encouraged finally to just step into the aisle and speak her speech, which she did, shouting the Brother down in gusts and sweeps of historical, hysterical documentation of mistrust and mess-up, waxing lyric over the hardships, the oatmeal, the food stamps, the diapers, the scuffling, the bloody abortions, the bungled births. She was mad as hell and getting more and more sober. She was righteous and beautiful and accusatory, and when she pointed a stiff finger at the Brother and shouted, "And when's the last time you fed one of them brats you been breeding all over the city, you jive-ass so-and-so?" she tore the place up.

Since then I've been made aware of the national call to the Sisters to abandon birth control, to not cooperate with an enemy all too determined to solve his problem with the bomb, the gun, the pill; to instruct the welfare mammas to resist the sterilization plan that has become ruthless policy for a great many state agencies; to picket family-planning centers and abortion-referral groups, and to raise revolutionaries. And it seems to me that once again the woman has demonstrated the utmost in patience and reasonableness when she counters, "What plans do you have for the care of me and the child? Am I to persist in the role of Amazon workhorse and house slave? How do we break the cycle of child-abandonment-ADC-child?"

It is a noble thing, the rearing of warriors for the revolution. I can find no fault with the idea. I do, however, find fault with the notion that dumping the pill is the way to do it. You don't prepare yourself for the raising of super-people by making yourself vulnerable—chance fertilization, chance support, chance tomorrow—nor by being celibate until you stumble across the right stock to breed with. You prepare yourself by being healthy and confident, by having options that give you confidence, by getting yourself together, by being together enough to attract a together cat whose notions of fatherhood rise above the Disney caliber of man-in-the-world-and-woman-in-the-home, by being committed to the new consciousness, by being intellectually and spiritually and financially self-sufficient to do the thing right. You prepare yourself by being in control of yourself. The pill gives the woman, as well as the man, some control. Simple as that.

So while I agree to the need to produce, I don't agree to the irresponsible, poorly thought-out call to young girls, on-the-margin scuffiers, every Sister at large to abandon the pill that gives her certain decision power, a power that for a great many of us is all we know, given the setup in this country and in our culture. I'm told, though, by women in the movement that movement women shouldn't use the pill because it encourages whorishness. That shocked me at first. The first group I'd thought would rally around the yes-pill position were the Sisters actively involved with revolutionary work. But given the inbred, cultlike culture that can develop in any group with messianic impulses, given the usual ratio of men to women in the organizations, given the "it's unfeminine to be ideological" undercurrent that makes the Sisters defeated and defensive, given the male-female division chumpbait we've eaten up of late via a distortion of our African heritage—given all this, perhaps these women should stop using the pill because they are, I've been told, reducing themselves to pieces of ass. Perhaps the abandonment of birth control will produce less cruising, less make-out, less mutually exploitive sexual hookups, and more warmth in the man-woman relationship. That's playing a long shot, it seems to me. But I can see the point. And after all, it's through the fashioning of new relationships that we will obliterate the corrosive system of dominance, manipulation, exploitation.

Fortunately, while we Black women have often been held in

contempt, we have never been irrelevant—as irrelevant, say, as the middle-class woman in the Latin culture. We've contributed too much to the household, to the social fabric, to the movement, been too indispensable and productive and creative to be invisible, overlooked, laid aside, laid aside as, say, the upper-caste women in feudal Asian society. We've been too mobile, too involved with the larger world outside of the immediate home, to be duped into some false romantic position of *the liberated woman,* as romanticized, say, as our Vietnamese and Guatemalan Sisters who were told to stay home and did; told to pick up the gun and did; and after the fight is over, they will be told to return to the mattress or to the factory or to wherever the Brother needs them. So while we've hassled and become divided from time to time (often with the help of the parochial social scientists who keep telling us we're in-fighting), while the Big Put-Down has had to suffice as the love link, our relationship has never been thoroughly fragmented, mutilated. Together under fire. So there's hope in dialogue. Hope in the idea of establishing a viable hookup. There's hope that we can shed yesterday's evil Black bitch and shiftless jive nigger and pursue a new vision of man and woman. She as something more than Amazon, breadwinner, domestic, mammy, as an intellectual, political vanguard being who has a voice in calling the shots about pregnancy because she's prepared. He as something more than sucker, trick, buffoon, slickster, abandoner, as an intellectual, political vanguard being who has a voice in calling the shots about pregnancy because he's there and is responsible.

It is revolutionary, radical, and righteous to want for your mate what you want for yourself. And we can't be rhapsodizing about liberation, breeding warriors, revolution unless we are willing to address ourselves to the woman's liberation. So what about the pill? Does it liberate or does it not? Will it help us forge new relationships or not? Does it make us accomplices in the genocidal plot engineered by the man or does it not? Does dumping the pill necessarily guarantee the production of warriors? Should all the Sisters dump the pill or some? What's the Brother's responsibility in all this? Who says the pill means you're never going to have children? Do we need to talk about communes, day-care centers, pregnancy stipends?

Personally, Freud's "anatomy is destiny" has always horrified me. *Kirche, Kusse, Kuche, Kinde* made me sick. Career woman vs. wife-mother has always struck me as a false dichotomy. The-pill'll-make-you-gals-run-wild a lot of male-chauvinist anxiety. Dump-the-pill a truncated statement. I think most women have pondered, those who have the heart to ponder at all, the oppressive nature of pregnancy, the tyranny of the child burden, the stupidity of male-female divisions, the obscene nature of employment discrimination. And day-care and nurseries being what they are, paid maternity leaves being rare, the whole memory of wham bam thank you ma'am and the Big Getaway a horrible nightmare, poverty so ugly, the family unit being the last word in socializing institutions to prepare us all for the ultimate rip-off and perpetuate the status quo, and abortion fatalities being what they are—of course the pill.

On the other hand, I would never agree that the pill really liberates women. It only helps. It may liberate her sexually (assuming that we don't mean mutually exploitive when we yell "sexual equality"), but what good is that if in other respects her social role remains the same? And it is especially doubtful that the pill can liberate her in these other areas—note how easily the sexual freedom has been absorbed into the commodity framework, used to push miniskirts, peekaboo blouses, and so forth so we can go on being enslaved to consumerism. But the pill gives her choice, gives her control over at least some of the major events in her life. And it gives her time to fight for liberation in those other areas. But surely there would be no need to shout into her ear about dumping the pill if the Brother was taking care of business on a personal plane and analyzing the whole issue of liberation on a political plane. Men are invariably trying to create a woman who will answer their needs, assuage their fears, boost their morale, confirm their romantic fantasies, lull them into the comforting notion that they are ten steps ahead simply because she is ten paces behind. And this invariably makes her not very true to herself. Women who've thought about this whole question have my support. The Brothers who merely rant and rave set my teeth on edge.

It's a sad thing that we haven't really looked at the education of our women. That they grow up knowing that our men were not the dragon slayers and the giant stalkers and that the only men who did do those gloriously grim storybook things are the greedy corporate kings and the bloody beef emperors and the six-gun generals and the chairmen of the boards of overkill cartels—none of whom they could ever love. And so they read instead those other story-books, those sepia-tan love confessionals of summer boat rides and blue bulbs and belly rub and big belly and cut-out and heartbreak. And shorting out on the celluloid Prince Charming and the minuet, they wallowed in those lost-my-man-loosin-my-mind and no-matter-how-you-mess-with-me-ain't-goin'-to-give-you-up-doo-ahh songs we've been hammering out for years. And they fashion a very defeated, strung-out, hung-up, lousy sense of worth/notion guaranteed to land them always on their asses, wigs askew, mind awry, clothes every which way, at the bottom of the heap, weeping about how some slick dude took them off while he in turn is crying about how the man done him in and it ain't his fault. As drama—hardly enough to keep the mind alive. As a lifestyle—not likely to produce tomorrow's super-people.

I bring it up, this grotesque training, this type of girl eager to cut a tragic figure simply because she is the only type of woman at these meetings who cheers on the Brother burning the little packet of pills, telling me in breathless ecstasy that it's very revolutionary having babies and raising warriors, conjuring up this Hollywood image of guerrilla fighter in the wilds of Bear Mountain with rifle in hand and baby strapped on back under the Pancho Villa bullet belt. And given her suicidal glamorizing, that was enough to make me: one, worry about those kids she was dreaming of having; two, think unwholesome thoughts about those Brothers standing on the stage addressing themselves to an anonymous house of Sisters; three, want to write the whole thing off as another dumb comic book.

I agree it is a sinister thing for the state to tell anyone not to have a child. And I know it's not for nothing, certainly not for love, that b.c. clinics have been mushrooming in our communities. It's very much tied up with the man's clinging to that long since refuted "10 percent" when so many census agencies agree that we more than likely comprise 30 percent of the population. But. Let's talk about murder and about these Sisters who rise to the occasion. Seems to me the Brother does us all a great disservice by telling her to fight the man with the womb. Better to fight with the gun and the mind. Better to suggest that she use all that time, energy, money for things other than wigs, nails, and clothes to ensnare the Aqua Velva Prince of her dreams who always turns out to be the ugly ogre who rips her off and rots her life anyway. That time, money, energy could be invested in taking care of her health so that the champion she plans to raise isn't faced from the jump with the possibility of brain damage because of her poor nutrition; could be invested in a safe home, so the baby isn't hazarded by lead poison in the falling plaster and by rats; in the acquiring of skills and knowledge and a groovy sense of the self so the child isn't menaced by stupidity and other child-abuse practices so common among people grown ugly and dangerous from being nobody for so long. The all too breezy no-pill/have-kids/mess-up-the-man's-plan notion these comic-book-loving Sisters find so exciting is very seductive because it's a clear-cut and easy thing for her to do for the cause since it nourishes her sense of martyrdom. If the thing is numbers merely, what the hell. But if we are talking about revolution, creating an army for today and tomorrow, I think the Brothers who've been screaming these past years had better go do their homework.

"Raise super-people" should be the message. And that takes some pulling together. The pill is a way for the woman to be in position to be pulled together. And I find it criminal of people on the podium or in print or wherever to tell young girls not to go to clinics, or advise welfare ladies to go on producing, or to suggest to women with flabby skills and uncertain options but who are trying to get up off their knees that the pill is counter-revolutionary. It would be a greater service to us all to introduce them to the pill first, to focus on preparation of the self rather than on the abandonment of controls. Nobody ever told that poor woman across the street or down the block, old and shaggy but going on longsuffering and no time off, trying to stretch that loaf of bread, her kitchen tumbled down with dirty laundry and broken toys, her pride eroded by investigators and intruders from this agency or that, smiling and trying to hold the whole circus together—nobody ever told her she didn't have to have all those kids, didn't have to scuffle all her life growing mean and stupid for being so long on the receiving end and never in position even to make decisions about her belly until finally she's been so messed with from outside and inside ambush and sabotage that all the Brothers' horses couldn't keep her from coming thoroughly undone, this very sorry Sister, this very dead Sister they drop into a hole no bigger, no deeper than would hold a dupe. And what was all that about? Tell her first than she doesn't have to. She has choices. Then, Brother, after you've been supportive and loving and selfless in the liberation of your Sisters from this particular shit—this particular death—then talk about this other kind of genocide and help her prepare herself to loosen the grip on the pill and get ahold of our tomorrow. She'll make the righteous choice.

The Black Social Workers' Dilemma

Helen Williams

Many Black social workers today, and I am one, are faced with the question of whether it is compulsory now that all Black people hate all white people. This issue generates a special kind of misery. We fear the irrationality of it all. But we seem to fear even more, rejection from a potentially evolving Black elite society, the militant separatists. We seem to fear being called white-oriented, white middle-class-educated Blacks. The ambivalence renders us sometimes mute and sometimes we begin to use the professional lingo, "acting out," which is simply an overt behavioral reaction to internal stress, in this case the stress growing out of the dilemma of Black social workers to choose an appropriate role in the militant movement. The muteness converts into immobility, inaction, and silence, while the "acting out," the vituperation of whitey, pro-Afro-Americanism and advocacy of Black extremism, could be viewed as deviant behavior, were it not for the justification in the very tenor of the times.

How to extricate oneself, how at least to be professional, so as to do the best job for which one was trained, to practice the method of social work with "all people and all communities who are in need of it" has become a problem. The problem relates to the past experiences of Black and white people, and this relationship, for the most part, has been impressionably negative. Consequently, Black social workers are torn between their loyalty to the profession which would accept people as people, regardless of color, and their own personal need to identify with the Black struggle.

Today's climate tends to add to the ambivalence. It is extremely difficult for the average Black professional to ignore social group pressures and function merely as a professional. One is no longer encouraged to accept basic premises that weaknesses, strengths, and needs are common to all people, regardless of color. One who differs at all with the Super-Black is likely to become the victim of Black isolation, chastisement, and/or reorientation to a peculiar brand of "Black thinking" that is based on the assumption that any degree of intellectual and logical thinking about human issues automatically represents "white brainwashing."

The scales of justice now beginning to shift in the direction of Black people seem to have imbued some professionals with a newfound sense of power and omnipotence. The utilization of this new power ostensibly seems to be purposeful, but its subjective, narrow, ethnic orientation renders it useless. An example of the positive use of power in relation to intergroup conflict would be to focus on developing in Black and white group members alike that kind of awareness and that degree of comfort and ease which would enable both to function cooperatively and effectively in meeting client needs. The situation now seems to be that some Black professionals are so concerned with confronting, acting hostile, and drenching themselves with the psychology that only Black people can help Black people, that primary goals of mutual growth and mutual understanding, which would move them toward the paramount goal of helping the client help himself, becomes secondary.

A case in point. The counseling staff of an outstanding university of which I am a faculty member was faced with the problem of a lack of communication between its Black and white faculty members. Since communication was vital to the smooth operation of a cooperative project involving a predominantly Black student body, it was decided by both Black and white faculty to engage the professional services of a therapist to conduct group sessions. Although the primary problem was communication, the compensatory gain would hopefully be the development of optimum relationships among staff and students. From a behavioral viewpoint, the sessions were more frustrating than therapeutic, in that they became the battleground for personal and racial vendettas; places to release years of pent-up hostility against seemingly vulnerable whites; and a means through which insecure Black male professionals sought to destroy at any price the Black matriarchal image presumably existent in any situation involving Black males and females. As a result, open season was declared on anyone fitting the aforementioned categories.

The blackness of the therapist only served to make the group meetings caustic. He identified with the Black majority, lest he be considered "integrated." Consequently, the white members as well as moderates such as I were ineffective and squashed. Carte blanche was served on sensitivity. Group and gripe alliances were openly and freely formed by those who ostensibly shared like feelings. Fair-skinned Black members, for example, who had exclusively associated with white faculty members prior to the student revolt, became, interestingly enough, the severest critics of white racism. Self-awareness, intuition, insight, and sharing became secondary to satisfying personal ego-needs. "Tell it like it is" comprised the group catharsis. There was little respect for individual differences, for personal feelings of any staff member, particularly if he were white. Drawing blood became the order of each session. Bitterness, hatred, invectives, accusations—professional ethics and courtesy were forgotten. After explosions of "nigger" and "bigot," we would leave the sessions drained, wondering what had been accomplished.

The key to understanding others is to understand oneself. If the Black professional cannot divorce his own needs from the professional self; if the Black professional has little knowledge of human motivation; if the Black professional has little knowledge of the objective and subjective aspects of feelings; if the Black professional passes judgment on others without being aware of his own biases; if the Black professional cannot hear for talking; if the Black professional cannot accept others because he cannot accept his own personal image—then how can he hope to help his Black brother who has all of these limitations?

Black social workers, like all professionals seeking continued growth in their fields, should continue educating themselves by their experiences, by re-evaluating themselves, and by continually restudying the principles and concepts established by the profession. For an example, the simple principle of "listening and beginning where the clients are" could very well be the key for reopening the doors of communication between Black and white professionals. It is simply a matter of our reaffirming our faith in the profession and in ourselves.

Doing this is not so simple. I shall never forget the dryness in my throat when I alone resisted a clique of my colleagues who wanted to impose, without total group consent, a regulation requiring constant attendance at the Black-white group sessions. (Experience in group dynamics has taught me that people join groups for many reasons, so groups have different meanings for different members. And the success or failure of them depends largely on that fact.) Although acceptance of the ruling was not vocally approved by the staff, many members, fearing the wrath of the Black majority, went along with it. When I dared to state that I did not know if I wanted to be a part of a group that so quickly wanted to impose regulations before I had time to explore and consider whether the group had some meaning for me, I was attacked. The severity of the attack taught me that there was no place for individuality within this group. Acceptance was based upon total and unquestioned Black identification, rather than on one's life experience and philosophy. I was being snobbish; I felt the group could teach me nothing; my age indicated a generation gap (at this point one member suggested the insensitivity of this last charge).

The point missed entirely by all was that my experiences and insights and maturity could be usable for the group. But what my stance ultimately accomplished, with the support of the therapist, was to establish a climate so that others could feel free to think as individuals, or perhaps they were always thinking so but did not feel comfortable enough to express individuality.

An element of doubt exists as to whether general concepts and principles of the profession can be made applicable to Black people and Black situations. And the doubt is reinforced by those "Black cats" who boast they get action without the services of the "professional change agent" as heralded by Lippitt, Watson, and Westley in the *Dynamics of Planned Change*. It is the authors' contention that people living in a modern world are forced to change. In given situations where change is difficult, people often seek the professional help of a change agent: a community organizer, a case-worker, a psychologist, etc. The antithesis to the authors' contention would be those extremists who by threats and the advocacy of violence are able to effect change to some extent. The relative effectiveness of this method of threat prevents them from considering the necessity or the possibility of professional help. What this group does not understand, and we are at fault, is that the skills of the Black professional, complemented with his sense of identification, his experience, and his ability to communicate, enable us to study situations and problems, make diagnostic evaluations, and embark upon treatment or self-help programs with Black groups, mobilizing and utilizing their resources, thereby motivating them toward a "normal" process (in the sense of being nonthreatening) of growth and development. As Black professionals we cannot afford to prostitute our skills and ourselves by being duped by their (the extremists) fast results, and jettisoned into the "all-Black, hate-whitey" fray. Nor must we be frightened into getting into the "all-Black, hate-whitey" act merely because we fear the demise of skills, white-endowed though some may be, but all of which were so painfully acquired in becoming professionals.

The pains we suffered in the acquisition of social-work skills should be our pains of commitment. And for those of us who are committed to the transmission of these skills to the Black revolution per se, pain is not new. Nine years ago when I was a student in the school of social work, it was revolutionary for Black students to remind the almost total white student body and white faculty that basic social-work principles had relevance to Black situations also; therefore Black illustrations should be included in developing points. Because we believe in the basic tenets of humanitarianism, we made deliberate pacts not to exclude ourselves from any social or academic situation which involved the general welfare of all people. Thus, we picketed such stores as Woolworth's, protesting the lack of Black personnel in its Southern stores. We picketed Rochdale Village demanding the hiring of Black construction workers. Whatever the social issues, we Black students had the same freedom of choice and involvement as the whites. There was never coercion from faculty or peers to force participation in any movement or support of any issue. One was left to his own conscience.

I find it now incredible as both an individual and a professional that I no longer have that freedom of choice—that thinking and acting as a person subjects me to social and academic isolation. There is, of course, some satisfaction in being excluded from the "struggle" many of my colleagues are presumably engaged in. For the fight in effect seems to be nothing more than a move toward security in conformity, the goal of which, or so it seems, is to cover up academic, professional, and personal shortcomings while professing that only we can service our people. Not only is this dishonesty, it is betrayal. How can a professional be of any service to the Black movement if he cannot critically evaluate himself, his stance, his role? And so an isolate I remain.

Instead of critical judgment (a white middle-class skill, evidently), my colleagues adopt a stance that repudiates anything white and demonstrates their desire for acceptance by the in-Black group which is, to our professional frustrations, composed mostly of grass-roots people. The repudiations are ironic considering the titles and positions held, the salaries earned, and the mode of living; the lifestyle blatantly speaks for itself. The rejection of values, part and parcel of the "hate the establishment" trend, becomes ludicrous when one diagnoses the core national problem today as the unequal distribution of value symbols. Can we really afford to be a part of those groups which reject those things which social workers, Black and white, have fought so long and so hard for, *the common goods and services for all* and *equal citizenship for all?* If we cannot, then toward what goals and standards do we as Black people aspire?

The summarized report of the National Advisory Commission on Civil Disorders says:

A new mood has sprung up among Negroes, particularly the young in which self-esteem and enhanced racial pride are replacing apathy and submission to the system. What the rioters appeared to be seeking was fuller participation in the social order, and material benefits enjoyed by majority of American citizens. Rather than rejecting the American system, they were anxious to obtain a place for themselves in it.

The report confirms the "fox and the sour grapes" incongruity of the extremists, as well as confirms the fact that the Black movement like the national student movement is largely made up of young people. How much this fact relates to or induces feelings of guilt on the part of many of us older professionals, one cannot say. But the fact is that teenagers are doing what professionals should be doing: guiding and shaping the direction of the Black revolution.

Why are we not involved? Why are we not useful or usable? Some of us, so fearful of rejection and hostility from our Black colleagues if we dare express principles that are perceptually different from the group, are paralyzed. That many Black professionals use color, as have most whites, as an index in measuring the degree of identification and depth of one's commitment to the group, splits us. And some of us, unfortunately, have accepted the inferior status assigned us and are crippled. Others have personal though often subtle investments at stake, and use the movement as an opportunity to further them.

I don't know about others, but I can hardly encourage my brothers in the street to burn, loot, and destroy, leaving themselves homeless and destitute while I reap the benefits of their actions in the form of bigger jobs, juicier offers. Frequently students and faculty have discussed this issue—here we all are benefiting from the "white peace offerings" as college students, college faculty, benefiting from the climate produced by the vociferous militants which put our skills in demand. Personally I find it difficult and do not want to be in a position to attribute my professional progress to my color rather than to my preparation, or gain professional cooperation from whites with a pose of anger and militance rather than through understanding and agreement. Perhaps I am unduly suspicious of many of my Black colleagues' "Blackness" because too many of them are males who scream "bigot," "racist" at their white co-workers on Monday, having "done their thing" with white women over the weekend.

There is still, perhaps, another reason we aren't more involved. Some Black social workers, like white social workers, feel helpless in attempting to utilize seemingly outmoded skills of a profession which at the outset professed to give no concrete answers or solutions to problems, but relies rather upon individual intuition, personal conviction, and personal commitment in the application of its principles. The current climate, the gaming and hustling, is confusing. So we hesitate. Because we hesitate, the children lead. And consequently, we become lost in the tumult of ankhs and dashikis, sinking deeper into the plush of our denials and assuming few if any real roles of responsibility.

We must ask ourselves to which drummer are we listening? Is it the drummer who beats out a "hate-whitey" theme faintly reminiscent of our need for self-expression, prestige and recognition, subtly, but always at the expense of the Black masses? Or have we become so confused in the rolling of the drums that we cannot perceive a likeness between Black dictatorship and white, Black exploitation and white, or Black deception and white? Are we seeking basically to fulfill at any price the theoretical concept of self-actualization through Black separatism and Black exploitation? Black social workers cannot afford to answer affirmatively to any of the above questions. This is not to say we must be super-professionals, with no common human needs to be met, but merely to say that implicit in professionalism, as perceived by social work, is the concept of self-awareness, the superego of the professional self, the watchdog of our limitations and desires and the scale for measuring our assets. We must be ego and image builders, not destroyers, standardbearers, not followers, innovators and not mimics or drifters, blending indiscriminately into the hate parade.

If Black professionals are uncomfortable in assuming positive roles, perhaps some consolation can be found in the social-science literature in which social theorists state almost conclusively that every individual has specific internal and external needs which must be met. If these needs are not met, the individual is deprived and thwarted. It follows that the primary goal of that individual is the fulfillment of his needs. We must ask ourselves, then, are the needs of our present stream of Black leaders sufficiently fulfilled so that they are then free to be concerned with the fulfillment of the needs of the general Black masses rather than with the fulfillment of their own?

There are those who indeed are committed to the goals of the profession to the extent that they will never attract publicity. They are quietly and effectively aiding in bringing about change. They wear no magic coats to shield them from their experiences with racial prejudice. They grind no personal axes and have no vendettas to settle. Yet, what they stand for creates all kind of guilt feelings in the consciences of the bandwagon followers. The followers seek to relieve their feelings through projection. They call these others emulators of the white middle class; they label them "white-brainwashed"; they call them "Uncle Toms."

It behooves us to critically examine our own motives and own needs to see these "other" professionals, as they are: achievers, integrationists, and mature people who were not afraid to become standardbearers or to be individuals, and who have made it in spite of being the "other American" in the American dilemma. For did not the Commission on Civil Disorders see as its goal the realization of common opportunities for all within a single society? Should we then as Black professionals allow ourselves to hate the "good life" or hate the holders of it merely because it is not yet proportionately within our grasp?

Black separatists argue that ethnic groups obtain power only to the extent that they are isolated together. The argument carries plenty of weight. But it is difficult to get a true picture of oneself, one's group, or one's community without a preconceived model or contrasts. All growth and progress is largely determined by comparison with established standards. As much as we may dislike the fact that standards have been set by the establishment we cannot magically overnight wipe them away by pretending that they are not or never have been present. Our knowledge of individuals, groups, and communities should pave the way for interpretation, and transmission to Black people of what isolation can do to a people. And perhaps, if we allude to a quote by the noted Black sociologist E. Franklin Frazier, the argument for isolated segmentation would carry less weight. He says:

> The church is an institution which the Negro has made his own. It reflects in its ideologies and practices, as well as its organization and leadership—whatever is unique and peculiar in the Negro's experience and outlook on life. To discover how isolation and inferior status affect the personality of the youth, one must study the Negro church.

Dr. Frazier seems to be saying that the organizational structure and leadership of the Negro church has been little influenced by white America. Yet, it seems to have irreparably damaged Black youth philosophically and ideologically. For, instead of the Black church focusing on current ways of handling the "now" problem of the racial crisis, it has sought in many cases to placate and to accommodate its philosophy to the social conditions while focusing on the afterlife.

Black separatism with its attendant "hate-whitey" discipline has most assuredly been well motivated by white racism. And it is reasonably easy to understand group attractiveness by those Black individuals who have been severely exposed to and damaged by its venom. And this does not exclude Black social workers! We can accept the possibility that those of us most damaged might react within the framework of our learned experiences. However, we must suspect that what is being preached and accepted by some of us as separatism is merely a cry for Black cohesion. This we, as professionals, can applaud. But are we as Black professionals healthy enough to ask ourselves these questions: Will the common bond of being Black, with the built-in requisite of hate, generate Black cohesion? Or can the common bond of being Black without the emotional requisite, but with stated goals and objectives, common experiences and interests, and the proper utilization of skills, generate it?

If hate is the requisite for affiliation with some of the more militant groups, can we as Black professionals, merely because of our badge of identification, and in spite of our knowledge and insight as to what makes individuals in general hate, allow ourselves to be sucked into what is becoming a national illness?

If we are to survive, as most of us would have it, as solid, Black citizens in a total society, we must, yes, we must, through unity and cohesion, become an integral part of that fabric. And so it seems to follow that if we are to become a cohesive ethic group in the fabric of American society, the "quality of attractiveness" which must touch all groups and appeal to all groups must be *humanitarianism,* or, as the late and beloved Dr. Martin Luther King Jr. would perhaps prefer, love for one's fellow being.

As the militant groups currently stand, can we as Black social workers afford to join—afford to hate?

Ebony Minds,
Black Voices

Adele Jones and Group

Several young women at the Harlem University (City College of New York) formed a Woman's Workshop at the Onyx Society's Malcolm X Conference in 1969. One of their activities is the rap. The transcription presented here of a tape made on the campus includes some of the members of that workshop and several other friends. Adele Jones got the group together in the nerve center of the strike headquarters of the university during the month of occupation by the Black and Puerto Rican community. The participants were: Adele Jones, Dorothy Randall, Cenen Moreno, and Sally Matthews, and later Renee Foster, Joyce Green, and Callie Harvey—T.C.

Adele—What do you see when you look around at the Black woman?

Dot—Well, I'll tell you. I see a lot of phoniness. I was saying the other day, I'll be glad when the afro goes out of style, then the people to whom it means something can still have it. I was in a department store the other day and two girls were buying dresses, talking about going to a dance. One girl says to the other,

"How you wearing your hair tomorrow?" The other answers, "I'm wearing mine afro; everyone else is." "OK, I'll wear mine like that." I was sick.

Sally—They're the same, I think, as the women in the past except they're wearing their hair differently. A lot of so-called Black women are still hung up on clothes and having a college-educated man and all. Same old stupid bullshit. Everybody looks at the hair first to see if she's Black. They don't yet check out the person and what she has to say. When we get on that level, we'll know what a Black woman is.

Cenen—It's really interesting about the hair and white girls, though. Before a white girl could come up and grab your man any time she wanted to. But suddenly we have something they don't . . . the hair. These girls are going through changes. And now the Black man sees something in himself he likes and in her—the hair. Kinkiness draws the line, helps us to define what it is we're about. The dark skin, broad nose, what-have-you.

Dot—Another thing. The white girls find that white men are attracted to the afro hair too. I've been in elevators with them and I've felt my hair being touched and ain't nobody in there but me and white people. They want to know how it feels.

Sally—It's soft and they're shocked.

Dot—It's funny how we go back and forth. We can emulate the white people—straighten the hair and bleach the skin. We can wear the same clothes. But the hair thing. Just blows their mind. "How did you get your hair that way?" They get frantic.

Adele—Right, and then, "How can I do it?"

Dot—Like white people have nothing of their own. Can't identify with the American culture. Can't sing old country tunes. So they latch onto ours. Take from everybody else, these young white kids. See them wearing Indian clothes, buffalo boots. Try to get an afro. Start wearing a dashiki. Everything from everywhere but nothing of their own. This afro is really messing up. They got a Grecian wig now with all these little curls. But they can't make it.

Adele—Cenen said something before about the natural being in effect a way to pull your mind into your own color, into your own being. When I got mine years ago when few naturals were around, I went through some changes. I'd be walking down the street and I'd be called a boy and things like that. And though it's a fad now, it's still identified with Black nationalism. We can't use that connection. Though the wigs are a drag 'cause that's the man co-opting the thing.

Dot—Yeh, that fashion stuff is too much to take. I do associate it with Black nationalism. And I still can't get over them girls in the store. "How you going to wear your hair tomorrow?" That's how it affects some Black people. By the time my sister got her afro my mother could say it was nice. But my sister delivered Avon to this lady and she said that if my sister had come to her door with hair like mine, she would not have let her in. No wild people were coming into her house. 'Course if your hair is short and neat, that's OK with the white folks.

Sally—You know what's interesting. I work at a children's center which is run by the Department of Social Services. The other day I saw a sign up saying something like, "If a child comes in here with an afro, he must have permission from his parents." You need permission to be natural.

Cenen—You know the whole thing is funny when you see the male and female draw closer together because her hair is like his hair. It makes them aware. They're struggling for the same thing. And it's telling white people that we're not going to allow them to tell us what they want—hair cut short and stuff. It's also telling them to watch out. We're not perpetuating slave-mindedness.

Adele—Well I think that if we all went into our reasons for having a natural, we'd find that underneath was the whole act of like this is me. Nothing's going to stop me, from parents on down. I have a girl friend whose mother actually went into fits when her daughter walked in with an afro. Laid down on the floor and cried.

Cenen—I can see that. I don't see why she didn't beat her daughter up. The natural is sacrilegious.

Dot—That's the exact word. Especially if you come from a Southern background where long hair was it. Long hair was sacred. So I cut it. My mother said, "You didn't consult me." She was hurt that I had cut my own hair.

Adele—Well, it's disconnecting from the society . . . cutting yourself off as far as they're concerned. Parents understand that.

Cenen—They're afraid for us. Afraid of the reaction against us.

Dot—Right. They're afraid you won't be accepted, won't get a job. They're looking out for you in their way.

Cenen—Like being a slave and bowing your head. When the slave said no, he'd be killed. Parents are fearful of that, of you being hurt.

Adele—Like when my mother used to sit and braid my hair, it hurt and I cried. But you had to be presentable. Burn your scalp, you take it. But the natural begins to change your perspective.

Dot—Self-respect. Like when you walk into stores, you no longer feel the clerk is going to be insolent. You have the upper hand and you say, "I want a blouse." You tell him firmly what color you want and you don't want no bullshit. It's a whole thing with pride in yourself. You're sure of yourself and no one can tell you a thing.

Cenen—I think of that a bit differently. You've gone against the rules and are on the defensive. So you become defiant and come on very aggressive and say, "This is the blouse I want and the color I want and don't tell me nothing about my hair." You know you're no longer "presentable" so you have to assume an I'll-fight attitude. But nobody blows you down. No bullet creased your body and no insult passed your ear. So you figure, if I can stand up for my hair, I can stand up for my person. It makes us aware and obligates us to be more aware.

Cenen—The white kids gave out a paper today that read, "We are SDS, we wreck colleges for fun and profit. Support us and we'll be happy to smash yours. Signed—Students for the Destruction of Society. Columbia University, May 1969."

Adele—That must be somebody cracking on SDS.

Cenen—No, I checked.

Dot—You mean this group is making fun of themselves?

Cenen—They're not making fun of themselves. They're serious about this. All this time we've been searching for a way of getting into their society, and they see no worth in it, want to destroy it. That's why so many white kids want to get into the Black movement; they want to relate to something that has value.

Dot—And there is a certain segment of Blacks bent on destruction. I wrote an article on so-called revolutionary phrases and how they don't have any thought behind them. The whole idea is, "Burn the motherfucker down." Like if you want to sound militant you say, "This university is not gonna grant our demands so we're gonna burn the motherfucker down and then the whole country." We were talking about all that yesterday, about how people don't check phrases out. They scream back, "Right on."

Renee—Phrases are a way of galvanizing people, not even dealing with the projection, just dealing with the momentum at the moment.

Dot—Who wants momentum with no direction. People get all

stirred up at a rally and are ready to smash, burn, kill, rape, murder, anything. But when you talk about direction, ask the question "What can I do?" You get some irrelevant comeback like "Relate" or "Get on the case."

Dot—When you're friends with a man, you can be honest. There's not the competition there is being friends with a girl. I can't take the pettiness and bitchiness of the majority of women. A man you can at least talk to before you tell him no I don't want to go to bed with you.

Joyce—Perhaps it's that when you rap with a man about your problems, the chances are he'll help you if he can. Rap with a woman and she says, "Oh yeah, you got that problem," or "Good for you, I don't have it."

Renee—Or else, "What are you telling me for?"

Adele—We've allowed that to be the case, competition with each other. I've been at parties with a sister and like you both spot the same brother at the same time, and all the rest of the party the two of you are on edge. Meanwhile the brother hasn't approached either of you. I think it's kind of ridiculous. We perpetuate that sort of thing. I can sit here and say this to you, but we'll go to a party and do it all over again.

Dot—The competition I can stand, that's natural. But the bitchiness.

Cenen—Why must we be bitches to each other?

Dot—I'm not.

Sally—Oh wow.

Dot—I'm talking about walking up to a sister and the first word out of the mouth is a nasty comment. I've never done it.

Adele—Oh stop.

Cenen—We don't have to say anything. We can act it. But why?

Dot—You are talking to an innocent bystander who is a victim of many bitches.

Sally—The first thing you think is that the other woman is a threat to you, gonna take your man. A Black woman cannot feel that the man is hers entirely. He's gonna look around.

Dot—That all goes back to what we were talking about before. It's a whole undefined area about this Black womanhood.

Joyce—You mean you could go out and support a man and not be a bitch? You wouldn't attack him because you realized it was the system and not his fault he can't find work and so forth?

Dot—Yes.

Joyce—Well, never mind all this talk about the poor man. What about the woman? I have this girl friend—it's only one sort of situation, but—and she's pregnant now and her ole man is into this Black Man thing going with some other chick, white chick. So my friend would bring it up and he'd go into this thing about, "Well, after all, she's a very sweet person, not bitchy." Then went on raving about what a drag Black women are—domineering, emasculating. You know, hiding behind that Poor Black Man Done In by Everything.

Dot—Yeh, men do use that.

Adele—That goes back to what we were saying before about the family, how the woman used to get out there and work and hold the family together. Now people screaming about how she done the man in. White sociological bullshit to shift the blame from the white system to the Black woman.

Dot—I think she should have provided him with a little extra something because he feels bad enough about not working. Now if the woman's gonna harp on that, he's gonna feel completely shattered.

Adele—So because of this "failure" of Black women in the past, we have to make up for it now. That seems kind of ridiculous.

Renee—It's like a recurring pattern, each generation making up for the last's mistakes. I'm not gonna make the same mistakes my mother made.

Joyce—That's why you can't relax in your womanhood, because you're always trying to make up for something in the past.

Adele—We seem to be conceding so much and not living up to our womanhood. Even though we have our naturals and take the pill and are independent and we TCB and we're always there and—why do we do it?

Sally—We figure wow, my man's got his thing together and I've got to keep up with him.

Dot—That's not what I see. It was the woman all along who was the motivating force, who got the man together. And even now, a woman going through her womanhood changes is not as bad as a man going through his man changes. Manhood with a Black man is a really big thing.

Callie—You're saying women are more together. I don't see that. When brothers be sitting in a room and another brother comes in they say, "Salam," or some greeting. But sisters. I was really not prepared for the atmosphere in here when I came in. You all are so friendly. Usually sisters check you out with a "What are you doing here" and shun you.

Sally—But I don't remember Black men being this together with each other in the past. It makes me aware of what we should be doing. It can't be a thing where the Black men are moving and the woman ain't.

Adele—Why can't women begin to move as women? All this mistrust and competition, bitchiness. Is it something we can correct? Is it something that can be corrected by getting together as we are here? Why do we have to wait for the man supposedly to do something before we make a move?

Callie—Men are our leaders, you know.

All—Uh hunh.

Cenen—Can I say something? I started to think about how up to now women have always been fighting to get the vote, to wear short dresses, to get an education, to go to certain places, to become political thinkers—and they've always had to fight men in order to achieve anything. Why? It boils down to the need to suppress someone. That's the way it's always been in this society. Our men go out to get a job and the white man there treats him like dirt. So he comes home and does the same thing to us. So we might take it out on the kids. Now that she's on a sort of equal level, the man sees her capable and productive and feels he's no longer a man in terms of sexual need and the old way, but a man in terms of ideology. Like before girls helped them across the street. We gave them this and gave them that. We were stupid. Suddenly women are saying to men, "I'm not trying to take away your masculinity. On the contrary, I'm demanding that you be more of a man than ever before." That's a big order for the man. When he says, "I'm going to do such and so," we don't say "Yes, honey, I think you should," we say "I'm going to do that too." And even if he doesn't do it, you're going to do it. So he has to move.

Dot—He doesn't have to, he can find another woman. The man thinks, "Am I ready for this?" He often says no. That's why there's so much frustration.

Callie—We're having a thing down at my school like a "No sisters allowed" at meetings. They put us out with that this-is-man's-work routine.

Cenen—The work includes us but we're not allowed. In spite of the fact that this business could mean our life or our death.

Adele—That's a white thing and a shame. We should be about defining new lifestyles.

Renee—The question is how do we get away from the society that continually faces us to create new values.

Dot—Well, female bitchiness is a thing in the total society. But I think we can certainly change that, address ourselves to that issue.

Renee—Why can't we look at the roots of the bitchiness? When I grew up in Harlem my mother put into my mind that there are certain types of women: loose women that do certain kinds of things and this is the kind of person I don't want you to turn out to be. The friends I had were all the same; our parents had the same sort of values, so we would talk about other kids. That's where it starts. And even in that game if-you-black-stay-back, the whole thing got ingrained when you were very young and weren't concious. Then later I said, like wow, all this happened to me and now I have to get out of it. I'm trying to change that now.

Dot—I was thinking of another thing. I work with kids and they are the nastiest, bitchiest people you ever want to see. They say things to each other that we would have to curb. Like, "We're forming a club. You can't come in. We made the club just so you can't be in it." Wow. Some kids grow out of it. Some kids just develop a subtler vocabulary.

Cenen—We're injected with all kinds of things that separate us, that make us move against each other, that keep us from thinking, growing, moving together. Divide and conquer. You run around in a circle worrying about tight skirts and low-cut dresses and crazy hairdos and plush cars, petty stuff. Then one day you wake up and realize there is something else. That what you really want is freedom to act, to do, to create. But something's always there to stop you. That makes you really wake up. That's why we have the welfare mothers organized and fighting. And that's why we need narcotic centers to teach them that they don't have to shoot in order to live. . . . You know, Puerto Rico is like some 8,000-odd square miles. And out of P.R. America the Beautiful takes out 700 million dollars annually. It all goes back to what we were saying about being bitchy to each other, fighting over men, being bourgy. Then when we realize it doesn't matter how you dress, it's how you think; it's not what year Cadillac is that, it's where you're going. It's not what college you're at, it's what you're learning. And you realize the thing is to go and create a society. Not just here, all over. But something out there is controlling us, throwing bones at us so we fight one another instead of attacking that which is really choking us. Same in P.R.

Sally—Amen.

Dot—Now what happens when you come to this state of mind Cenen is in. You become different. You become the woman you ought to be and because of this you are no longer accepted in your old crowd. They're sitting around talking about a party, and Cenen is talking about Vietnam. I think this is a long process. I don't even know how it would start.

Renee—It starts with getting involved thoroughly and then sitting back to assess what you've done or been trying to do, what you've learned and what you've become.

Dot—But it has to get down to me personally. What can make me change so I would not be concerned about getting a dress to wear?

Callie—You'll be able to do it when you can say you don't care what someone else may feel about you if you don't have on the latest dress. When you can say, "Here I am and that's enough."

Dot—That also takes some changing. On that level, you're secure and can keep yourself company. But if you're not on that level, you can't even say, well fuck everybody.

Adele—I think we're going to have to end. I really think we need another conversation.

Joyce—What we need to consider soon is at what point and to what degree we go into ourselves and hide out when we talk.

Poor Black Women's Study Papers by Poor Black Women of Mount Vernon, New York

Pat Robinson and Group

These are the working papers of a group of women in New Rochelle and Mount Vernon committed to Women's Rights and Power to the People—ideas that are not, cannot be, mutually exclusive or antagonistic to a revolutionary people. Their work consists of, among other things, using criticism and analysis in written form to clarify their own observations, and then using these working papers to further the awareness of other sisters with whom they come in contact. The working papers of Patricia Robinson have appeared in Lilith, one of the Women's Liberation Front journals.—T.C.

Letter to a North Vietnamese Sister from an Afro-American Woman—Sept. 1968

Dear Sister:

We know full well that the power structure of our country is so threatened now by you, the great vanguard of this historical period, and after Chicago, by a rapidly awakening minority of U.S. citizens. It will strike out and we blacks with our historical memories of the reconstruction period gird ourselves along with the knowing oppressed whites.

In the 1880's and on we were slaughtered by the petit-bourgeois whites, those frightened fascists in white hoods. We don't overestimate or underestimate the enemy. We know his pattern and ours as well. We gave up; we submitted to what we saw as overpowering force. We were disorganized slaves. We went back to the land we did not have the power to own.

In 1920, a large group of us, mostly petit-bourgeois blacks who had trekked from the South, almost physically starved, decided in our new semi-opulence of the Northern cities (we were eating) that we could not gain power in this country and we wanted power and affluence. So we would go to Africa and become "kings and queens" over the natives there. Liberia had already been established. The government had helped groups of Afro-Americans to establish one of the first U.S. neo-colonies in Africa.

But this was a different historical period. The great white entrepreneur denied his new wage slaves and consumer market the opportunity. Marcus Garvey, the famous Black nationalist, was summarily done away with, jailed and dropped from history. We permitted this. We did not go to Africa; a few were left to dream about it.

The historian and intellectual W. E. B. Du Bois formed the elite thinkers of a Negro movement. This movement developed into the NAACP, a bourgeois organization with which you are familiar. It exerted the kind of pressure, integration, that the well-versed imperialist could deal with.

The international capitalist had learned from his experience of colonization how to deal with rising expectations. Let the small middle class integrate, school them well in the role of puppets, and they will make excellent overseers— hence the Supreme Court decision of 1954 to integrate schools.

Meanwhile he persecuted those bourgeois, like Du Bois and Paul Robeson, who were not taken in. Those were the middle-class Black radicals who had analyzed the system as the enemy but had not the resources or followers to unite with the poor Blacks. Like Nkrumah, they saw the opportunities socialism could offer their people.

In the late fifties and early sixties a new generation of Blacks without historical awareness and seduced by the prospects of education and integration moved forward on the backs of the poor Southern Blacks in Birmingham, Alabama. The great bus strike provided the opening for the opportunistic Southern middle-class Negro to move forward on the results of their nonviolent marches. Martin Luther King was brought in by the less charismatic Negroes to lead the movement. The capitalist system was not supposed to be overturned, just reformed so the Negro caricatures of a middle class could enjoy the crumbs of what the U.S. pillaged from Latin America, Africa, and Asia.

The international capitalist wisely supported this movement while the weaker and more lower-class domestic capitalist saw his social and economic interests threatened. The local oil interests, progenitors of LBJ, the labor monarchs, now a labor elite able to socialize occasionally with big industrial leaders of the East and the white lower middle class, made semi-affluent through war contracts, fought this rise of the Negro middle class. Du Bois, too long persecuted by the U.S. government, escaped to Ghana, where he died a Communist. Nkrumah would be overthrown in 1965 after the publication of his book, *Neo-Colonialism, the Last Stage of Imperialism*, exposing the new European and U.S. colonization of Africa and the need for African unity under socialism. Mrs. Du Bois would flee to China and Nkrumah to semi-socialist Guinea.

The petit-bourgeois Black in the North, who had by now turned to bustling and had been educated in our great Black universities, "whitey's jail," modified his Back to Africa dream. The Nation of Islam or the "Black Muslims" would have their separate state here. The lower middle class and their domestic capitalist supporters saw the opportunities such separation would give them. The class-race struggle would diminish and they would have a colony, with a small and crippled capitalist economy they could exploit—much like "The Fraud of Separate Development, Feathering the Nationalist Seat," analyzed by Govan Mboki in *South Africa, The Peasant's Revolt.*

... with the establishment of *Bantu authorities*, the government could try and break down by forcing the chiefs to comply. Many have been the techniques that the chiefs have employed to implement government policy against the will of the people, but they have not broken popular resistance and their conduct has increased it.

But Malcolm X, a brilliant Black humanist, revolted from this essential betrayal of the oppressed, his damned brothers and sisters. He began to teach, educate, and awaken thousands of Black North Americans, to the wider factors in our oppression, the international oppression by the U.S. of poor dark people and their rising revolt. He reflected our depth, our human wealth and beauty. He gave us back our roots, our history, and he connected us with the world revolutions. When he turned inward to the monster and identified him as the real enemy, he was assassinated.

Many had heard Malcolm X from all classes, both Black and white. Another generation had come forth more historically aware and with eyes turned both toward the world revolution and the monster counter-revolutionary oppressor in whose belly they had been born. They began to analyze, to study, write and act to confront the monster, the United States. The young Black man thought unity necessary to the freedom of the Black colonies or ghettoes. We are still in the period of trying to bring the middle class and the poor Blacks together in a united front.

Meanwhile the moderate Negro middle class, now more sophisticated through its integration struggles and, like the labor unions of the thirties and forties, intent on keeping its hard-won, petty privileges, moved to co-opt the awakening Black poor. Martin Luther King moved into the struggle of the poor laborers in Memphis, Tennessee, to unionize themselves. The lower-middle-class whites would not stand for this incipient social and economic competition. They assassinated King.

The Black United Fronts and Black Power, at this point in our history, are in reality a historical continuation of an elite group of moderate and petit-bourgeois Blacks attempting to gain power over the existing urban Black communities. The Black poor are the main population of these neighborhoods. Thousands of Negroes have been able to move out of the center-city slums to the suburbs where they are semi-integrated or have all-Black enclaves of well-kept homes. Black Power is actually power over the poor Black communities, not the more middle-class neighborhoods.

Ideally the exponents of Black Power imply that the poor Blacks can achieve a more comfortable life through the leadership of elite Blacks who will gain for them better housing, education, medical care, and jobs through the manipulation of the white capitalists. Consequently, they threaten to be the new puppet exploiters, moving out the present white-skinned small businessmen, educators, and professionals and installing themselves. Developing an interest in keeping their privileges, they can become like those puppets who in Africa rule the "natives" in the interests of the United States and Europe. In capitalist societies, after all, the profit motive and material incentives motivate individuals, not human need.

The rich and internationally minded capitalists believe this maxim absolutely, as does the labor aristocracy in certain socialist countries; they, therefore, support not only the Black Power Conferences but the new school decentralization schemes with limited community control, actually limited and controlled by them.

What Nixon calls the "forgotten American" or the seriously threatened new rich and new middle classes, are again feeling oppressed and sacrificed by the big industrialists and their intellectual university parasites. It is this "taken-for-granted group" that has always directly confronted the rising Negro classes and is beginning to do so again. This group has shown itself to be like all fascists—nondialectical, antihistorical, anti-analytic, and more prone to hysterical reactions to threats from below to its hardwon small social and economic status.

Yet it is strong enough in numbers at certain historical periods when revolution really threatens capitalism to be the necessary class to sustain the imperialists' interests. Correspondingly, this class which oppresses openly increases revolutionary rage and fervor across class and ethnic lines. Hopefully it will force the discipline, patience, and unity to create a revolutionary ideology and party and a base for a real revolution in the United States.

At this point in our history many Black and white women are forming their own class and historical analysis of capitalism. The poor Black woman is the lowest in this capitalist social and economic hierarchy. A few are beginning to see their oppressors as those who mean to keep them barefoot, pregnant, and ignorant of male oppression. But the fact of white male oppression has already been exposed by certain groups of middle-class white women. Poor Black women have close contacts with middle-class white women through their jobs as domestics, health and social welfare programs, education, etc. They live the reality daily of Black male oppression. Now they fight back in a silent warfare of guerrilla wits and homemade weapons. Some have begun to move toward smashing the myth of Black female social and economic dominance over the Black male. The middle-class white female sees the oppressor as maleness gone mad, the technocrat, cybernetically programmed, nonhuman God. This is the warfare state, a dynamic capitalist power requiring periodic wars to survive. Out of a long history of worldwide oppression North American women are being moved by historical forces and exalted out of their slave mentality.

We must speak out at this time from the belly of the monster to all the oppressed throughout the world to tell them whence we have come to join them in the struggle for a new world and a new people.

Please send this to our great and courageous sisters in your country and tell them we embrace them and will do all that is necessary here. First, we must smash the myth of white supremacy. Then together we can work toward smashing imperialism and capitalism.

Let us hear from them soon, if possible, because some of us as individuals do not have much time and we want to pass on the message to those who will take up our weapons.

We salute you and ourselves, in love and courage.

Onward to the world revolution.

On the Position of Poor Black Women in This Country

It is time to speak to the whole question of the position of poor Black women in this society and in this historical period of revolution and counter-revolution. We have the attached analysis of their own perspective and it offers all of us some very concrete points.

First, that the class hierarchy as seen from the poor Black woman's position is one of white male in power, followed by the white female, then the Black male, and lastly the Black female.

Historically, the myth in the Black world is that there are only two free people in the United States, the white man and the Black woman. The myth was established by the Black man in the long period of his frustration when he longed to be free to have the material and social advantages of his oppressor, the white man. On examination of the myth this so-called freedom was based on the sexual prerogatives taken by the white man on the Black female. It was fantasied by the Black man that she enjoyed it.

The Black woman was needed and valued by the white female as a domestic. The Black female diluted much of this actual oppression of the white female by the white male. With the help of the Black woman, the white woman had free time from mother and housewife responsibilities and could escape her domestic prison overseen by the white male.

The poor Black woman still occupies the position of domestic in this society rising no higher than public welfare, when the frustrated male deserts her and the children. (Public welfare was instituted primarily for poor whites during the depression of the thirties to stave off their rising revolutionary violence. It was considered as a temporary stopgap only.)

The poor Black male deserted the poor female and fled to the cities, where he made his living by wife-hustling. The Black male did not question the kind of society he lived in other than on the basis of racism. "The white man won't let me up 'cause I'm Black." Other rationalizations included blaming the Black woman, which has been a much-described phenomenon. The Black man wanted to take the master's place and all that went with it.

Simultaneously, the poor Black woman did not question the social and economic system. She saw her main problem as described in the accompanying article—social, economic, and psychological oppression by the black man. But awareness in this case has moved to a second phase and exposes an important fact in the whole process of oppression. It takes two to oppress, a proper dialectical perspective to examine at this point in our movement.

An examination of the process of oppression in any or all of its forms shows simply that at least two parties are involved. The need for the white man, particularly, to oppress others reveals his own anxiety and inadequacy about his own maleness and humanity. Many Black male writers have eloquently analyzed this social and psychological fact. Generally a feeling of inadequacy can be traced to all those who desperately needed power and authority over others throughout history.

In other words one's concept of oneself becomes based on one's class or power position in a hierarchy. Any endangering of this power position brings on a state of madness and irrationality within the individual which exposes the basic fear and insecurity beneath—politically speaking, the imperialists are paper tigers.

But the oppressor must have the cooperation of the oppressed, of those he must feel better than. The oppressed and the damned are placed in an inferior position by force of arms, physical strength, and later by threats of such force. But the longtime maintenance of power over others is secured by psychological manipulation and seduction. The oppressed must begin to believe in the divine right and position of kings, the inherent right of an elite to rule supremacy of a class or ethnic group, the power of such condensed wealth as money and private property to give to its owners high social status. So a gigantic and complex myth has been woven by those who have power in this society of the inevitability of classes and the superiority and inferiority of certain groups. The oppressed begin to believe in their own inferiority and are left in their lifetime with two general choices, to identify with the oppressor (imitate him) or to rebel against him. Rebellion does not take place as long as the oppressed are certain of their inferiority and the innate superiority of the powerful, in essence a neurotic illusion. The oppressed appear to be in love with their chains.

In a capitalist society all power to rule is imagined in male symbols—and in fact, all power in a capitalistic society is in male hands. Capitalism is a male-supremacist society. Western religious gods are all male. The city, basis of "civilization," is male as opposed to the country, which is female. The city is a revolt against earlier female principles of nature and man's dependence on it. All domestic and international political and economic decisions are made by men and enforced by males and their symbolic extension, guns. Women have become the largest oppressed group in a dominant, aggressive, male capitalistic culture. The next largest oppressed group is the product of their wombs, the children, who are ever pressed into service and labor for the maintenance of a male-dominated class society.

If it is granted that it takes two to oppress, those who neurotically need to oppress and those who neurotically need to be oppressed, then what happens when the female in a capitalist society awakens to this reality? She can either identify with the male and opportunistically imitate him, appearing to share his power and giving him the surplus product of her body, the child to use and exploit. Or she can rebel and remove the children from exploitive and oppressive male authority.

Rebellion by poor Black women, the bottom of a class hierarchy not heretofore discussed, places the question of what kind of society will the poor Black woman demand and struggle for. Already she demands the right to have birth control. Like middle-class Black and white women, she is aware that it takes two to oppress and that she and other poor people no longer are submitting to oppression, in this case genocide. She allies herself with the have-nots in the wider world and their revolutionary struggles. She has been forced by historical conditions to withdraw the children from male dominance and to educate and support them herself. In this very process, male authority and exploitations are seriously weakened. Further she realizes that the children will be used as the poor has been used through history—as poorly paid mercenaries fighting to keep or put an elite group in power. Through these steps in the accompanying analytic article she has begun to question aggressive male domination and the class society which enforces it, capitalism. This question in time will be posed to the entire Black movement in this country.

So few men, even among the proletariat, realize how much effort and trouble they could save women, even quite do away with, if they were to lend a hand in "woman's work." But no, that is contrary to the "right and dignity of a man." They want their peace and comfort. The home life of the woman is a daily sacrifice to a thousand unimportant trivialities. The old master right of the man still lives in secret. His slave takes her revenge, also secretly. The backwardness of women, their lack of understanding for the revolutionary ideals of the man decrease his joy and determination in fighting. They are like little worms which unseen, slowly but surely, rot and corrode. I know the life of the worker, and not only from books. We must root out the old "master" idea to its last and smallest root, in the Party and among the masses.—Lenin, 1920

A Historical and Critical Essay for Black Women in the Cities, June 1969

*Pat Robinson
and Group*

It is time for the Black woman to take a look at herself, not just individually and collectively but historically, if she is to avoid sabotaging and delaying the Black revolution. Taking a look at yourself is not simply good tactics. It is absolutely necessary at this time in the Black movement when even Black radical males are still too insecure about their identity and too full of insurrectionist fantasies to dare reach out to the Black woman in revolutionary love—to urge us to begin to liberate ourselves, to tell us the truth, "Black women, you are the most oppressed and held down of us all. Rise up or we as Black men can never be free!"

No Black man can or should think that he can liberate us. They do not have our economic, social, biologic, and historic perspective, which is from the very bottom of the value structure of the West. The irrational scorn and fear of WOMAN, ANIMAL, and BLACK in Western culture keeps us in reality out of history. We all know, except for certain "house women," that history is made only by men. The word "animal" is a male's epithet for hated and feared underdogs. We Black women are considered "animals" by North American Black and white men who summarily overevaluate their brain power with its pregnant offshoot, reason and "soul." From their head regions they grow a culture of materialistic white and Black power backed by gods in their own images. What a shock it is to these males that so often they have to come down from Harlem and Wall Street to go to the bathroom! How they struggle against the fact that they are born of woman and from the moment of their leaving our wombs, they begin to die! Yet we Black women in our deepest humanity love and need Black men so, we hesitate to revolt against them and for our own human freedom.

If we Black women are slightly affluent, sucked and seduced by our own field-nigger families who only wanted to be house niggers, our anger and frustration must go underground, lest we endanger our few social and economic gains. We become nervous-nagging-narrow murderers of ourselves and our children. We distort our madness into other channels and against other Black women and our own oppressed white sisters, where it can emerge far from its source and appear rational and reasonable.

If we are poor Black women—one night in the street we explode. The small razor cupped in our fingers slashes his hated Black face, that mirror of our own; we sink the knife deep into his chest. Murdered by our own acceptance of the myth of male supremacy—the American Dream—we become murderers of our own threatened and frightened Black man.

If we feel ourselves to be enlightened and politically aware, we become common opportunists, affecting the role of some fantasied

"African Queen," as if we would rule just below the robed and haughty Black kings. No matter that our own feudal period in Africa was oppressive to Black women and peasants, that this warring and exploitive period was only interrupted by the European colonialist. We need this imagined power to nurse our own deep sense of inadequacy where, "Lo! We at least rule over the poorer classes!"

Those of us caught in the myths that were meant to keep us exploited and oppressed are frightened; yet enchanted by the white world of male gods. We hold tight to that little capital (clothes, furniture, and bank account), lest its loss would symbolize that we are "nothing" again. We are terrified of that gargantuan phallus—that big Dick, the war machine. But how we laud its power at the same time.

Myths galvanize people and direct their form of culture. They are the fullness and depth of the people. They are the projections of their learned fears, anxieties, frustrations, hopes, and the deepest unconscious contradictions of a civilization. In them is found not rational, linear thought but the inner contradictory reality of the human being. The American Dream is the end of a long, circuitous route away from the *animal body, the land, woman,* and *black* to condensed wealth (money, machines and property), cities, man, and white. It is time now to break out of these deathly myths and this culture built on the oppression of women and Blacks.

The Western world was built on much more than colonialism and imperialism. It was built on the long-standing mythical split of male and female, as well as the split of body and mind. All things having to do with the animal body were repressed unconsciously. The repressed reality of life, like oppressed peoples, never stays repressed. It always threatens to rise and cause trouble to those who *need* to control others and themselves.

Men who controlled the making of myths and culture after the overthrow of women saw to it that women were eventually relegated to the darkness, pressed down into that infamous, anarchic hell of the fables. Animals, women, and Black become the underground witches and demons in men's minds, their own feared, chaotic animal femininity. This split enabled the male head to soar to the celestial heavens, there to be worshipped in countless Apollonian symbols.

The woman's body, which receives, hosts, and gives forth the future of the species, had to be suppressed when the phallic aggressive male decided he needed power over others and that soft, feminine part of himself. Some thousands of years ago, the female was considered the Goddess of the Universe, from which heaven and earth sprang. Certainly, the myth conforms to reality; out of one comes two. The female births both male and female. The Adam and Eve myth turns that reality on its head. The female now issues from the male. Hence we know how terrified the male had become of animal reality to establish such a perversion of the truth.

Briffault in "The Mothers" traces the first animal family to the first human family and notes that the male's only role early in human history was insemination. Then he drifted off, leaving the female to take care of herself during pregnancy, birth, and the nursing of the young. When men and women began to live together, what can be called culture began. But women controlled the first fruit or surplus, the child, by reason of its long need for protection before it can take care of itself.

This was concrete power over the child and the male in those places with a warm climate and food and water readily available. There was no real need for a male procurer, a hunter. When the child came to have parents and an extended family in a culture, the childish vitality was inhibited by all manner of rituals and folk stories in order that it could be controlled and socialized. The primary oppression is that of the child; but that is an analysis I will leave to the revolutionary children.

Today in the time of the cities, cybernetics, nuclear power, and space exploration, white men have developed a man-made body, the self-regulating machine of manless factories and laboratories. Man has now projected and sublimated his "holy" head into electronics and soared in "Apollo" to the moon. He struggles to perfect artificial insemination and a machine host for the human fetus. At last man has done away with the practical need for his own body. Now he must turn his attention to the danger the woman's body has always posed to his rule. He concerns himself with the biological control of reproduction of the species—as necessary to his sustained power over others as his present concentration on the reproduction of capital rather than the production of goods.

The notorious subjugation of human beings with black skins to the "other world" of dark hell and slavery took place rapidly as the Semites, Christians, Moslems, and the middle-class industrial capitalists secured their conquests. Outcast Black men and women were the menial slave laborers and the scavengers of the waste of the city. They were also the receptacle into which white male conquerors and their ladies could cast their own fears and guilt for this murder and rape; and how they trembled inwardly behind their armies at the expected retaliation of the havenots. The long, neurotic, historical process by which these descendants of the hunters and the herders attempted to deny their biological reality was achieved through the projection onto others of what they could not stand in themselves. They were animals who were born and died.

But through symbols and capitalism they could live forever. From this oppressed humanity they brought forth huge profits. The raw fruits from the earth were molded into vast monuments and empires of condensed wealth. Through interest money could actually grow. And on top of it all they stood tall with their heads in the clouds; beneath the Black bending bodies did not stir. From the pyramids to the cities, we are stuck with these monuments and great surpluses built on man's fearful need to be God.

In the Kalahari Desert in Southwest Africa, where remains of the tiny bushmen driven southward by constant tribal wars still live, there are legends that tell of men, women, and animals in equilibrium, each performing their appropriate tasks of hunting, fishing, collecting. There is no strong matriarchal or patriarchal emphasis. All the environment is sacred—the animals, the sky, the earth. The main social problem to this day is living harmoniously together while hunting and gathering enough food and water in this vast desert to which few outsiders go.

In that desert are mountains with almost inaccessible caves, and on their walls, the animals and the men and women of the hunt. Women, unlike the men, are not masked. The human figures are almost sketchy compared to the care taken in drawing the animals. The figures of women, usually nude, and simply standing, are sculptured. "Many are extremely obese, emphasis is on the great loins, the pubic triangle and the nourishing breasts." Some of the women appear to be hunting with spears in their hands. Joseph Campbell in his series on mythology believes that "in the earliest ages of human history the magical force and wonder of the female was no less a marvel than the universe itself and this gave to woman a prodigious power, which it was one of the chief concerns of the masculine part of the population to break, control and employ to its own ends."

When a group must be controlled, you always take away from them their gods, their very reflections of themselves and their inner being. But first you must use force.

In the days when all the forest was evergreen, before the parakeet painted the autumn leaves red with the color from his breast, before the giants wandered through the woods with their heads above the tree-tops; in the days when the sun and moon walked the earth as man and wife, and many of the great sleeping mountains were human beings; in those far off days witchcraft was known only to the women of Onaland (Tierra del Fuego, South America). They kept their own particular lodge, which no man dared approach. The girls, as they neared womanhood, were instructed in the magic arts, learning how to bring sickness and even death to all those who displeased them.

The men lived in abject fear and subjugation. Certainly they had bows and arrows with which to supply the camp with meat, yet, they asked what use were such weapons against the witchcraft and sickness? This tyranny of the woman grew from bad to worse until it occurred to the men that a dead witch was less dangerous than a live one. They conspired together to kill off all the women; and there ensued a great massacre, from which not one woman in human form escaped.

The legend goes on to describe how the men waited for the little girls to grow up so they could have wives. Meanwhile they plotted how they would have their own lodge (secret society) from which all women would forever be excluded. They would be frightened into submission by means of demons drawn from the men's imagination.

This is only one of thousands of such legends taken from all parts of the world that indicate some crisis occurred in which leadership was wrested from the woman, either by force or seduction or both. Certainly there was great fear of women and a sense of being oppressed by their inner and reproductive powers. The great earth mother could bring forth life and inexplicably take it away. This was one kind of power. In fact, it could only be overcome in most of the folk stories by tools of war in the hands of muscular men—the murder of the women and the great earth goddess by the phallic aggressive men, determined to have their external power over nature and its symbolic representative, woman.

In highly organized hunting societies with their sacred animal totems, women were separated and confined to the domestic role. The great hunters occupied those areas where there was much large game and the efforts required were herculean. Africa, North and South America, Asia have great historic legends of the mighty hunters and horse herders, the determined individualists and the male supremacists. The split of the male and female is well documented during this paleolithic period. Fortunately, some figurines of the female form from that time remain to this day. Women were but driven underground.

Even though hunters roamed the banks of the Congo, agricultural communities arose there. The plant as well as the animal were the main sources of food. In those villages where the women produced food by planting, both woman and the earth were valuable. The woman who tilled the land came to own it. Man was almost superfluous except for his sexual mating role.

Anthropologists describe this period as the famous matriarchy when woman, owning the land and having much to say about the distribution of the surplus, had not only sacred power but economic and social power as well. In West Africa, particularly, secret male councils were formed in reaction to this female dominance. Unlike the more aggressive hunting societies, males were elected to such lodges. Men from other tribes were encouraged to join so that a secret council might spread through many tribes over a large area. The sacred divinities were still often female. The moon, symbol of the Great Mother, was a basic part of their life. These secret societies did not absolutely exclude woman. She was kept symbolically among the group gods.

These lodges gradually developed into councils of chiefs or elders and the communal village was eventually ruled by a male tribal aristocracy. In *Some Problems of the African Village* (Spark Publications, July 30, 1965, Accra, Ghana), Vladimir Jordansky describes the class culture of the rural society before colonialism.

At the top of the traditional society were the elders and the chiefs. Everywhere custom released them from a direct part in agricultural work and gave them administrative duties. The elders saw to the redistribution of communal land, maintained order and handled relations with neighboring villages. Their privileges were extensive and their authority indisputable. The division of land and labor within the commune was once a means of uniting the members in an integrated labor process.

By the above-described period, which was the Iron Age, when metal discoveries allowed for more complex labor production, the women had been assigned less "lofty" tasks. Men worked the metal while women made pottery and did basketweaving. In the fields men would clear the brush and women still did the planting and caring for the crops.

Whereas about 7500-3500 B.C. the Great Goddess "was the focal figure of all mythology and worship, the mother and nourisher of life and receiver of the dead for rebirth," by the time of the Iron Age, about 1250 B.C., much of what the great mother symbolized was displaced by the aggressive gods of the hunters and herders. The more complex villages of Africa and the Near East were overrun by these restless men, and female shrines were gradually displaced by male monuments and objects of worship. With polygamy women and children were finally subjugated and exploited by a male aristocracy, as was most of the lower strata of the African village. It was on this feudal development in African society that European feudal states were able to build a cooperative venture with African chiefs for the beginning of the slave trade.

In the rise of the cities the suppression of the female is concrete and complete. Cities developed out of this surplus produced by the countryside. It is on the increase of this surplus that the growth of cities depends. Cities fed by an economic surplus are essentially not needed and superabundant. Control of the surplus, whether it be of children (labor), food, goods, leads to special privilege and prestige for the elite of a society. The root meaning of "prestige" is "deceptions" and "enchantment." No force of arms can control whole peoples forever. Deceive the oppressed into believing you are a god. Make them believe that you are supernaturally powerful and they will offer themselves up to you, at least all those who have learned to despise and hate themselves through their lowly defined class position. Finally these lower-class people have only labor as their wealth, not the products of their labor. This is the alienation in which the male industrial ruling class took root.

From the early times the surplus has been given to the gods, male and female, and to their earthly representatives. The rest was divided communally and later stored. Those who could specialize and increase the surplus might have the power to raise their social status in the hierarchy. Through deception and enchantment, the tactics of the shaman, the trickster, the medicine man, the class hierarchy grew rigid and power over the poor and women was made concrete, first by force and then deception and seduction. The prestige of the aristocracy (kings) and the upper classes (the entrepreneurs) is maintained on psychological power which developed into sacred and religious power. As the ruling classes' religious and psychological enchantment of the oppressed is weakened by shifting historical forces, they must revert to their original force of arms to protect their huge surplus and to hold down the rebellious people.

The village was a communal gathering place in basic equilibrium with itself and its surrounding. The walled-in city was a separation from nature. From the fields and forests the city attracted men who felt the need for great expression of physical prowess and control over others in daily life. The hunters and herders entered the cities, bringing their individualism and male supremacy. Sacred temples, where gathered the money lenders, are the base of our banks and where metallurgy was turned into wasteful ornaments to adorn the new rulers of the world, men. The city became the religious monument of male gods, springing from yet in opposition to the village.

Cities represent the mythical power of kings, gods, money, and gold. They represent the male's psychological need for the "higher" life, away from the human body and away from the human female, the peasant, and that view of life. Man began to assume superhuman proportions symbolically. Concretely, he was the exploiter of lower-class human beings.

The city is primarily masculine and reflects that revolt against the feminine principles of connection with nature that began in the paleolithic period with the northern hunters and the southern herders. The revolt was decisive with the wide acceptance of Judeo-Christianity and the Moslem religions. Women, now no longer in the image of the great gods, became decisively powerless.

James Boggs in an unpublished manuscript writes that "Black men from the time they were captured back in Africa with the help of tribal chiefs lost their domination over the Black woman. For a long period in Black slave society in the United States there was no domination of the female by the male. Both were entirely dominated by the whites. African male domination continued in the

African bush, where hardly touched by the white settlers, African elders could continue their male supremacist customs and control of the land."

Essentially the white master controlled the Black slave family and slave groupings by superior force of arms. The main responsibility of the field female slave was to produce male babies—the labor commodity needed for the master's fields. Male field slaves were used as studs. The stories that come down to us by word of mouth from our slave great-grandmothers tell of stag pens throughout Virginia and South Carolina where "black bucks" were made to copulate with indentured white females from England.

This arrangement was a good basis for establishing faithful house slaves to look to the physical comfort and entertainment of the master and his family, since the master controlled the children from all Black unions. He usually allowed these lighter-skinned Blacks in the big house and slowly created another class of slaves in addition to the house slaves. This one was based on color as well as social position in the slave hierarchy. The children from the master's union with the slave women were a part of this class. Many from this group became educated, multilingual parlor entertainers, in the images of the feudal court jesters.

The first form of solidified relations between Black male and female was generally decided by the master, who thought that a certain Black was so good he ought to settle down, usually with the cook. In order to keep a good male house servant "tame" he gave him a Black woman for a permanent mate. They could both imitate the master and his lady and achieve social prestige. This could be carried on among field slaves as well in order to have responsible field foremen, slave-quarter guards, and Black bounty hunters who returned escaped slaves to the plantation for money. This slave hierarchy developed by the master plantation class for its own support decreased the need for constant force against the slave population.

The master had the right and practiced it freely to have sexual freedom even with the Black woman he allowed the Black male. At anytime he could countermand the Black slave's orders to the Black female. At best the house servant or field foreman was sharing "his woman" with the white master.

Among the field slaves the master could not control the male-female relationship to the extent he could control the house slave's relationships. Among field slaves, man-woman ties were very unstable. The male could be sold, beaten, killed for reasons bearing on the productivity of his laber—e.g. his age, his speed and usefulness in the fields, the number of children from his matings, the degree of submissiveness to the slave role. His brutal oppression and distance from privilege and social status planted the seeds of hatred and revolt. The master could be paternalistic to the house slaves but was forced by the fear of retaliation to be hostile and sadistic to the field slaves.

The field woman was a laborer beside her man, a begetter of children who was let out to the other plantations for breeding. She was responsible for cooking, feeding, and care of the slaves, midwifery, and finally in old age, the mammy for other slave children. If she rose in social status then she became a mammy to the white children.

The Black male slave's position under slavery in the United States was similar to the position of the male during the early agricultural stages of history when women owned the land and controlled the surplus. He had no responsibility for an extended family unit beyond the sexual act and conception—which he ofttimes had to steal if he was not assigned. The family unit was, as in earliest history, the mother and the children, but usually for a limited time.

Extended family units were not helpful to increased production and judicious use of labor.

Those Black women who worked in the big house and the fields acted not as a dominant factor over the Black male but as his protector and savior. Her primary strategy was to allow herself to be sexually used, often to save the life of the Black male. She could speak out to the master and to the white boss if she pleased him with good food, good sex, good care of his children, a role which the master's own woman was seldom allowed to pursue. White women were the vicarious display of the master's economic and social position, his property as well. A vocal link between the white man and the Black man, the Black woman often forced opinions and bargained successfully for whatever pitiful reforms were possible under slavery.

The male house slave early became a caricature of his white slave master, aping his rituals and manners and after emancipation assuming education to be a vehicle to power. The female more subtly transferred much of her feeling of deprivation in this patriarchal society to the benign Protestant male God provided by the conquerors to support their system. Aping "Miss Anne" gave some comfort but no strong reflection of human worth, for the white woman was a female and every female was dangerous to male rule.

The famous Black Madonna disappears from North American Catholicism (except for Mexico) and under capitalism emerges more as a fertility cult in eastern Europe, parts of France, and Italy, Spain, and England. She has been traced back to the Egyptian goddess Isis and very possibly she is the submerged and underground prehistoric Great Earth Mother. But she could not appear in the United States, where white male power was still so tentative over the land of the American Indian and the Black slave population. The Black woman would have to be denied even this Europeanized reflection of herself, as was the male denied his black God.

Among all freed slave society there was a loose family relationship but most particularly among field slaves, who, still tied to the land they could not own, were only nominally free. But with the rise of industrialization after the defeat of the South, he could hire himself out as a hired hand. Whites receded from direct domination to indirect domination. Black males still had to accede to the white boss on whom they depended for a job. But the Black woman was still the farm worker anchored to the land, much as her African sister is to this very day. In the towns she could be a domestic and a little higher in social status. It was only during World War II that she, like the Black male, was allowed into the factories, and then only as a desperately needed semi-skilled laborer, earning smaller wages than even the Black male.

Generally the Black male looked upward toward the master, his boss, and his material possessions, property, e.g. the white woman, the land, the factories, education, or culture and its material extravagances. But the highest piece of personal property, the white woman, was off limits except in the North, where a few Black men could get a white woman descended from indentured slavery and usually economically and socially oppressed herself.

After emancipation the Black man got his Black woman but his range of domination was only in the home, not in the public arena. The white woman could still counter his orders to the Black woman by removing him from a job, a home, or from the land. Only in the small arena of the Black family could the Black man hit back during slavery, after emancipation, and up practically to the present time. The use of the Black woman as a whipping post reflected the stigma the Black man carried within himself and from the ruling white society, that of a whipped person, a cur dog.

Because this tortured Black animal can't beat the master, he beats his Black woman, that bitch dog. She retaliates by any means necessary, and the cycle continues as both are unable to bring the contradiction to its logical explosive conclusion and synthesis—confrontation with THE MAN. It is understandable, for so many Black males and females have grown to love the white man's money, property, military prowess; and assuming the master's possessions are power, they tremble in envy as they dream of taking the master's place.

But the bitter joke is that money and property and machines are only projections and sublimations of the power in the body, not power itself. These physical entrapments were the adornments and possessions of inadequate kings and queens and later rich merchants, absurdly wearing the masks of a Protestant God. They could only rule over the lower classes if the latter believed they were gods and awesomely powerful. It does take two, after all, to oppress—the oppressed have to be seduced into the supernatural belief by these symbolic representations of power so that they give up themselves, their labor, and the products thereof.

The long patriarchy and aggressive male rule is also based on the illusion of male power suffered by exploited and self-hating Black and white women. Historical movement charts the struggle of the repressed dreams of oppressed peoples to rise and return to their proper equilibrium. Social unrest, wars, and insurrections loosen the inner binds of the individuals and the outer binds of exploited human beings. It is said that true revolutions begin from the bottom up and from the inside out. There is such a great power in the lower recesses of our people and deep within us all. Perhaps our struggle is to radiate it rather than to possess it.

The American Dream is a bold, heady, ruthless dream—away from the Black woman, the very image of the Great Earth Mother and the Black Madonna. For us Black women, "motherfucker" is now a definitive, historical term symbolizing the first murder, the murder of the Great Earth Mother repeated endlessly to this day. Perpetrated by Black men first and later by white men and then taken up by Black women, the murder becomes the murder of ourselves; as if this could somehow defend us from our fearsome but inevitable historical duty, to overthrow oppressive male authority and its system.

In the Black world, the Black man could only be a man at the Black woman's expense. In the Western world, the white man could only be a man at the Black man's and the white woman's expense. All of it seduction and trickery, a prestige game, dying myths, absorbed by us all. We vomit them up!

Revolutionaries are the smashers of myths and the destroyers of illusions. They have always died and lived again to build new myths. They dare to dream of a utopia, a new time of equilibrium and synthesis.

Patricia Murphy Robinson for

Robin	Lenise
Marilyn	Dale
Carrietta	Saundra
Maureen	Donna
Aretha	Linda
Celeste	Wanda
Denise	and their beautiful brothers

but most of all for Vilma Sanchez and Norma Abdullah, courageous women and brilliant theoreticians.

The Black
Revolution
in America*

Grace Lee Boggs

The subject on which I have been asked to speak is "The Black Revolution in America." Not "racism," not the Black "movement," or the Black "struggle," or Black "power," but the Black *revolution*. My first task, therefore, is to define the concept of revolution as precisely as I can, particularly because nowadays the word is used like a TV commercial, to turn thought off rather than to turn it on.

A revolution, first of all, involves a rapidly escalating struggle for power, culminating in the forced displacement of the social groups or strata who have held economic and political power, by another or other social groups who have hitherto been ruled by those in power. Secondly, a revolution involves the destruction of one form of social organization which has been developed to meet the needs of a given society but which has obviously failed to meet

* No. 6 in the series "A Black Look at White America," University Center for Adult Education, Detroit, Michigan, Nov. 12, 1968.

[269]

the needs of a significant section of that society, and its displacement by another system or form of social organization which purports to meet these needs.

These two conditions are not all that is involved in a revolution. But without these two conditions, what we are talking about may be a revolt, a movement, a rebellion, but it is not a revolution. The central question therefore becomes: "Is there a Black revolution really developing in this country?" And, if so, what kind of revolution is it, i.e., what social strata and what forms of social organization are in conflict?

I do not pretend to have the definitive answers to these questions. I would not be so presumptuous because I believe that what is involved at this stage in human development is a transformation of human activity at least as profound and radical as that which took place when men stopped being nomads and began to settle down to plant food and domesticate animals. All I can do is attempt a systematic and unrhetorical analysis and projection—which can then be rejected, criticized, modified, or hopefully used as a foundation on which to build.

Looking back at the Black movement over the past thirteen years, it is possible to discern a historical and logical development which is characteristic of all revolutions: namely, a movement toward involving ever deeper layers of the oppressed masses whose grievances are deeply rooted in the nature of the system and who are ready for increasingly desperate actions against it. In this respect, it is important to bear in mind that the contemporary Black movement is only thirteen years old, a relatively brief period in the lifetime of a revolution from infancy to maturity.

To get to where it is today, the Black movement has gone through two clearly discernible stages. First there was the stage of reform or the struggle for integration, which began with the Supreme Court decision and lasted for approximately eleven years.

Now we are at the beginning of the stage of Black Power or Black Nationalism, which first achieved the dimensions of a popular movement with Stokely Carmichael's cry on a dusty road in Mississippi in June 1966.

It is not strange that the Black movement began with a reform stage. Great revolutions usually do. Masses of people usually begin by seeking rights or the satisfaction of needs into revolutionary struggle in the specific sense that I have defined when the reforms they seek are not granted, or, having been granted, only whet their appetite for more.

Thus the black movement began as a struggle for civil rights or a struggle to achieve for Black people the rights which every other group in this country already had. The indisputable leader of this stage of the movement was Dr. Martin Luther King, Jr.

King's great contribution to the movement was the clarity with which he stated his goal and the consistency with which he pursued his strategy. His goal was *integration* but his strategy was *confrontation*, and in the actual struggle the first was turned into its opposite by the second. The strategy of confrontation, or disciplined demonstrations in search of reform, systematically exposed both the pitiful inadequacy of the reforms and the bestiality of the whites with whom the demonstrators were seeking to integrate. Thus, while King's professed *aim* was civil rights legislation and integration, the *means* of confrontation taught Black people that all the civil rights legislation in the world could not solve their real grievances and led them to question whether, after all, whites were good enough to integrate with. As the saying goes, "Why fight to get into a burning house?" or "Why integrate with cancer?"

King did not draw the dialectical conclusion of his movement. This was the historical contribution of the young blacks in SNCC who pursued his strategy in every state of the South. Thus in 1966 the movement arrived in practice, before the eyes of the whole nation, at the concept of the *struggle for Black Power* which Malcolm had been developing before black audiences in the North since his break with the Muslims.

Malcolm's theories, unlike those of King's, had developed out of the day-to-day experiences of Blacks fighting just to survive in the ghet'oes of the North. When the movement came North following the Birmingham riots in 1963, Malcolm began to find it impossible to accept Mr. Muhammad's concept of Black Power, which was based not on conflict but on an apocalyptic or religious prophecy of the doom of White Power and its replacement by Black. Malcolm had come to the conclusion instead that Black Power could be achieved only by a *struggle for power,* or by what he called the Black Revolution. Hence his famous phrases, "by all means necessary" and "by ballots or bullets." Having come to this conclusion, Malcolm spent the brief period following his split from the Muslims in establishing links between the Black revolution in the U.S.A. and the world Black revolution. He was assassinated before he could give organizational form to his revolutionary perspective.

Between 1964 and 1968 the Black masses erupted in a series of spontaneous rebellions in virtually every Northern city. The biggest of all the rebellions, the rebellion which erupted in Detroit in the summer of 1967, established Black Power as a national phenomenon and laid the basis for the movement to enter a new stage in which Blacks were not just shouting "Black Power" as a slogan but exploiting the fears and panic of the white power structure to gain certain facets of power for themselves.

After the summer of 1967, Black Power became so respectable that practically everybody in the Black community from coast to coast became a Black Power spokesman. The result was twofold. On the one hand, Black Power was reduced to its lowest common denominator, i.e., a definition of Black Power as Black Consciousness, Black Pride, and Black Identity, symbolized by the wearing of afro hairdress and clothing. In effect, this meant that Black Power became identified with Black Culture. Secondly, each social grouping in the Black community began to put into the slogan the content which best expressed its particular grievances, aspirations and capacities, or what came most naturally to it.

In the course of each social layer in the Black community doing its own "thing," it has become clear that instead of being a homogeneous entity, the Black community is actually made up of distinct socio-economic layers. The divisions and splits now taking place inside the Black movement reflect these social and economic differences. These splits are actually a healthy development and a sign of the movement's growing maturity and search for political clarity rather than a cause for demoralization. All great revolutionary movements have developed through splits. Their positive significance can best be understood by speculating on what might have happened to the black movement had Malcolm not split from the Muslims.

At the present time there are three distinct social classes represented inside the Black Power movement. These are (1) the Black middle classes; (2) the Black student youth in the universities; and (3) the Black city youth on the streets.

The Black middle classes, which include Black businessmen, Black politicians, Black professionals, and Black preachers, are generally taking advantage of the upsurge in Black Pride and Black Consciousness and the tremendous fears aroused in the white power structure by the spontaneous ghetto rebellions, to obtain funds and support for what they call "building black economic and political power." Doing their "thing" means setting up projects for economic development, job training, voter registration, social welfare and education.

These Black middle-class elements are the ones now being celebrated as "Black militant leaders" by the mass media, which is doing its best to co-opt them into the smooth functioning of the system just as yesterday it built up and co-opted integrationists into the system as "Negro leaders." The aim of the white power structure is, frankly, to build a Black middle class, i.e., to bring as many Blacks as possible into the mainstream of American society, and in the course of this to create local power groups or puppet Black administrations who will be too weak to overthrow the white power structure but strong enough to contain and pacify the Black masses. At the end of the road, if Operation Co-optation could succeed, the Black community from coast to coast would be balkanized into little Black bailiwicks resembling the tiniest neo-colonialist nations in Africa but if possible with even less independence and power than these nations.

Just below the Black middle classes are the Black university youth, some of whom are simply preparing themselves individualistically to be co-opted into the system but many of whom are carrying on struggles for facets of Black power in the university and seeking to make it and themselves relevant to the Black community. Meanwhile, university power structures from coast to coast are trying to anticipate demands and yield concessions to these student youth as fast as they can, hoping that by so doing they will produce more candidates for co-optation into the establishment and deprive the Black university students of any excuse for struggle.

Actually, Operation Co-optation cannot succeed because none of the projects organized by the Black middle classes, even with million-dollar subsidies from the white power structure, can incorporate or contain the third, deepest, and fastest-growing layer inside the black community, the layer of Black city youth. The end-product of three hundred years of an American racist-capitalist society and more specifically of a system of education organized by and for the white middle classes, these youth have recognized that they have become expendable to a highly automated and cybernated society and that they will have to destroy this society or be destroyed by it. Some of these city youth are still in school, some are working in the unskilled jobs which even now could be automated out of existence (if the power structure did not need them for pacification purposes), large numbers are in the armed services, and at least one-third is just unemployed.

These are the youth for whom and to whom the new Black poets speak:

> There they are
> Thirty at the corner
> Black, raw, ready.
> Sores in the city
> That do not want to heal
> —"In the Mecca" by Gwendolyn Brooks

In every Northern city new organizations are springing up to give political direction to these Black street youth. Among these the best-known and the only one which has achieved a form of national organization is the Black Panther Party for Self-Defense. Locally the best-known is probably DRUM (Dodge Revolutionary Union Movement), an organization of young black production workers at the Dodge plant in Hamtramck who are demanding what amounts to Black control of the industrial plants inside the Black community. A parallel organization, FRUM, has been formed at the Ford-Rouge complex. But these are by no means the only organizations. Almost every day you hear of a new group emerging among high school youth, among unskilled Black workers, and even among Black GIs in the armed services. The names they choose—Black Liberators, Black Guards, Black Brothers Onward, Black Students for Defense—indicate their revolutionary orientation.

These groups have certain characteristics in common:

(1) Unlike the Black middle classes, who dream of *building* black economic and political power with the support and cooperation of the white power structure, these youth organizations see themselves as engaged in continuing *confrontation* and *struggle* for control of police, schools, industry and employment, housing, health and welfare, indeed, every institution inside the Black community.

(2) Their struggles spring from very real grievances, the everyday abuses and hardships suffered by the great bulk of the Black community on the job, in the streets, in the schools, at the welfare office, at the hospitals, grievances with which their elders have learned to live but which these young people refuse to tolerate any longer.

(3) They also recognize that although a particular struggle may be precipitated by an individual incident, their struggle is not against just one or another individual but against a whole power structure comprising a complex network of politicians, university and school administrators, landlords, merchants, usurers, realtors, insurance personnel, contractors, union leaders, licensing and inspection bureaucrats, racketeers, lawyers, policemen—the overwhelming majority of whom are both white and absentee, and who exploit the Black ghetto the same way that Western powers exploit the colonies and neo-colonies in Africa, Asia, and Latin America.

(4) They are for the most part consciously anti-capitalist in the sense that they have no use for anyone, Black or white, who makes a profit off the Black community and generally believe that the elimination of the profit system is a necessary condition to Black liberation.

(5) They are also consciously anti-imperialist in the sense that they are against the U.S. efforts to dominate the Asians, Africans, and Latin-Americans. Following in the footsteps of Malcolm but also as a result of their own reluctance to die abroad for a self-determination denied them at home, they are against the U.S. war against colored peoples and identify with the world Black revolution.

(6) They are also consciously anti-liberal. Having assimilated the experiences of the civil rights movement, they distrust the white liberal, recognize the futility of reform legislation, and are ready to pursue their struggles by all means necessary—which they usually interpret as armed struggle. To an extent that it is difficult for most adults to understand, their fundamental attitudes toward struggle have been shaped, first, by their own daily battles to survive, and now by the death by violence of Malcolm and Dr. Martin Luther King, Jr., and even of the Kennedy brothers.

These attitudes, taken as a whole, amount to a repudiation not only of the American racist-capitalist system but of the vehement anti-communism or anti-egalitarianism which is deeply rooted in most Americans. The average American's profound antagonism to communism stems essentially from the benefits which the great majority of whites have received from the American way of life as a system of social mobility for the individual and for successive ethnic groups on the backs of others. For the average Black street youth, this concept of America as a land of opportunity and peaceful progress is not only a fraud but an insult.

America
Is a fairyland fraud
Where democracy is pronounced,
Dippity—do
Ten times on a T.V. commercial—
Insulting my
Black mother,
My black sister,
My black wife,
   My black self.

—Bobb Hamilton

Nevertheless it would be a mistake to consider these Black youth as influenced by the Socialist or Communist parties. Quite the contrary. For the most part they reject the ideological paternalism of white radicals who tend to regard Black militants as unfinished products who will eventually arrive at the Marxist understanding of racism as a product of capitalism and of the working class as the irreconcilable foe of capitalism, and who must therefore in the final analysis accept the white radical program of Black and white workers uniting to overthrow capitalism. This analysis completely contradicts the historical and daily experience of Blacks, and the refusal of white radicals to repudiate it openly and honestly demonstrates how "invisible" Blacks remain in the white radical's picture of the world. The analysis is also completely unscientific because it applies the formulas developed by a European a hundred years ago to an American capitalist society which has had its own specific historical development. The appeal of George Wallace to blue-collar workers is no accident. It is the culmination of the historical process by which American capitalism accumulated its first capital from the labor of Black slaves and then successively exploited and integrated white immigrant workers of various ethnic groups to defend the system and to keep the Blacks in their place at the bottom of the ladder, scavenging the old jobs, old homes, old churches, and old schools discarded by whites and thereby contributing to the overall capital of the country.

On the kind of social organization which Black Power would put in place of the "American way of life" these young Black revolutionaries are not so clear. *This is perfectly understandable since there are no historical models for a revolution in a country as economically advanced as the United States.*

All the successful revolutions of this century, with the possible exception of Russia, have been in countries which had been systematically damned to underdevelopment by Western imperialism. The fundamental contradiction driving these countries to revolution has been the contradiction between the material needs ("rising expectations") of their populations, on the one hand, and their extreme economic backwardness and therefore inability to satisfy these expectations on the other. The main task before the new revolutionary governments has therefore been rapid economic development. This could not be achieved by private enterprise. It could be achieved only by a socialist government, a government representing peasants and workers and with the authority and power to organize and plan industrial development. Socialism in the sense specifically defined by Marx in the middle of the nineteenth century, as a stage *between* capitalism and communism, in which workers take power for the purpose of developing the productive forces, has therefore been the natural goal for the revolution in these countries.

The United States, on the other hand, has essentially solved the problem of developing the productive forces. Objectively, as far as economic development is concerned, this country is riper for communism, in the sense defined by Marx as a society in which each gives according to his ability and receives according to his need, than it is for socialism.

What, then, is the fundamental contradiction driving toward resolution or revolution in this country? Because a revolution does not take place in a country unless there is a contradiction in its development which can be deeply felt by and nags at the society as a whole. Essentially it is the problem which for the last twenty-three years, ever since the dropping of the atomic bomb, has been posed over and over again as "How can this country cope politically with the crises posed by its technological revolutions?" Or as I prefer to phrase it, "How can it resolve the contradiction between its extreme economic development and its extreme political backwardness?"

If this is the contradiction, then the task of the revolution is to create a political system that will be adequate to deal with the specific American reality of a world in which machines can now easily do the work which men used to do and do whatever society wants done, if only society could find a way to decide what it wants done.

That this country is economically and technologically the most advanced in the world is obvious. That it is politically backward and underdeveloped is proved by the support and tolerance which the great majority have shown for racism over the centuries, for the Vietnam war over the past few years, and most recently by the instinctive response which George Wallace has aroused all over the country.

All these phenomena can no longer be considered accidental. Instead they should be recognized as a logical result of an ingenious political system which has made a virtue of social irresponsibility on the part of the individual citizen and has encouraged each individual to believe that if he voted his ignorance, his confusion, his indecision, his weaknesses, his ethnic and sectional prejudices, and his personal self-interest, this gigantic lottery by some magic or miracle would produce a winner for the country. No matter whom you voted for last Tuesday, you must have had some doubts not only about the adequacy of the candidates but about the historical relevance of a political ritual in which some 75 million adults in the most advanced country in the world had only the choice between lesser evils and in which the predictable winner was a man whose public image—of being the least of the evils because he had no clear-cut position on any issues—had been carefully manufactured by professional image-makers.

What we are witnessing in 1968 is the breakdown of a political system which is proving itself as obsolete and backward for political decision-making as a stick is obsolete for plowing up the land for planting. In the same way that the new nations need rapid economic development, the United States today urgently needs a rapid development of another method of political decision-making. And what is needed for the rapid development of political skills, even more than for the rapid development of economic skills, is not just a change in institutions (e.g., monkeying with the electoral college or the primaries or the national conventions), but a rapid change in people, their attitudes, their values, their level of awareness, and their level of commitment. The political activity of people must play the key role in changing the institutions, not vice versa. Otherwise we will be perpetuating the evils of the present system in which the institutions render the individual powerless.

It is by penetrating into the essence of the present outmoded political system that we can begin to discern what is essential to a new political system. The essence of the present system is the social irresponsibility of the individual. By its very operation, including the privacy and secrecy of the vote, its involvement of the citizen only once every few years, and its preoccupation with the personalities of candidates, this system undermines the average citizen's sense of social responsibility, systematically destroying any feeling on his part that his values, his social judgments, and his political actions are socially relevant. It also destroys any relationship between himself and a community. Instead what he thinks and the individual himself-are reduced to a number on a machine, to be counterbalanced by another anonymous number, all of which are calculated on computers, the results of which can be announced even before the citizen goes to the polls.

Conversely, insofar as his judgments and actions are canceled out by the judgments and actions of anonymous others, this system breeds in the citizen a sense of social impotence, a respect for and dependence upon the authority and power of others who actually run things, and eventually a readiness for the great Fuhrer who will solve all his problems for him.

Any fundamental change in this system must begin with the concept of the individual as a maker of history, responsible for creating his social environment, convinced of his actions as historically significant, and therefore of how he thinks, feels, and judges and the positions he takes on social issues as not only personally but socially relevant.

This sense of one's own personal-political value cannot be developed in private or in secret. It has to be developed (a) in relationship with others with whom one feels a sense of community; (b) in the course of actual and continuing struggle and conflict with those in power; (c) over issues in which positions taken or decisions made can be evaluated in terms of their consequences; and (d) with the perspective of finally taking the power which will bring both the authority *and* the responsibility to create new forms of social organization.

It is because these elements of a new politics are rapidly developing in the Black movement, which is itself strategically located at the heart of the institutions whose collective failure constitutes the so-called urban crisis, that we can call the Black revolution the heart and core of the American revolution.

In the first place, Black Americans and particularly young Black Americans do not have that misty-eyed, coming-to-a-salute blind superstition about the rituals of American democracy or that Founding Father complex which characterizes the average white American. The latest proof of this is the response evoked throughout the Black community by the demonstration of Tommie Smith and John Carlos at the Olympics in Mexico City.

Secondly, in the last two years the combination of the spontaneous rebellions and the slogan of Black Power have brought Black Americans to the point of believing in themselves as the makers of ongoing history, of themselves as part of a community, and of that community as needing and having a right to power to control its own destiny.

Thirdly, as a result of the development which the Black movement has already gone through, from the reform to the Black Power stage, and also because of their own objective circumstances, young Black Americans are organizing for a struggle to take power from those in power. At the same time, as I have pointed out, their demands for power are rooted in very real and concrete grievances which are shared by the great bulk of the black community and which strike at all the issues involved in the urban crisis. For that reason they are able to pull into the struggle large numbers of Blacks who up to now have played practically no role in the Black movement and even pull back into the struggle some Black middle-class elements who were prepared to settle for peaceful (neo-colonialist) co-existence.

For example, Black teachers and parents are now organizing to support Black students in the demand for community control of schools. Black police are organizing to take a stand against stop-and-frisk and to persuade the Black community that they too are brothers. Black architects and urban planners are supporting demands by Black citizens against Negro-removal and for citizen control of urban renewal. Black doctors and hospital workers are beginning to support demands for community control of health services. Black social workers are organizing to support demands that the dehumanizing welfare system be replaced by a Well-faring system. Older workers in the plants, who in earlier years learned to adjust to their second-class positions vis-à-vis white workers, management, and union, are being forced to re-evaluate their stand under the pressure from such organizations as DRUM and the Concerned Transportation Workers in Chicago. Even Black professionals, who are presently enjoying the amenities of the project director-consultant-conference jet circuit, can be expected at some point to come down to earth and make a distinction between motions and movement.

Because all these struggles are for control and power, implicit within them and growing increasingly explicit as the struggles intensify is also the drive to redefine the goals and methods of the institutions whose failure can no longer be questioned. Thus, even if Black parents join the struggle for community control of schools with the aim of raising the reading achievement level of their children to that of white children, they are being led in the course of their struggle to challenge the fundamental philosophy and methods of contemporary education. In the course of fighting city housing and planning commissions for control over model cities construction, Black homeowners are faced not only with the question of how this country can build the millions of homes needed to meet the elementary requirements of shelter but with the fundamental question of the role of the city itself in the last quarter of the twentieth century. How should the various elements that make up the physical environment of a city—homes, schools, streets, shopping centers, promenades, factories, cultural centers—be built in order to meet the human needs of the community and to make possible creative interactions between human beings in the various phases of their development from infancy to old age? Or how can we create cities which will bring technology into line with human purpose rather than vice versa?

Thus, in the course of the struggles for Black Power, there are beginning to emerge the elements of a new vision of society in which all the institutions of twentieth-century America are completely transformed. Without such a vision and without the perspective of taking power in order to realize the vision, you have rebels but not revolutionists, rebellion but not revolution.

The presence of these elements does not, of course, guarantee the success of the revolution. That depends upon the development of a revolutionary strategy which will shape the enemy rather than be shaped by it, in other words, which will confront the power structure at its weakest points and the revolutionary forces' strongest points, rather than at those mass media, the courts, and frontal physical battle. But these are all questions of strategy, to be evolved and decided by the revolutionists themselves. My aim tonight has been to help you to see beyond the color of the Black Revolution to the revolution which Blacks are leading *inside* America.

Looking Back

Helen Cade Brehon

What is it like? A Black woman in "white-America," a capitalistic democracy, experiences love, hate, fulfillment, need, pride, embarrassment, and confusion. Each phase and each era presents a different picture in the total retrospection.

In the early twenties in most any and every apartment hung a sign that quietly announced, "Christ Is the Head of this House." Black women were a deeply and profoundly religious group—it was part of the Black heritage. However, the Black woman of that era was without a doubt the "earthly head" of the house (and she would have pitched-a-bitch had you called her "Black"). The dining room was the family room in those days and the table had a special significance. It was here that the family gathered for prayer, reprimands, praise, celebrations, the ironing out of family problems, and the reading of the evening papers.

One Saturday night as the women sat around knitting, crocheting, darning, they discussed in hushed tones the woman that had made the front page—a Black woman on the front page! The conversation embarrassed some of them. Some millionaire had married a Negro girl and because of pressures was trying to have the marriage set aside. He claimed, rather his lawyer claimed, that he did not know she was a Negro. Her lawyer had her disrobe to the waist to prove to the Court that her "fine brown frame" was brown. The names of hotels on uptown Broadway were mentioned as places where they had spent weekends before marriage.

They also retold a story about Annie, one of the old women's daughters. (Those women weren't really old but when you are nine, anyone who doesn't go to school is old.) Annie was visiting in Atlanta after having spent several years in Chicago. The motorman had told Annie that she could not get off "by the front door" of the trolley. She did not argue the point but stood tall, all five feet, twelve inches of her six feet. She walked back to her seat in the back of the car (where else?). As the trolley car crept along, Annie watched the passing scenery—modest frame houses, all with flower gardens in the front yards. Some houses were freshly painted and some were badly in need of repair and paint. When the Fair Street trolley passed Spellman Seminary (as it was called in those days), Annie walked to the front of the trolley, grabbed the unsuspecting motorman by the back of his neck and the seat of his pants, and put him off the car—front door. She walked hurriedly along Greensferry Avenue, mumbling to herself (my mother is still known as the Amazon of the Henderson clan). They all gave a hearty laugh and then began to make plans to go to Rockaway Beach a week later. Basket-lunch menus were planned and all arrangements were formulated. Bathhouses did not welcome Blacks but a few enterprising Blacks who lived in Rockaway had accommodations in their homes for one to change clothes and there were showers in the backyard. So we Blacks "made out."

Fall came and I was delighted. "Second only to religion is the importance of education," I was told almost every day. "For Black people it is the saving grace." (Whatever that meant.)

P. S. 27 (now occupied by the Central Commercial High School) had as many Black teachers as there were Black students. One of the Black teachers had the habit of making a Black pupil the butt of his racist quips. This always got a hearty laugh from the class, and he laughed loudest. This was his way of winning the approval of his white colleagues—he thought. I despised him.

During the high school years at Washington Irving I remember no unpleasant incidents. I also remember no Black teachers. Negro girls were well represented in the executive officers of the General Organization, the Arista, the monitors, and some of the clubs. Black girls were not too welcome in the swimming club. Many of the Black graduates of Washington Irving in the late Twenties and early Thirties entered Lincoln and Harlem School of Nursing, Southern universities, and City College Evening School.

Meanwhile up in Harlem many creative people were "doing their thing" and won worldwide acclaim. The Harlem Renaissance or the New Negro Movement it was called. The daughter of Madame Walker was fastly becoming the number-one hostess. Intellectuals and pseudo intellectuals gathered at her parties to hear the latest poems of Langston Hughes, Countee Cullen, and others. Madame Walker had been the first legitimate businesswoman in the United States to make a million dollars, Black or white. (We have no record as to how many women bootleggers or whores made a million.) Madame Walker made the money—A'lelia, her daughter, enjoyed it. And we younger ones simply envied it, but we wished her well. Many women owe a debt of gratitude to Madame Walker, for not only did she do much to enhance the appearance of the Black woman, she opened up a vast new field of business enterprise. Beauty culture was and is a booming business. There are more than forty thousand beauty salons owned and operated by Black women in America today. (Pity they don't do afros.) A'lelia

Walker's party brought many notables from the downtown while "select set," even royalty. The talented Blacks were also on her guest list, and Harlem was the "in place."

Many co-op apartment houses were opening up in Harlem. The largest of these was Rockefeller's Dunbar Gardens. In one of these co-ops lived a family that became lifelong friends. Mrs. Groves had been one of the businesswomen with a lot of charm and know-how. She had owned a restaurant downtown, convenient for the redcaps and porters from Penn Station. It was with her daughter, Queenie, that I shared many of the happy experiences in Harlem. Often we watched the lines of chauffeur-driven limousines on Lenox Avenue, outside the Cotton Club. Blacks were neither wanted nor welcome at the Cotton Club. The entertainers were the best of the Black artists. One such artist was a shimmy dancer, Louise Cook, who wore her hair "au naturel" long before the Black Renaissance of the Sixties. We went dancing at the Savoy, where the best bands came sooner or later.

The "Renny" was the place on Sunday night. The best basketball teams in the country—dancing after the game—then Chinese food at "The World." Mr. and Mrs. Groves often took us to dances given by "The Bellmans," one of the many social clubs in Harlem. Although we Blacks are supposed to be "born" dancers, I can't remember ever seeing my parents or any of their friends of their generation dance, not even pat a rhythmic foot. We went to beaches—even then at Pelham Bay and Coney Island the bathhouse was still a problem for the Blacks. A new phase . . . a new era had come uptown . . .

The Scottsboro incident brought a new breed of whites to Harlem. Many were members of a then recognized and legal party—the Communist Party. The grapevine insisted that young white girls were sent by the party to induce young Black men to join up. (Or was it seduce?) I sometimes wonder if the party didn't fail simply because it underestimated not only the significance of the church, but the importance of our women in the Black community.

The Catholic Church came to Harlem to recruit members and to give instruction. The Catholic Church, much like the Cotton Club had neither wanted nor welcomed Negroes up to this point. This was the beginning of the depression—an old situation, a new name, "depression." Blacks joined the Communists, Blacks joined the Catholic instruction groups, and the motivation in each case was almost always the hope of employment through the party or through the church. Thousands of hungry, angry Blacks came up to New York from many areas of the South. Many of the poor Black women were forced by desperation and hunger to resort to the "hiring market" in the Bronx. Here, women gathered early in the morning, with hunches and work clothes, and neighborhood housewives could come out, look them over (much like in a slave market), and hire the one of their choice. The salary was twenty-five cents an hour. The work included scrubbing walls, scrubbing floors, washing (without benefit of washing machines), ironing. No lunch, no carefare. Legislation for the poor of the nation helped the Blacks. There were many new agencies that helped one way or another, either employment or welfare.

Out of Sayville about this time came Father Divine and his Peace movement. He coordinated the talents of his followers and the general Black population profited. For two dollars, one of the "kingdom" dressmakers would make a dress—no matter how complicated the pattern. For twenty-five cents, one could get a haircut in one of the many barber shops. His restaurants were spotlessly clean and in each was a table set for Father Divine. A good "soul-breakfast" or dinner was served for as little as twenty-five cents. "Peace, brother" became the salutation of the day.

Because of the nondiscrimination policy of civil service, Black women were taking whatever examinations came along whether it made full use of their educational background or not. It was a job and that was what was wanted. Legislation created new agencies and new hiring policies were introduced. The WPA, the NRA and numerous others all helped the economy of the Blacks.

When the incident at Pearl Harbor sent us headlong into war—this was the phase of my life when I met up with many problems confronted just by being a black woman. The war left the home front short of manpower. All those tests for civil service jobs (some as long as six years back) began to pay off. Large department stores sent out letters to white customers asking how they felt about Black salespeople. So many supervisors of many of the newly opened jobs were not "briefed" on the handling of the new Black personnel and many failed hopelessly. If you were not insulted, humiliated, or harassed at least once every hour—that was a banner day. Shifting population made housing impossible. Attitudes of landlords were hopeless. The armed forces were having their problems with segregation in the army and we were having the housing problem on the home front. The school system was feeling the shortage of teachers and Black teachers began to appear in larger numbers. The school system as a whole stood still, while progress was being made in other areas. Helen Meade and Mildred Johnson were a godsend to parents who were not satisfied with the New York school system and didn't have time to fight city hall. The Little Brown School House and The Modern School served the community well.

Black women are a hale and hearty group. With the odds so against them, they managed to excel in many fields. The news media only present those in the theater, politics, or the criminal element. They represent a small percentage. The ones in theater rely on publicity. The ones in politics, if they are doing anything at all, will at least get a by-line. Black women became involved in politics, and names like Bessie Buchanan, Bertha Diggs Warner, Dollie

Robinson, Ruth Whitehead Whaley, and Anna A. Hedgemen may not be as familiar as Black stars of the stage, but they fought to get into these offices they held, and fought for causes that they thought were just. In her quiet way, Mrs. Roy Wilkins served as Secretary to the Department of Welfare, a social worker for the department for twenty years. One Negro woman of extreme vision bought trucks and kept buying trucks until after good business management, she owned a million dollars' worth of rolling stock in Pennsylvania. The Negro doctors don't get front-page billing, but we have many. As early as 1912 Black women were in the medical profession. And there are over ten thousand Negro nurses in the United States. In the field of education, top billing goes to Mary McLeod Bethune. She was also an organizer of women's clubs.

Closer to our generation are names like Augusta Baker, storyteller and author of "Books About Negro Life for Children," or Dr. Aurelia Toyer or Jean Blackwell. Before Marian Anderson made her debut at the Metropolitan Opera House a Negro dancer, Janet Collins, got a star role. Every Negro and even a few whites know that Althea Gibson was the first Negro woman to play in the National Tournament at Forest Hills. She became an international champion. How many know that the owner of the Newark Eagles Baseball Club was a Negro woman, Mrs. Effa Manley? If you read the story in one of the national magazines, "See How They Run," or if you saw the movie, *Bright Road,* made from the story—your author was a Negro woman, Mary Elizabeth Vroman. So many Negro women work almost behind the scenes, doing the thing they can do best with endless drive and knowhow. Mrs. Julia Jackson, who works diligently in one of New York's municipal hospitals, also operates two shoe-repair shops in *two* different boroughs. The union appreciates her talents; for a few years she was shop steward for the union. This is the kind of directed energy that has made the Black woman as respected as she is by industry today.

Problems were mounting as they went about their creative endeavors. Problems kept mounting—not enough housing, a collapsing school system, segregation in jobs, in housing, and for the Southern Black . . . segregation everywhere. The Black veteran had put his life on the line for several years only to return to hopelessness. When he returned he found less democracy than when he left. Moving into new suburban areas caused new problems in the previously white schools and formerly all-white neighborhoods. One shoe-repair place in Jamaica was run by a white shoe repairman and there was no other "help" in the shop. He let it be known posthaste to new Negroes moving into the area that he did not fix nigger shoes. This I thought was as absurd as the dog cemetery in Hartsdale that doesn't bury dogs belonging to Negroes. Of course having a dog cemetery is an insane idea as far as I am concerned.

A few veterans were lucky enough to purchase homes under the G.I. Bill. Many of their homes were bombed, crosses were burned on the lawns of others. Children on the way to school were harassed by neighborhood mothers—not the children. Children have a way somehow of adjusting. Legislation was being written—and that's where much of it ended, on the written page. On the job, if you worked in an integrated office, much group whispering was done. Co-workers became a bit distant. Emmett Till was lynched and the situation became more strained. Occasionally whites jumped up when you sat by them on the bus or subway. There was an old woman on the job who made a point of cutting out any article that concerned a criminal act of a Black. She would put these on the bulletin board.

As the do-nothing legislation kept passing and the Supreme Court kept upholding the laws there was greater tension in the air. When things started happening in Alabama that "great day" that the old folk sang about seemed nearer. After the bus incident—and once more the Black woman triggered that movement, a standing ovation for Rosa Parks—the tide turned for the Black man and woman in America.

Martin Luther King, we forever salute you. The marching, the boycott of the buses, the singing, the praying, the nonviolence, were great, truly great, but greater than all these was the new image created for the Black man.

To Malcolm X—a twenty-one-gun salute! You told it to them "like it is." You gave to the Black man and woman a new feeling of pride and security. An assurance that you thought like the masses and let's not turn the other cheek; not nonviolence, but self-protection.

Thanks to SNCC, CORE, the Rap Browns, the Stokely Carmichaels, the Huey Newtons (did I leave out anyone?). We need all of your talents.

Before Martin Luther King organized the Southern Christian Leadership Conference—what was the church doing? Where were all the spiritual leaders that preach brotherhood, love, to "all God's children?" What was the World Council of Churches doing to end the social, economic, and political situation of America's Black populace? They should have led the fight many years ago, not lagged along in the rear. In 1954 the Second Assembly of the World Council of Churches went on record as urging the churches to renounce all forms of segregation within the membership, and to work to abolish segregation and discrimination within their own life and within society. It is not enough to renounce by writing. . . . Conferences, reports, and speeches are "stalling" devices.

There are enough Negro women's organizations in America to put pressure in the right areas to gain unlimited rights and privileges. The National Council of Negro Women and the National Association of Colored Women's Clubs are the two largest and most effective. Negroes are instinctively "joiners." The Negro or Black woman has gotten together with other women with common interests to pray, sing, dance, sew, teach others, save money, or whatever the common interest. Let them now get together to set a course for a new America. The Negro or Black woman has caused heads to turn to watch her progress. They make their voices heard. There is power in organizing and strength in joining with other groups with the same goals, no matter what the route. Clear out the old out-of-date ideas; clear out the old mental attics.

After looking back over the years I am certain that the greatest strides, the greatest changes, will be seen in the South. The people in the South have tolerated more, so they are more fed-up, disgusted, and will act. The best jobs, the best homes, the most freedom will be in the large Southern cities. Change had been relatively faster for them than in the Northern areas, especially New York. (I'm not so sure we aren't going backwards.) Nothing is more irritating than to hear some middle-class white who pays less income tax than I remark, "What do they want?" Other pet peeves include: "It's not time yet!" "I don't want them in *my* neighborhood!" (My?) "They are so dirty! lazy!" In answer: The "time" was years ago; you may own a house, you do not own a neighborhood. Dirty—I find dirt and laziness know no color lines. Other pet peeves include the white male who wants to integrate by jumping in bed with me— and the white girl who tries to "make" conversation and forces "small talk," afraid you may not be able to discuss current shows, books, political issues . . . whites who honestly believe most Blacks are on relief and all people on relief are Black.

Looking back—no more! To what shall I look forward? Chaos, revolution, more love, hate, fulfillment, need, pride, embarrassment? After the "Great Day" I do hope I'll be able just to hail a cab—Utopia!

From the Family Notebook

Carole Brown

I'm a natural blonde with light-gray eyes. Based on my skin color and the color of my hair, I am oftentimes "mistaken." White people attach a lot of importance to natural blond hair. As is evidenced by the Clairol ads—"Blondes have more fun." To be Black with blond hair and only be able to trace white ancestry back to a great-grandfather is difficult indeed. I've been determined ever since four years old when I accidentally blurted out in a fashionable New York restaurant, "Daddy," to my brown-skinned father, that I would never let my color become a problem that I could not deal with. With this firm commitment to myself, I set out in the world braced for whatever would happen to me.

I grew up in the age of the invisible Black. The age in which conditions in which Negroes lived were an accepted pattern of life. This age left its imprint on many of us then—some who didn't even survive to tell the tale.

My grandmother migrated North to New York with an armful of five children in the early 1900's. Being a widow, Black, with children to support, her pattern followed many, many strong Black women of such stock. Seeking a better life for her children, she headed as far North as her money would take her. Now Grandma was not educated, but she possessed a keen awareness of life and strength of purpose which helped her succeed in raising her children. I can still hear the words now: "If I ever catch you in a white woman's kitchen, I'll kill you." My mother died when I was three and my brother seven. My father, a young widower at the time, felt it was better if Grandma raised us.

The trip to Birmingham was to forget the tragedy. There was something else for me to never forget. The one-room log cabin that was called a "school"—and the fights from school to home with the little white children. There were the fights home from school with the children who thought that because of my color, I thought I was better than they—little did they know how I suffered inside as I defended myself and beat them up. There was the time in Sunday school when a little girl called me a white bitch. I turned around and called her a black bitch—I was the one whom the Sunday-school teacher punished by making me stand in the corner. For in those days to call a Negro black was something that just wasn't done.

I attended what is termed today, by many sociologists, and poverty warriors, a "culturally deprived school." The schools in which children, pent up in crowded homes, sought refuge each day, but were only to be greeted by hostile apathetic teachers. Teachers, who because of their attitudes, became the victims of these children's misdirected hostilities, which had been ignored for too long.

Junior high school was a new experience for me. It was here that I met an individual who was to have a profound impression on my life. Miss Anita Fraser was a most remarkable woman. Her majestic mahogany-hued face, with its high cheekbones, was framed in an afro hairdo. This was 1954, and Miss Fraser was not only Black and beautiful, but brave; for this was a time when Black women had not discovered their natural beauty and sought to emulate their white counterparts. Miss Fraser was the essence of Black womanhood. I only hope that her students of today can derive and absorb from her brilliance a message, that which was almost but not totally comprehended by the Class of 1954. Miss Fraser had the same attitude that I had. I know she must have heard the snickers from the class when she walked in. The girls especially would whisper, "Doesn't she have enough money to get her hair pressed?" Negroes at that time were impressed with the Lena Horne type of beauty—the chiseled features, the "good hair," and every "model" was hailed as another Lena Horne. Miss Fraser was herself, and I was myself, and through her I was able to mold myself into my own individuality.

In the eighth grade, I competed in and successfully won the Hi-Y Quiz for Negro History Week. One of the questions was, Who was James Weldon Johnson? Even the judges debated my answer when I said that he wrote the Negro National Anthem—they did not know that we had one.

Upon graduation from high school, I was counseled into a job at an insurance company—I lasted four months there. Thanks to the typing I learned in junior high school I was armed with a marketable skill. I set out for California in 1960, after working as a clerical and then a secretary. My job at a major TV station in New York sent me to shorthand school. I was, in 1961, the only Black in a twelve-story building in Los Angeles, California, which employed approximately five hundred persons. Since that time, I understand that tokenism has set in. My schooling has continued at night; my major is sociology.

Many of my contemporaries sought careers as models. This appealed to them because not only was it glamorous, but education had not been stressed in school, so rather than work unskilled as a waitress or in another service-type occupation, modeling was a way out for the Black girl. Dorothy Dandridge was at her prime at the time. Every Black girl aspired to emulate her, identify with her. Miss Dandridge was the first Black woman who had come on the screen since Lena Horne, who had already held her position for at least three decades.

It never ceases to amaze me that I am mistaken by my own. White people I can forgive their ignorance, but Blacks I cannot. There is a special way of walking, language, culture of Black people that erases skin color. But I have been mistaken by my own on more than one occasion. Probably the most ridiculous one was the time Malcolm X mistook me. I chuckled to myself.

In 1963, I returned to New York to visit with my family. The visit lasted six months, as I got "involved" with working for the Poverty Program in Harlem. New York Blacks were at that time getting militant—the Nouveau Noir had emerged, replacing the negative, complacent Negro, who never really existed. Leaders were popping up all over the place. Pickets all over Harlem, the shake-up of the Black Bourgeoisie—the invisible Negro. A construction company was being picketed (and when last heard, still is) because although the hospital was in the heart of Harlem, serving Black people, there were no Black workers assigned to the crews. Malcolm X was there. I came within one foot of him. I was later told by my companion, one of the youth from HARYOU, that Malcolm had scolded her, "Sherron, don't ever walk up to me in public like this with a white girl." Malcolm spoke at one of our youth meetings—he spoke to young Black youth regarding their future. And then he spoke in the square at 125th Street and Seventh Avenue—that famous square in front of the Hotel Theresa in the soul of Harlem. And then the rain came. Everyone ran for shelter—a cloudburst of rain poured forth. Malcolm had spoken.

The March on Washington was coming up on August 28. All of Harlem was preparing for the trip. The crippled came—the young who couldn't yet walk. It was a sunny bright day in Washington, D.C. On my side of the Lincoln Memorial, I looked up to see a thousand faces pour into place—the features were not visible—all I could see was a throng of Black bodies slowly move into place. That day could have been my proudest, if it hadn't been for July 4, 1963.

I had always thought of Maryland as being a fairly moderate semi-Southern state. After all, it was just below Pennsylvania, and just above Virginia. The Freedom Ride to Baltimore, Maryland, on July 4, 1963, was co-sponsored by SNCC and CORE. I had mixed emotions about going. I felt I had to go, but at the same time I didn't feel I had to sit down next to a white person. The theme of the ride was nonviolence, and we were to integrate an amusement park. As the bus pulled up—I got nervous. Indecision as to whether I should be arrested or whether I should picket. My fourteen-year-old companion, who had been cursed, chased, beaten in many areas of the South, helped me to make up my mind. As we departed the bus and headed for the park, a band of whites came forth; the hate on their faces gave a purplish hue to their skin. As we entered the park we were greeted by the police. We refused to leave—the sit-in began. One by one we were herded into the paddy wagon. Shouts of "the Irish made it," "You've got to deserve it" permeated the air. I did not feel fear; in fact, I never felt as strong as I did that day.

About three years ago, I appeared on KNXT's "Images and Attitudes" show. The topic of discussion was racial passing, and I was one of the participants who contributed to the show. The theme of the show was the problems of fair-skinned Negroes. When queried if I've ever been tempted to pass because of my coloring, my answer, unrehearsed and expressing my deep feelings, was, "Why should I try to assimilate myself into a hostile society when I have a rich culture of my own?"

What does all this mean to me? The advent of the Black Revolution, which was to reach its height in 1964, made me reflect on my past. The injustices in school—the apathetic teachers who discouraged me from going on to college, who had a job as a clerk in an insurance company carved out for me . . . "no skills needed, just a high school diploma." My excelling in French in high school but no honor upon graduation even though I received a score of A on my four-year regents.

There is another teacher who stood out in my life. Each time I met Miss Ecker in the hallway she would query me as to my ancestry. I assumed that having gotten her degree to teach, somewhere along the line she would have taken biology and known that hybrids are the result of the fusion of mixed genes from mother and father. The dregs that our schools got for teachers! The misfits who would punish me by putting my hair in an inkwell; and the idiotic one, Miss Ecker, I still remember her name, who asked me more than once what my ancestry was instead of how my studies were coming along. There was no one to turn to. Little black children took, and still are taking, abuses from underqualified, insensitive, patronizing teachers who got their degree from, and still react to the psychology of the institution of slavery.

Thinking About the Play <u>The Great White Hope</u>*

Toni Cade

Ignoring flaws for just a moment—*The Great White Hope* is a fine play and it is a fine production and it is a fine lesson. It combines a sense of history and a sense of immediate relevance. At the moment, that seems to me to be the criterion, the standard by which our attempts (ignoring for the moment too the author) to compile a canon of nationalist literature need to be judged.

Since the beginning of the current "renaissance," there have been many and will be many more works that will be important for the movement in that they reappraise the past, re-evaluate where we've been, clarify where we are, and predict or anticipate where we are headed—vital statements for the moment, applicable, usable, but hardly immortal. For as has been not often enough pointed out by our writers who have taken the trouble to distinguish between

* Reprinted from *Obsidian* magazine, October 1968.

the two aesthetic traditions, Western and Black, our tradition tends to be dynamic. Our art is not a separate entity, reflecting the immortal aspects of the human condition, the "universality" of man; it is, rather, a literate attempt to offer up an ample moral vision, to articulate that life that fluctuates from day to day. It is, then, timely rather than "fixed." For our needs and our perspective shift.

Blues for Mister Charlie, for example, which had its feet firmly implanted in the historical (Emmett Till as archetypal) and its head and voice in the present, was something of a powerhouse in 1964. Today, we might be a little impatient with the pitiful-po'-me intimations just beneath the stormy invectives. We might also be unmoved by the rally atmosphere that is provoked primarily because of the presence of the white witness. The impulse of *Blues* is to enlighten and move the conscience of white America. Very shortly, that motive will prove not only sickening, but thoroughly fraudulent as a dramatic thrust. And *Blues* will seem a woeful period piece.

Pitiful-po'-me for generations has been the terms of our survival as illustrated and nurtured by our blues—survival music. We are somewhere else at the moment. "I got the blues this morning, lawdy lawd," "I lost my man, 'bout to lose my mind," "why the world wanna fall on po' po' me" are simply not the terms on which we base our struggle. The blues idiom now seems to be informed by another spirit: "I wish I knew how it would feel to be free," sung not in the twine-groan school of the Delta, bent knees and longsuffering, but with the demand and power of a Nina Simone or a Novella Nelson; "I have a right to be me," not delivered in the Tin Pan Alley idiom in which it was written but sung in the blues idiom with the insistence and determination and you-better-believe-it of a Letta Mbulu. There is combined in the presentation of most of our present songs both a judgment on the past, and a restatement of survival terms. So much of our current music, like other current cultural production, is like a survey course in art, history, attitudes, stances. So much of the Howard Sachler play is survey too.

Several things in the production of *Hope* link the past with the present, creating the epic dimension that gives the play its sense of importance. The piled-high hairdos and minimum make-up of the Black women in the cast link the Pre-Rose Meta days with the contemporary *au naturel*. The Black man/white woman syndrome, that has become something of a preoccupation in our letters (Baldwin, Cleaver, Jones, Austin Clarke) and something of an obsession in general, stresses the sense of continuity. There is already a voluminous list of theories regarding the Black man/white woman relationship. I may as well, what the hell, add my two cents. A cursory glance at the career of many of our national super-Blacks, or even the neighborhood national, reveals a white woman somewhere along the line. And it has always struck me, when I have allowed myself to be nosy enough to be struck by other people's private lives and when I have the heart to ignore the pathology inherent in such hook-ups, that in many ways the Black man who moves beyond the quest for hi-yaller and hooks up with a gray lady awakens sooner to the fact that he is indeed Black, is somehow freer to fashion his blackness than the dude fantasizing his life with some nucoa babe equally deluded. The Black cat and the nucoa gal can always convince themselves that they are white; they reinforce each other's deception. But the cat with the white woman is constantly being bombarded with reactions to the interracial aspect. To a great degree, the mutual attraction depends on the fact that he is Black. He is expected to interpret Black news, to be a jazz expert, to have the final word on Karenga's latest quotable. You try pulling some Black cat's coat and saying "How come you always got some very, very light-skin, straight-hair, freckleface sister?" He'll nut out on you. The other cat'll at least respond; it's on his mind. Suppose the various LeRoi's had gone ahead and married the fair-skin quasi-model-plus he'd been groomed for? He'd be manning the back-yard barbecue pit in an apron from George Jensen and a fork from Hammacher-Schlemmer, not manning the barricades in a dashiki.

Hope tends to trigger a lot of coldblooded thinking about issues that concern us still. Jack's hassles, the traditional harassment and exile for any Black man who says fuck you, is tied to the current period of repression in which we find wherever a visible and vocal Black organization exists—offices raided, files confiscated, communities occupied and intimidated, the leadership muzzled, jailed, coldly offed. No matter how we may have viewed Jack and his escapades, we are seduced to sympathize and agonize with the on-stage character, for we are not ambivalent about the systematic harassment that goes unchecked these days in the name of law and order.

The Scipio character ("How much white are you into?") is a survey in charisma—combination prophet, Tiresias, Marcus Garvey, Noble Drew Ali, Malcolm, and present-day nationalist sooth-sayers. His appearances on stage, darkly sinister but righteously enlightening, help the play to operate in that historical framework. And, too, the convention of asides—several characters boldly addressing the audience, breaking through any fixed time—keep the hook-up of past and present fluid. But most important to carry the thing off is the textual role of Jack Jefferson and the craft and artistry of James Earl Jones.

Jones has always been able to create a larger-than-life aura on stage. His Macbeth and Othello were olympian. His other characters, sometimes mangling the script, have always had an air of the legendary about them. In this play, he is as much Watusi warrior and John Henry as he is Jack Johnson and Mohammed Ali.

But the time hook-up is accomplished more by what he does with his lines. When he's playing Dufus, for example, lapsing into cotton patch, breaking into a mask grin, he seems at once several people through several decades—the contemporary Black actor commenting on the way a Negro actor in the forties might have compromised himself in those Tom lines while still trying to goof on the Fetchit character as ole Charlie views him, never knowing whether the prototype might have been a bad nigger having fun, goofing on Charlie and Tom at the same time for survival's sake and for the sake of a little private irony—all in one beat. It is amazing to behold. It is doubly amazing that the script and direction were wieldy enough for that kind of playing. Rare. But I stress that it is the artistry of Jones rather than the competence of Sachler and Sherwin that accomplishes this feat: the crucial assembling of historical jigsaw.

At the same time, it is the artistry of Jones that diverts us from some of the flabby features of the text (but what play can really stand up under a great deal of scrutiny? That's why pace is so critical. Why we bother to see it done rather than read it) and points to the other flaws—flat characters. Edwin Sherwin's pacing shows that he knows all about nerves, but little about sinews. And the third-gear-ride-herd-over-the-audience direction squeezes out what little plasticity the other portraits might have had in original conception.

The sense of the mythic, the epic, of timeless history, of world travel, the very globe, is accomplished by the thrown-open stage, Jones as the Black Colossus, the booming voices, the cast of thousands (read sixty-five), the starkly drawn good/evil issues, the graphic black/white scenes. The built-in problem in this kind of History with a capital H is characterization. We see Jack often enough to get varying aspects of his self both public and private. There is always some telepathic, unnameable, supra-human something or other that is brooding, defiant, cunning, gentle, primordial—there is an ambience as well as a person that strikes us; it is familiar to the gut, but we've seldom seen it with our eyes. Jones' man becomes a great deal more than fiction. Johnson and Ali are no fiction, after all, but super-people.

Eleanor becomes in spurts a little more than pasteboard. The "no dick mothergrabber scene" never went well the three times I saw it, but it does round the character out nonetheless. And too, there is ample opportunity to see Eleanor as fighter ("no dick"), feminine ("you rosy, I'm cozy"), loser (death scene). Goldie's role, its tensions and tearings, is not so much written as it is indicated by the very fact that be, a white, is allied with the big bad nigger.

But Clara! The one-dimensional portrait can barely contain the energy of Marlene Warfield. Nor can that bluntly drawn salty harpy hope to express Black Woman—which is, whatever the arguments to the contrary, exactly what Clara must represent in a work approaching myth, utilizing a cast of elemental types. It is what Clara must become since Mrs. Jefferson is obviously served up as Black Mother (another undernourished, short-shrift portrait). Clara is rarely a dramatic character, although her impulses do propel much of the action and her ugly drive must contrast the Jack-Clara idyll in the early part, and she is used to punctuate scenes. She is a tool, but not a character. Merely a notion, a motion, a swoop, a pounce, whatever Warfield can jam into the role. But never a character so much as a piece of the antagonist, a part of the anti-forces that hound and victimize the giant and try to lay him low.

To say that there is so much more to be said about Clara, her drama, her passion, her victimization, her unwitting role as the Man's accomplice—is to say nothing at all. We know all that. Obviously we will have to wait for some other play for the obligatory scene: two promethean powers lighting each other's fires and either illuminating the world or shorting each other out. The pyrotechnics would have been a really fine contrast to the other love relationship, so necessary a contrast, so obligatory a confrontation—what with all the other fireworks in the play, that the absence of a good Jack-Clara scene seems criminal in emotional and historical shortchanging.

I wonder how long it's going to take our dramatists and novelists to produce a really live and complex Clara. And then how long before we see how the seven-eighths of the fireberg hidden beneath the surface motivates her in her relations with a Jack. And then what an understood Jack and Clara mean in terms of our liberation from synthetic and superficial Jack and Clara types. I don't doubt for a moment that one of the reasons the Evil Black Bitch is so entrenched in our stock types is that men have never had the heart or the intelligence to find out what she's all about. And women, who do know better, are forever lying, keeping the guard up, shielding the vulnerable spots. It's a pity women have never trusted their ability, and therefore never developed the technique, of talking with each other. Half the sense of inadequacy and conviction that something is wrong with us would disappear if we were honest. For we would find that it's not us at all, but It—the expectations, the image, the breezy assurance on everyone's part that nigger women ain't worth a damn.

Many critics, in their hasty-headed zeal to get the copy in, have called *The Great White Hope* a Black play. It is not. It is what it is, a remarkably workable script mounted well and cast with several strokes of genius (Fargas as Scipio, for example), written by someone with a good ear for idiom and a rare sensitivity for the subject. It is the least harrowing example I know of of whites hustling Black material. And for the first time in my experience of white-on-black theater, it was the drama of the playwright that captured my attention, rather than the comic-tragedy of the Black players trying to cope with bullshit without losing their credibility as either actors or Black people. Half the time we sit there, in the theater or in the movie house or in front of the TV, keeping our fingers crossed and shuddering "Oh God" or "Oh brother" as we watch our thespians losing ground, bartering what they know to be the truth about this line of dialogue or that cut of character for that "other" truth, that stage truth, getting the worst of a bad bargain.

Some critics have called the play the great hope for the white liberal, offered as they are a chance to flagellate themselves and perpetuate the guilt-ridden nightmares, offered as they are still another chance to raise the standards for still another non-white hero—which is the only kind of hero liberal America has had since W.W. II except for the Kennedys, who are running low. Of course it doesn't cost anything to cheer the innocent beast/transhuman archangel in the dark of the theater. And it doesn't pay us much, I fear, to have the liberal conscience pricked (since the other white bastards let the lesson roll off their backs like so much molten lead which they ignore as they ignore their death).

And most critics have hailed it as the hope for the great white way (not named for naught), dramatic fare there being what it is, predicting a long successful run—which it well deserves. But that some have already labeled it. The Great Black Hope is as inevitable, I suppose, as it is stupid. We have great Black playwrights who can write great Black plays. Most of the reviews ignore completely, or rather are totally ignorant of, both the reactions Blacks at that time had of not only Johnson, but of the loner, the unaffiliated, the go-for-yourself celebrity who makes it perfectly clear that he doesn't give a one-minute shit for his people, and the reactions of Blacks at this time, carefully mapping out what is "correct" for the man of "advantages" who is in position to advance the course of the group.

Back then, the community was boldly paraphrasing "Look Away, Dixie" when they triumphantly sang "Jack Johnson II Whip Jim Jeffries, Hooray, Hooray." But in the kitchen they'd suck their teeth about "all those white gals" and mumble about the "way he throws his dough around—chile—humph." It was not merely that they envied Jack, or even that they put him down, or worshipped him. They were torn. They wished to claim him, but he repudiated them. They wished to rally around their hero; he rejected the role. Champ was the title that concerned him—or at least that's what the newspapers led us to believe.

And now, one of the major stumbling blocks for the Movement is—what do you do about the lone wolf, the individual, the "non-committed," the uncorrect brother? Muhammed Ali of course puts the play and the questions into perspective. He was a champ for the group and for himself. But I suspect that there are bloody days ahead, wasteful days of brother moving on brother, charges of "counter-revolutionary" and "renegade" (updated versions of "Uncle Toms"), before we really find out how to even pose the question correctly. It's not: What do we do about the super-hustler brother, go-for-yourself politician, who got into office and didn't do right? Didn't have the interest of the group? No sense of the struggle? What do we do about that drop-out from our organization who no longer espouses our philosophy but is now becoming a TV celebrity and taking backhand slaps at us? Or writing critiques of us for big bucks? Or going on speaking tours as the authority on the struggle? The question should be: Who is the enemy? Who is the greater and more immediate danger—the individualist, self-centered, selfish brother who's embarrassing us or cooperating with the foe or who is likely to become agent material, or the blind, deaf, headless engine of demonic white America prepared psychically and technically to blow us all away? If we can get basic and be clear about our priorities, we might be able to get basic and be clear about our possible allies.

Are the Revolutionary Techniques Employed in <u>The Battle of Algiers</u> Applicable to Harlem?

Francee Covington

In the past few years the works of Frantz Fanon have become widely read and quoted by those involved in the "Revolution" that has begun to take place in the communities of Black America. If *The Wretched of the Earth* is the "handbook for the Black revolution," then *The Battle of Algiers* is its movie counterpart.

The problem of successful revolt in the U.S. is a difficult one that will be solved only in the actual process of trial and error during the course of struggle. It will not be solved on these pages or in this book. The fact that this material is printed is a direct indication of how deeply we are actually into the revolution.

The American society is a unique amoebalike structure that can not only absorb some of the most adverse elements in it but can also co-opt the ideas of those elements to such an extent as to make it profitable for the society as a whole. Co-optation includes having cigarette commercials in the latest Black jargon and a "revolution" taking place because people have changed their tastes in wine. America has the best shock absorbers of all the countries in the world. Her resiliency to the only civil war she has had, two world wars, the McCarthy era, and the Vietnam war protests has left her virtually unchanged from the time of her independence until now. The Constitution is the same, the government system of so-called checks and balances is the same. And the attitudes of the majority have changed painfully slowly. France does not have this same absorptive character. The independence of Algeria caused the downfall of the Fourth French Republic. Numerous factors would have to come into play before that would be true of the U.S.

Every revolution is different of course, but it is undeniable that there are certain factors common to all that can be utilized by those seeking methods of implementation. The Chinese Revolution, the Russian Revolution, and even the Kenya Revolution labeled "Mau Mau" have not been given the attention that the Algerian Revolution has. This is primarily because of the great extent to which the public has been made aware of this specific revolutionary instance through the writings of Fanon and the more graphic motion-picture illustration, *The Battle of Algiers.*

One of the basic problems of this kind of mass aeration of the Algerian struggle has been to further over-romanticize the concept of struggle—real struggle. To read Fanon three or four times along with Mao to the extent of having paragraphs memorized is not the

essential thing. When someone says "Freedom by any means necessary" and someone else suggests that the earnings of prostitutes be
used for procuring guns—that's by any means necessary. Or "If the
Administration does not accede to our demands, we're going to
burn the motherfucker down!" How many state capitols, police sta-
tions, and college campuses have been burned down by Black people? These are clearly cases of our rhetoric being far, *far* in front of
our actions.

Revolution—the overthrow of a government, form of government,
or social system with another taking its place—is not an easy task
or an eight-hour-a-day, five-days-a-week job. This is not an attempt to point out the best way to overthrow the U.S. government,
but a study in the feasibility of revolution in this country based on
the techniques evolved in the Algerian war on the part of the
French and on the part of the Algerians. General talk on the subject
has been in excess. What are some of the reasons for the success of
the Algerian Revolution? Can those reasons be transported and
used in the United States, Harlem, Watts, Howard University?
What are the parallels between Algeria and Black America, between
the French colonialist army's approach and that taken by the U.S.
army and national guard?

The impression that the viewer gets from *The Battle of Algiers* is
that the war was decided and waged in urban areas. It was not. The
outcome of none of the major revolutions in this century has been
decided in an urban setting as would be necessary in America. The
bulk of the Black population is located in specific areas of the
major cities. In the event of the beginning of an insurrectionary
war, the first steps taken by the federal government will undoubtedly be:

1. To cut the insurgents off from any type of foreign assistance.

2. To destroy larger guerrilla groupings and regular forces (cells). This is achieved through the use of torture. The cell setup is such that a person goes out and recruits two more people, persons two and three, who are not known to each other but only to person one whom they also know. Then persons two and three recruit persons four-five, and six-seven, without telling person one who the new guerrillas are. The line of command of this pyramidal-type structure starts at the top without the person at the top knowing precisely who is at the bottom of the pyramid. The advantage of this is that if number one is captured by the authorities, under torture he can only reveal two names and not the names of all those involved in the cell. The standard and probably the most important order of the FLN was that in the event you were captured and tortured, then you were to summon all of your spiritual and ideological strength to hold out for at least twenty-four hours. This would give the FLN time to render any information you might have relinquished useless.

3. Communications and essential administrative and economic centers will be under heavy guard.

4. The government may undertake the task of mass resettlement of communities in order to prevent these communities from becoming bases for the rebel forces.

5. The captured rebels will be re-educated (brainwashed).

The above were the cases in Algeria. Things may be very different in the United States.

In open territory, as compared to city limits, it is a difficult military maneuver to maintain an electrified line of defense, but it can be done. In Algeria, the Morice Electrified Line was started by the French in 1957, to cut off the external rebel army in Tunisia. The line was made of two rows of electrified fencing and barbed wire with scattered minefields running from the coast some two hundred miles to the Sahara. It was defended by radar and scouting planes and flooded with light at night while troops patrolled in tanks and armored cars. In 1958 the effectiveness of the Morice Line was proven when a rebel leader attempted to get 1,200 men from Tunisia into Algeria, with the result of only ten, *ten*, reaching the destination. To increase the effectiveness of this line of defense, the population was evacuated from adjacent areas and these areas were designated forbidden zones where civilians could be shot on sight. In an urban setting this same kind of defense system would probably be 100 percent successful. The Black population in these areas would in essence be living under concentration-camp conditions while in their own homes. The area is well known to the inhabitants just as the mountain terrain was known by the Algerians and Cubans. But knowledge of the area is not enough. Guerrilla warfare cannot be waged in a laboratory-type setup. It is based on the ability of the guerrillas to move undetected from one place to another. There must be freedom of movement.

If such a line were established around Harlem, with adjacent areas evacuated, the search for rebels would then become just a problem of systematic searching in a control area. The operation could be carried out apartment by apartment, block by block. Photographs of rooftops, streets, and layouts of the sewer system are probably already in the possession of New York City authorities.

The existence of an external army in Cuba, Canada, the Bahamas, and Mexico would have the dual purpose of winning international support through propaganda and being at readiness for invasion and receiving munitions. Algeria received her munitions and stationed her external forces in Tunisia and Morocco, two neighboring sister Moslem countries. The feasibility of the above mentioned countries as external bases (especially for Canada and Mexico) depends primarily on the developments within these countries within the next few years. At the present time they are outstandingly pro-American in their policies, foreign and internal. It must be pointed out that we are definitely without the type of support that the Moslems of Algeria received from the Moslems of Tunisia and the Moslems of Morocco. What is our common denominator with the countries in close proximity to the United States? We don't have common history, common culture, or common language. And why should they risk their lives and homeland for a people with which they hold nothing in common?

One of the few things ever gone into in detail about the Algerian Revolution is simply: Why was it successful? What was there about the Algerian people that made them undefeatable?

Tradition seems to have played the most important role. Traditional aspects common to all Algerians were: (a) religion, (b) a sense of community and (c) geography. Religion, since it was invented, has been a unifying force for war. When religion is added to nationalism, the fight is going to be a fierce one. Orthodox Islam in Algeria, unlike watered-down Christianity in America, has the property of making all else seem insignificant by comparison. Political parties and material wealth are subjugated to moral issues. When Moslem Algerians must have independence, the issue is not only a political one, but a moral and religious one. As someone once said: "There is no true war other than religious war." With a strong sense of religion "brother" becomes more than just a salutation. Guerrillas are to be assisted because they are patriots *and* Moslems. Inevitably, a sense of community is already present because of the common bond of religion, which makes the task of winning over the population that much easier.

As early as 1940 the groups who agitated for Algerian independence were in the main orthodox religious groups. In the forefront of the independence movement was the Algerian Association of

Ulema (doctors of Islamic Law). Ferhat Abbas in 1935, the man who was to become President of the Algerian Provisional Government in 1958, was accused of treason to his own people because of his assimilationist ideas. In response he wrote: "If I had discovered the Algerian nation, I would be a nationalist and would not blush for my crime . . . However, I will not die for the Algerian fatherland, because this fatherland does not exist." His career of struggle for Algerian independence is an excellent illustration of the various Moslem attitudes from 1930 to 1960. In the beginning he regarded independence as unthinkable and wanted Algeria to be aligned with France. After much disillusionment, he saw it as a possibility and then finally as the only way to achieve true dignity for Moslems. This same experience will happen to many of our people. But it is our duty to bring the realities of the situation to the Roy Wilkinses of Black America.

The Association of Ulema was the first to attack Ferhat Abbas' assimilationist position. "We have examined the past and the present and have found that the Algerian nation has taken shape and exists. This nation has its history marked by deeds of the highest order. It possesses its culture, its traditions, and its characteristics, good and bad, as do all nations of the earth. We maintain further that this Algerian nation is not France, cannot be France, and does not wish to be France." The Association of Ulema was in the forefront with the slogan "Islam is my religion, Arabic is my language, Algeria is my fatherland." This was in 1936; independence was not achieved until 1962 (March, 1962). Religion can also be considered as the source of strength and convictions that the guerrillas exhibited. Religion can give a man that inner strength which is necessary to survive and not break under torture. What do Black Americans have that would be a strong ideological base for everyone from New York to Atlanta to Los Angeles? The major problem of any revolutionary movement is getting the backing of the population. As Peter Paret puts it: partisan warfare and psychological warfare=revolutionary warfare. The FLN, by taking the position that its leaders were responsible for the moral and spiritual wellbeing of the inhabitants of the country as well as their physical safety, immediately got those people who were vehemently opposed to the presence of the French on the grounds that the moral fiber of Algeria was being eaten away by the corruption of European ways. The Casbah was to be made a decent place again. There was to be no consumption of intoxicating beverages; drugs were to be outlawed as well as the occupation of prostitutes eliminated. The theory behind this was (1) we must clean up ourselves before we begin to clean out the French effectively; (2) no true Moslem would be against the return to the true values of orthodox Islam; (3) the most important in influential groups in the population, namely the religious leaders, stood behind this new approach. Everyone remembers two scenes from *The Battle of Algiers:* the first one showing children dragging a drunk down a flight of stone steps and the second showing a drug pusher being shot in the streets. At the top of our priorities list should be removing those obstacles to Black unity. Manpower is desperately needed. It's the one commodity that we must make sure we have plenty of. This means that our young brothers cannot go off to war in another part of the world. We must do everything in our power to protect their lives. The best way to do that is to make sure that they don't go. (By any means necessary.) This salvaging or stabilizing of our numbers has to include the eradication of those who would make us slaves to heroin. Eliminate them or their means to do business. "Off the pig" in this case means dope pushers.

For those who are so fond of speaking of "armed revolution," "armed struggle," and "protracted struggle" a war between Black people and those elements of the Mafia who control the drug traffic in our communities would offer all three of these. And if we cannot effectively deal with the Mafia and that organization's killing off of our most precious resource, our youth, within the next five years, then we had better forget about taking on the most militarily advanced nation in the history of the world. Coming to terms with organized crime in our communities would be a sort of apprenticeship for those who still have romantic notions about war. Messing with the Mafia is serious shit. And if we don't have it together, we won't live to tell about it. They don't take prisoners of war.

Religion is a key factor not only for unifying those of different political persuasions, but in the case of Algeria was influential in the type of insurrectional war that was waged. The French in their pacification effort put up a facade of respect for Islamic law and customs, such as the prohibition of foreign men touching the persons of Moslem women. This way women could go unaccosted through the checkoff points with concealed weapons to be used outside for terrorist activities. Islam also states that the woman must obey the wishes of the man to whom she is charged, thus if ordered to carry guns, hide insurgents, etc., she did so. Not necessarily because she was so politically aware, but because she was told to.

The major religion of Black people in the U.S. is diluted Christianity. Perhaps fifty years ago religion may have proved to be a good rallying point, but not today. Particularly among young Blacks. What then will our major unifying idea be? The combating of racism in America? Racism has become so subtle in most parts of the country that one must almost remind himself on a daily basis that it does indeed exist. It will be necessary in the near future to come up with a viable alternative to religion that will have the same unifying effect. The matter of geography is common to all revolutions. The land issue is inevitably linked with the independence issue. The land fought for is the same area that is in the hand of the colonialists. The problem is ridding the land of the colonizers, sending them back to where they came from with the revolutionaries remaining. In the cases of Kenya and Algeria, it was first the rightful owner of the land who had occupied it for centuries, then the coming of the settlers (the colonizers), and after the struggle, the return of the land to the natives. In the case of this country, this usual pattern would be broken. Which block of land are we fighting for? The northeastern United States? The southeastern United States? All of it? Then comes the problem of deporting so many whites to "where they came from."

I have tried to show thus far that the idea of importing the techniques of revolution that were successful in one place may prove disastrous in another place. That the main reasons for the success of the Algerian Revolution were (1) religion; (2) a sense of community; (3) land base; and (4) outside basis of support. And that none of these elements has emerged to any large degree among Black people in this country.

Notes on the Contributors

The author biographies below are presented here exactly as they appeared in the original edition of The Black Woman *in 1970.*

Frances Beale   Active in SNCC's Black Women's Liberation Committee, the National Council of Negro Women, and several Black women's study groups. Resides in New York.

Helen Cade Brehon   Active in Women's League of Voters and discussion groups. From Atlanta, graduate of Clark and Columbia. Mother of artist Walter Cade and Toni Cade Bambara.

Grace Lee Boggs   Active in Movement since first march on Washington. Has chaired numerous community-teachers conferences in Michigan. Co-authored with husband James Lee Boggs "The City Is the Black Man's Land" and "Detroit: Birth of a Nation." Resides in Michigan.

Jean Carey Bond   Frequent traveler to Africa with architect husband Max Bond. Author of *A Is For Africa*. Resides in New York.

Carole Brown   Active in anti-poverty projects in California. Hobbies include music and writing. Resides in Los Angeles.

Toni Cade   Works have appeared in *Liberator, Negro Digest, Massachusetts Review, Prairie Schooner,* several Black anthologies, and various high school texts. Currently at work on a collection of stories for children and a never-ending autobiographical essay, *The Scattered Sopranoes.* Currently on staff at Rutger's Livingston College, formerly of Harlem University (CCNY). Resides in New York.

Joanna Clark   Graduate of CCNY; opera singer; mother of Dion and Pia. Resides in New York.

Ann Cook   Traveled widely throughout U.S., Africa, and South America as teacher, counselor, linguist, researcher, visitor. Formerly of Harlem University's SEEK program. Currently on travel grant.

Francee Covington   Active member of Black student groups. Political Science major at Harlem University with a special interest in Africa. Traveled to Ghana in 1969. Resides in New York.

Nikki Giovanni   Graduate of Fisk, SNCC, and John O. Killens' Writing Workshop. Poet, short-story writer, editor, reviewer, currently on staff at Rutger's Livingston College, formerly of Queens College SEEK program. Author of *Black Feeling, Black Talk, Black Judgment,* and *Re-Creation,* distributed by Broadside Press. From Cincinnati to Delaware, currently resides in New York.

Joanne Grant   Writer, lecturer, participant in Black Heritage Series. Author of *Black Protest* and *Confrontation on Campus.* Working on a book on Ella J. Baker. Resides in New York.

Joyce Green   Active in community work with young children. SEEK student at Harlem University with an interest in Black literature and research.

Adele Jones   Active member of the Black Student Alliance, the Onyx Society, and *Utambuzi Newsletter*. A political student at Harlem University. Resides in New York.

Maude White Katz   Organizer and civil rights activist. Several of her pieces have appeared in *Freedomways*. Resides in New York.

Abbey Lincoln   Famed singer-actress of film, stage, and T.V. Is currently collaborating with Alice Childress on several dramatic productions for stage.

Kay Lindsey   Program producer for Pacifica Radio, currently working on a collection of poems, and research on oppression of Black women. Currently residing in the South.

Audre Lorde   Poet, instructor in SEEK program at Lehman College, conducted a writer's workshop at Tougaloo in Mississippi. Author of *The First Cities*, published by Poet's Press. Resides in New York.

Verta Mae Smart-Grosvenor   Actress, designer, cosmic force with the Sun Ra Solar Myth Science Orchestra. Author of *Cooking By Vibrations* (Doubleday). Currently at work on a million and one projects. Her piece on kitchens is dedicated to "miss K lindsey, mr c hayes; moonbeams, palm hearts, tangerine juice and to mr h p in appreciation of the good times we had in the kitchen in the spring in the year of the rooster." Resides in New York.

Paule Marshall   Former writer for *Our World*, author of novel *Brown Girl, Brownstones*, of the collection of short novels *Soul Clap Hands and Sing*, and of the current novel *The Chosen Place, the Timeless People*. Member of the Harlem Writers' Guild. Resides in New York.

Gwen Patton   Active in the Movement, formerly of SNCC; ex-student body president of Tuskeegee, former chairman of SNCC's Black Women's Liberation Committee, currently chairman of the National Black Student Association. Articles have appeared in *Liberator* and *Negro Digest*. Currently resides in Washington.

Patricia Peery   Organizer of Black women's study groups. Currently resides in New York.

Pat Robinson   "Woman—born 1926 of woman, Black and a mother, middle-class capitalistic programming—wife, B.S., M.S. S.W., psychiatric social worker, private psychotherapist, consultant Planned Parenthood, staff correspondent Afro-American newspapers.

> 'Ants on the locust tree assume
>   a great nation swagger
> And mayflies brightly plot to
>   topple the giant tree'
>
> —Mao Tse Tung"

Fran Sanders   Ski enthusiast with football knee. Graduate of Pratt, mother, freelance commercial artist—in real life—fine artist. From Montclair, N.J., currently resides in New York.

Gail Stokes   SEEK student at Harlem University, mother, journalistic work for *Focus*, *Liberator*, and other Afro-American magazines.

Alice Walker   Stories have appeared in Black anthologies and in *Freedomways* magazine. New collection of stories being published. Formerly of Georgia, now resides in Mississippi.

Helen Williams   Singer, playwright, musician, social worker, formerly with SEEK program at Harlem University. Resides in New York.

Shirley Williams   Works have appeared in several magazines including *Massachusetts Review*. Collection of short stories to be published this year. Resides in Fresno, California.